the ranch that was us

For Caroline

Becky Crouch Patterson
Stieler Hill   Comfort, Texas

The Ranch That Was Us

Text and illustrations by Becky Crouch Patterson

Foreword by Willie Nelson

TRINITY UNIVERSITY PRESS, SAN ANTONIO

Trinity University Press gratefully acknowledges the support of the following in the publication of this book

Kathryn N. Harrison of the Anderson Ranches
Chigger King of the KX Arbuckle Ranch
Michael Lawrence
Janey Briscoe Marmion of the Briscoe Ranch, Inc.
Christi and Tommy Moorman of the Moorman Brady Creek Ranch

For Oma Dora

For the gift of the lives
of those who have gone before me,
glory to God.

For those still here,
may God bless both you and your children,
now and evermore.

Der Herr segne euch,
Je mehr und mehr
Euch und eure Kinder.

—Psalm 115:14

Contents

HS

In our sleep, pain that cannot
forget falls drop by drop upon the
heart and in our own despair,
against our will, comes wisdom
through the awful grace of God.
—AESCHYLUS

[The sheep] still had some distance to go . . . and now, leading from the
sheep pen, they found a beaten trail that made walking a lighter business,
and responded to that small inquiring something which all animals carry
inside them, saying unmistakably, "Yes, quite right; this leads home!"
—KENNETH GRAHAME, *The Wind in the Willows*

ʜS

the ranch that was us

Foreword

WILLIE NELSON

Listen to my song and if you want to sing along
It's about where I belong. Texas.

I know Becky from the times at Luckenbach and the book she wrote about her dad, Hondo Crouch. My first introduction to Becky's family was in the early 1970s at Hondo's magical Luckenbach, before the song found it. Hondo invited me to the Luckenbach Domino Tournament, which consisted of only me and my partner Zekie Vernon, the owner of the pool hall in Austin that my mom and pop ran, against two eighty-seven-year-olds. Hondo had raked up the bottle caps in the dirt yard the night before and put a butcher-paper sign on the outside bar wall announcing the tournament. Even though he tried to keep it a secret, two thousand showed up. People were hanging out of the trees over our little table outside.

Shatzie Crouch, Becky's mother, brought food to share with the regulars in the bar, or she would throw a link of sausage on the woodstove. One time she brought King Crab legs all the way from Alaska, to the locals' delight. I went to Hondo's funeral in 1976. Later I came back to Luckenbach to play five Fourth of July picnics.

On quieter days I would find Hondo scribbling notes in a notebook he kept in his shirt pocket, to use later in his satirical writings. The most beautiful poem/song he ever wrote was "Luckenbach Daylight." I was one of the lucky ones to hear him recite it. As a writer, Becky is a chip off one of her father's whittlings. She has the same keen eagle-eye observations, as well as a poetic voice of clarity and truth.

One of the lines in Becky's book is from my song "Still Is Still Movin' for Me." *The Ranch That Was Us* will make you want to stop, be still, and read slowly. We live in a fast-paced cyber-landscape. Slow down with foreman Raymond where there are no phones—though he manages to stay in touch anyway. Atop Thunder Mountain at five thirty in the morning, on horseback, he said, "Since you don't talk to your neighbors much, about all I could do to check on them was to see when they got moving in the morning by watching when the smoke came outa their chimney. Everyone cooked with wood back then."

Shatzie Crouch is a durable branch from a family tree that thrived in rocky soil. They were rugged individualists. Only a few from the thousands of German immigrants, like Louisa Hellmann and Dr. William Keidel, were tough enough to survive the walk from the Texas coast to their designated Hill Country land. As Freethinkers and persecuted loyal Unionists, some lived through the Civil War here in German Texas. Shatzie's father, Adolf Stieler, experienced tragedies and setbacks, but he and his extended family were still key players in developing Central Texas.

Growing up in rocky soil—like the mountain laurel, which grows even in drought—develops character. The laurel's tap root goes deep and produces fragrant purple blooms. So it is with Shatzie Crouch, who put down her deep roots and thrived, devoting her life to preserving her heritage by saving its treasures. Because of her wind-worn pioneer spirit, she is truly a Texas treasure.

What defines all of us native Texans is our strong sense of place. We own where we're from, carry it inside us no matter where we go. Becky's book is about the Home Ranch in the Texas Hill Country, a physical place where you are born, leave, forsake, return, and still love. But more so, it's about home as a feeling, a landscape in our heart where we always feel welcome. No matter where we live, we take home with us by writing and singing about it.

Someone from the audience once threw a felt hat to me on stage, with ribbon lacing, a horsehair hatband, and a star punched in the crown. It was one of the hats Becky had made. I never took it off. But I take it off now to say congratulations on her great book about Texas—its land, stories, and people.

Pentimento

Mama was a handful.

I knew this long before the day I stood in a forty-five-minute-long line at the crowded bus station in San Antonio to buy a ticket to Houston for one of the three hitchhikers Mama had picked up two days ago. Still, it brought the point home. The other two had been arrested that morning for fighting at Mama's house, which she'd turned over to them for the night. We had even been robbed in that short time.

After losing pounds of adrenaline, we were left with just one hitchhiker—the one with only six fingers, who had previously worked for a drug lord in Colombia washing his cars. (In gratitude, he had washed mine with newspapers.) He turned out to be the good one.

Hector from Honduras had to catch a bus at 4:50 to make his connection with a Salvadoran down the line. I'd spent all day arranging the meeting, but then Mama, who was in her eighties but hadn't slowed down for a minute, took charge. I should have left her in the parking lot, but she'd already dragged the driver off the 3:30 Houston bus—not knowing it was not *our* Houston bus—to wait for Hector.

Mama had gone inside. I found her scooting Hector's heavy bags across the floor with her feet, as if she was pushing a sick sheep through a meandering flock of woollies in a pen. Her doctor had told her never to pick up anything heavier than twenty pounds after some surgical repairs she had had, and she did get her purse

5

down to four pounds after removing her hammer, screwdriver, hunting knife, furniture scrapers, and drill bits for T-posts. But she paid the order no mind. In fact, she still buys and carries dog food in fifty-pound bags, and this for a dog the size of a small piglet.

I patiently waited in line with another woman my age. She was buying a ticket for her eighty-four-year-old mother, who was behaving nicely, quietly sitting on a bench. Meanwhile, Mama had bustled her way to the front of the line. The aggravated ticket sales lady reprimanded her, saying that she was not allowed to cut in. But Mama wangled a ticket from her anyway, in her name and at a senior citizen price. Then, pointing to Hector, she said it was for him. The frustrated clerk said, "Oh well, since you're all the way from Comfort," and made a new ticket.

All the way home I lectured Mama about her bad judgment in undertaking these hitchhiker projects, even if they were in the name of mercy. This was not the first time she'd done this. "Everything in life is either illegal or in bad judgment," she retorted. "You just have to do what you think is right. Larry had blisters on his feet walking all the way to Amarillo. Besides, he had eyes like Kerry." Kerry, my brother, had agonized us with years of aimless hitchhiking. For his part, Larry, a hitchhiker from a project past, told me that Mama had the face of Jesus. The drifters' down-and-out stories cut straight through to our sympathy, no question.

⊢⊊

In the spring of 1981, Mama went into the Fredericksburg post office, where she disturbed another waiting line of silent customers. "Who has that kid goat out in the truck?" she loudly asked. All eyes turned to her commanding question. "That's my goat, Shatzie," a rancher answered. "It's poor, an orphan. I'm taking it to the auction." "Can I have it?" she asked. It was Eastertime, and she was thinking of an Easter Angora, not a rabbit but a goat, for her city grandkids in San Antonio. "Can't get it to suck a bottle," said the rancher. "I can get *anything* to suck!" retorted Mama. "I'll take it off your hands!" More heads turned.

My boys were enchanted with their new pet. We raised that goat in our backyard on Prinz Street until it got bigger, smellier, and rowdier and ate all the flowers. Then Mama relieved us of it as easily as she'd gotten it. She drove up in her truck to the Gillespie County Livestock Auction, the very one her father had started forty years before, with the pet grown goat standing proudly on her front seat, a place usually reserved for privileged sheepdogs. The livestock wranglers receiving stock got a big kick out of that. One of them said, "Who was *that?*"

"That was Shatzie Crouch, daughter of the Goat King," another replied.

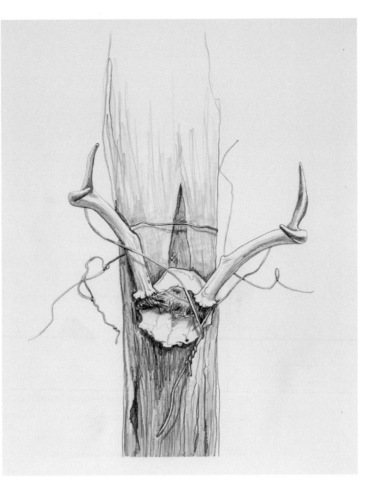

One Christmas morning, dressed in red silk and black wool, Mama drove up to the house at the ranch with a very rotten dead deer in the back of her truck. She'd noticed the buck on the highway days ago and thought maybe we could make something—door or knife handles, cup hooks, buttons, jewelry—out of the antlers. Mama was always a scavenger for creativity's sake.

"I thought I could just roll it up into my truck, but it was too heavy," she explained. "Johnny saw me from across the field and came to help me." She dumped it in our canyon with a warning: "If you see buzzards, they're just cleaning up your deer for you." "Mama, buzzards aren't here in the winter," I said. "You didn't need to have that on your list of things to do on Christmas morning!" When I commented on some blood on her hand as she was mashing away at the guacamole, she shrugged, "Must be from the deer."

That New Year's Day, Mama took in a helpless neighbor woman who was recuperating from migraine headaches and shoulder surgery. She turned her little two-room antique log cabin over to her for weeks, nursing her back to health. There the neighbor was, propped up on pillows in Mama's bed, in her sanctuary, in her room where she had her TV, books, and reading lamp, being waited on hand and foot with hot tea and even baths. "I'm going to stand by her through this," Mama stubbornly said.

My sister Cris and I were shocked, angry, and even a little jealous, protective of our mother, whose heart was too big for her own good. But Mama said she liked sleeping up in the attic, where you can't even stand up. She had to climb a steep ladder, and, at the top of the landing, she had to crawl over a pile of cut boards— might need those someday—and a big ugly potted plant that she had been trying to bring back to life. Her chamber pot during the night was a cooking pot, which she emptied onto the pitiful plant. "I feel like I'm sleeping in a basket," she said of the crumbly roof overhead. "I can still hear the taps, splits, chops, when they were making the cedar shingles. It lulls me to sleep."

Cris and I thought that Mama too often acted with no discernment, a little over the top. We worried about her energy limits, her "spells," although she insisted that she was stronger than most her age.

Now, every day, over the subject that binds us, Cris and I cry to each other about what to do, knowing full well no one's going to tell Mama what to do. Our only resort is to report all this behavior to her doctor, to intervene for us perhaps. "I get it. I get it. I'm writing all this down," says the nurse on the phone. "Incredible."

Mama's foolish wisdom and carefree compassion are what happens when someone is blessed with basic goodness that is then tempered by years of collective pain and disappointments. She still trusts everyone. She still has the rancher instinct, the loyalty to the almost obsolete Angora goat. The spirit of generosity, with its giving and sacrifice, the rescuing and loving the unlovely, the resourcefulness, saving everything, making do, the resilience, the taking charge, are all characteristics she learned from her Texas German family and from life on the Home Ranch. This place in the Hill Country has shaped us all, this ranch that was us—and still is us.

"I'm comfortable being uncomfortable," Mama says.

A few years ago, while at an artist's residency in Maine, I was painting over a painting I didn't like. The image kept bleeding through the gesso. "Isn't there a word for this," I asked, "when the old image keeps coming back?" The artist next to me replied, "That would be called *pentimento*. That means the painter repented, changed his mind."

The pioneer spirit bleeds through the pages of history. It remains. The ancestors, family, workers, stories, buildings, the noisy comings and silent goings of many animals—all left their subtle mark on this land. Like the old paint that almost disappeared, the ghostly traces fade through to the surface. As I live on this same ranch today, the ranch that was us, I am trying to see what is left here for me to learn, to cherish, to continue, or to change. What I keep. What I let go.

The Walk

They put olive oil on the bottoms of their shoes and began walking. At seven thirty on a drizzly wet morning, September 11, 2007, my sons Kit and Sky set out to walk the entire seven-and-a-half-mile perimeter of the old Home Ranch as seriously as if it were the ancient walls of Jericho. It took five hours, a lot longer than they thought, stopping along the way to rest, read, pray, and drink water. Prayer warriors, they'd come armed with lines of scripture. Carrying a bottle of olive oil, a symbol of the Holy Spirit, they would mark each corner post as they passed.

They started at the main entrance of the ranch, marked by its trademark tall cedar post-and-lintel gate. There, on Stieler Hill, they were standing at the highest point in Kerr and Kendall Counties, smack dab in the center of the Hill Country, in the very heart of Texas. Their great-great-grandfather Hermann Stieler was the first man to own the land, deeded to him by the state of Texas in 1876. It was once remote, but now Interstate 87 slashes through the ranch to connect Comfort to Fredericksburg, with Kerrville making an equilateral triangle that surrounds our spread.

The boys walked on the outside of the fence line along the highway, adding their tracks to many that had come before them. They walked the caliche divide. As high as it is, it plummets as low, dropping into spring-fed canyons with names such as Dietert Schlucht, Turkey Hollow, Washtub Canyon, and our own secret canyon, North Creek. They would never get to see the beautiful Turkey Hollow, sold years earlier. It's where Uncle Victor Keidel and Adolf rode horses in Washtub Canyon to hunt wild turkey. They would kill so many that they carried a packhorse with them with washtubs on both sides to hold the birds—hence the name of the canyon. They wouldn't return home until the tubs were full.

Kit looked at the first of the many carefully handpicked scriptures he had brought to read and said, "For the power of life-giving Spirit has freed me from sin and death."

The boys had never seen the ranch this way before. They passed huge rolls of rusty handmade barbed wire, twisted by a wire-making machine right there ninety-three years earlier by their great-grandfather Adolf and his brother Fritz. They were the first to stretch miles and miles of fence on this land. Replacing it now was a new

eight-foot-tall game fence put in by our neighbor, whose jet runway lies in view of our place.

Deer holes now perforated many parts of the fence. Others were so brittle and delicate they seemed to be held up only by large spiderwebs that glistened with trapped dewdrops like dreamcatchers.

Dozens of fence holes were patched with just brush and limbs. Kit and Sky saw them as fragile, cluttered, clinging to a definition of a once strong boundary. Repairs could come later. For now, this new generation was on a mission of obedience—of a spiritual principle. Theirs was an act of faith to walk the land, spiritually claiming it back with God's promises.

Sky read another one: "For You deliver me from the webs of fear and illusion. You deliver me from all that separates and divides." The boys knew nothing of the land. They knew only that it had been fought over, lost, sold off, that it lay silent, abandoned, and unproductive. All they saw now was diminished to old fallen-down fences and barns melting into the ground. They never saw it as a glorious but humble empire that thrived thanks to hard work, common sense, many hands, and family unity. Rocks, cedars, horehound, and thistles now replaced big flower and vegetable gardens, fields of maize, corn, and oats. They would never see the life this place once teemed with—sheep, goats, cattle, horses, dogs, wildlife, people. The boys would never have believed that the land was once carpeted with forests, thick with towering post oaks, now gone.

They could never imagine how a team worked together hard to survive tragedy and nature with such defiant spirits, with such resiliency and tenacity. This sprawling ranch machine was once a place called Home. But now the soul was missing.

They wanted to pray it back if they could. We had been exiled from this place for almost fifty years, and finally we had returned. Surely, with contrite hearts and anointing of oil, we would make changes to the place. We would change ourselves. With new intention, this place, like an old battleground that had seen glorious and bleak days, would return to prosperity, healing, and blessing.

"Faith comes by hearing, even if it's your own voice." Kit shouted, "I will praise the Lord no matter what happens!" He told Sky, "Speaking out loud births life." So they sang songs of victory and praise loudly, as if to yank down from the same old sky of 130 years ago strong confidence from what had been a godless vacuum. "The Lord will find you," Kit read, "and bring you back again to the land of your ancestors. He will bless you!"

Covering them like an umbrella, the misty rain washed the walkers, washed the air, washed the land. The boys praised the gray sky. They praised the cactus with all its tenacity and defenses. They praised the rocks that propelled and stumbled them forward. They praised the shoes that carried them.

Beauty of nature surrounded them on this walk of discovery. With new eyes, they saw silvery bear grass, reddish big blue stem, and canopies of oak trees—Spanish oak, blackjack oak, post oak, live oak. They crossed dry, rocky creek beds, the rocks of which are good for making patios. Surefooted, dodging cactus, they carefully descended a treacherous, steep canyon, a whole other world of high cliffs punctuated with little animal caves and draping ferns.

Down in the canyon they came across a tiny trickling spring. Someone had covered its eye with big flat rocks to protect it from the destructive hooves of the cattle. Although pitifully shallow, the spring bubbled up clean, cold, clear water. The source of water is always holy, and in this country water is always rare. There used to be twenty-five springs on the place, but now only three remain. The boys bent down to drink from the ground. Kneeling, Kit read, "The voice of the Lord echoes from the clouds . . . thunders from the skies. So powerful is His voice it breaks down the cedars. Our words are powerful too, Sky."

At the bottom of North Creek they saw a timeworn image of strength. The flood gap still remained, a battered fortress of vertical tin roof panels, cedar staves, twisted iron rods, brush, T-posts, all tightly wired together. It separated our turf from someone else's. The gap had fought and won battles against torrents of rushing water, brush, and debris that had threatened our boundaries. "You are my hiding place from every storm of life," Sky read. "Abiding love surrounds all those who trust the Lord." Looking up from the depth of the canyon, Kit read, "I will lift my eyes to the hills. My help comes from God!"

On their lung-taxing ascent out of the canyon, the boys found that the southernmost corner post was a huge oak tree that had grown and embraced the rusted strands of barbed wire fence. There they stopped to observe. Delicate spongy moss grew, and tiny flowers nestled in the protective roots at the base of the monumental tree of endurance.

Weary, their wet feet rubbed raw, the brothers persevered. Their spirits drove their wills. They wanted to open their hearts' eyes to truth and discernment. They were tired of hearing stories of loss from lawsuits, greed, tragedy, heartache, and mishaps.

From 1862 to 1999, there had been untimely deaths in every generation up to mine. Confederate vigilantes hanged Heinrich Stieler, sixteen, as a spy in 1862. A friend accidentally shot Adolf's twenty-five-year-old brother Emil Stieler while hunting in 1910. My grandmother Dora Stieler died in a car accident in 1936, at the age of forty. Walter Stieler died jumping into a silo to save others. Alfred Stieler had eye cancer and committed suicide. Wilbert Stieler, just twenty, was decapitated in a car wreck. My son Ren, nineteen, died in a car wreck in 1987. My brother Kerry was diagnosed as a schizophrenic in 1971, at the age of twenty-one, and committed suicide in 1999.

Not only were there curses of tragic loss needing to be broken. Agreements, lies told to our minds, also had to be canceled. Mama still recounts one of them. At her mother's funeral, when she was just a twelve-year-old girl, the preacher had said, "God needed her." Mama remains mad at God to this day, seventy-odd years later, even though she has lived a godly life. The truth is, God doesn't "need" anyone. What is truth or lie can stick with you for a lifetime, into the next generation.

With contrite determination they declared another promise. "No evil shall befall you, nor any plagues come near your dwelling."

This was spiritual warfare. Sky and Kit were fed up.

On this long zigzag trek they encountered many corner posts. Sky noticed one post in particular that had layers of rusted wire wrapped around it so many times so tightly that it looked as though a dead post had continued to grow and envelop the metal. "That wire sure is binding that post," Sky commented. "Remember, we're here to *bind* things," Kit said. "Bind demons, kick out fear. It's all about forgiveness. God said, 'What is bound on earth is bound in heaven. What is loosed on earth is loosed in heaven.'"

As Sky walked away from the last corner post, he looked back. The indelible oil had repelled the rain and remained. "At least we were here," he said, "and left these marks."

A Landscape of the Heart

Frozen feet brought my ancestor William Neunhoffer to Texas in 1870, a story I will tell you later. A broken heart brought me back to the Home Ranch in 1990.

I had lived there before, until I was five. Mama was already living down at the Camp Shack with Kerry, where Tomás's rock chimney stands like a sentry. What land she didn't regain by strong-arming it from her stepmother, I had to buy back. The ranch and house had been ransacked, and the homecoming was like a vacant empty dream. We called the ranch Rancho de Viudas, ranch of widows. It had all gone to seed. Digging in the waist-high thistles in the backyard of the main house, Mama found buried in the grass a tarnished silver baby spoon. It had been lost for forty-seven years. My name was engraved on it. "Here, Becky," she said, handing it to me. "This is an omen. This place will be yours someday."

The first 113 years of this ranch was about landscape—measured, fenced, grazed, cleared, plowed, built on, traded, bought, lost. The next twenty years would be about the landscape of my heart, windblown, with human droughts and tornados. At times I wanted to stay, dig in, restore; then, at times, to cut and run. The rooster weathervane on the shearing barn was knocked cockeyed from a hailstorm. I felt the same as the old weathered barns here, falling down and worn out. Do I get the wrecking ball out for both of us? The old barns are not just for one life. Neither am I. We can be resurrected, renovated, and changed.

But I rebel against change.

The ghostly old place was oppressive with absences, disappointments, losses. Ragweed, horehound, thistles, beggar's lice ruled, covered everything. I came back to Stieler Hill as a necessity. I felt anew the air, ground, rocks, fire ants, and even the hummingbirds' vibrations. To open a gate was to make several trips, lifting the rotten boards in pieces on hinges bound by rusty brittle baling wire, the chains and horseshoe latches the only thing holding them up. The wolves from 1916 were gone—that's another story I will tell—but the coyotes were back. Things once purposeful now haunted me: rusted, corroded sheep and goat bells with homemade clappers of nuts and bolts, broken shearing blades. Through these archaeological finds I could still see the work, life, living, planting, the animals beneath all this. There's the weedy landing strip that once brought Uncle Gene's Bonanza plane in, moss-choked water troughs, a piece of tin nailed atop a fence post to protect the end. I could hear the jovial voices of the shearers through their chalk-and-paint initials scrawled on the shearing barn walls. A barrier of cedar pickets at a gate once stopped stampeding stock but now only braced a gentle gust of wind from time to time.

Like the ancient hedge of fieldstones in the Highway Field, laboriously compiled to prevent soil erosion, I was here now to keep the local soil of my soul and memory in place. Returning to my childhood places, I felt the old comfort of belonging here. The most comforting were the smells of the dark musty feed room: the fresh green of the alfalfa and coastal hay, the sweet of the molasses in the cow cake, the earthiness of cottonseed, oats, and corn. In its dank darkness, sharp slivers of light cracked through the crudely handmade wooden doors. Dust motes floated in on shards of sunlight. Every time I ripped a string off a feedbag I thought of my grandmothers Clara and Mietze saving each one of them to crochet their dishrags and an entire tablecloth. It was here up at these barns, when I was five, that I saw a nanny goat struggle to give birth to triplets. I ran back to the house, screaming, "Something's happening to this goat!"

The nanny died from that struggle. We raised those triplet kids in the house. They jumped up and down on the couch and chairs in the great room along with us kids.

The boyfriend tree in the backyard was too big for me to sit on its lap anymore. But I used to sit on the curve of this young oak, hug, lean on, and caress the tree as if it were my boyfriend. Embracing the trunk, I dreamed of whom I might marry someday.

I remembered what wild invincible carefree kids we were. Nothing could kill us. We could jump higher, run faster, be meaner and tougher than any other kids. When my brother Juan was a young boy, he and his friend Mark Langerhans were so careless with guns when hunting that they both got shot. The first time they were in Opa's brand-new Scout in the Six Hundred. As they stopped at a gate, Mark decided to load his gun, and it went off. The gun shot a hole through the floorboard and a tire of the new Scout. "Gosh dang! I shot a hole in my new boots!" complained Mark. He took his boot off, dumped the blood out, and realized he'd shot his toe off. Juan didn't know what would be faster—jump out and change the tire, or run all the way back to the house for help. He ran.

On another hunting trip here at the ranch, Mark and Juan were in their truck. Juan pointed to a deer through an open window. Mark aimed out of the cab and shot. The bullet went straight through Juan's pointing hand. Juan was too embarrassed to tell our parents, so he doctored the black burned wound himself with a razor and alcohol.

We were immortal.

$$\vdash\!S$$

I read to my firstborn before he was born. Lorenzo Dow Patterson V, whom we called Ren, was a gift containing gifts. He was a free-spirited child, with an engaging generous smile, bright and beautiful from the inside out. Ren had talents in art that were light-years beyond those of his peers. He spoke poetically. In the summer of 1971, when Ren was three, we came home from Alaska to visit at my father's ranch in Texas. Ren had never seen a Texas-size sunset before. The sun that evening was a big red-orange ball that was quickly sinking across the field by the barn. "Come on, dogs!" he said with surprising enthusiasm. "Let's go get the sun!" Distance seemed nothing to him. By the time the eager toddler crossed a huge field with the sheepdogs, the sun had sunk behind the hills, and we had to go fetch him from his short and disappointing journey. But his innocent faith inspired his father, Dow, to write a song about it called "Let's Go Get the Sun."

Let's go get the sun! And bring it back when the day is done.
It's going down behind the hills.
It's calling me to come.
And the light runs through the meadow,
Turning leaves and grass to gold.
As I reach for things I surely
See but cannot seem to hold.
It's sad but true with passing youth
Some lose the will to dream,
Or chase a giant ball of fire,
Or ripples in a stream.
And when I think of all the things I've tried,
And never did get done,
I can still hear that small boy say,
"Come on, dogs, let's go get the sun!"

He called himself a bud waiting to bloom.

Ren had another talent. Inheriting his grandfather Hondo's swimming finesse, he was an All-American swimmer, in the top twenty-five in the nation in the butterfly and freestyle events. It earned him a scholarship on the nation's number-one swim team at the University of Texas.

I remember my last hug from Ren—that tall strong body with long arms, that winning smile—under some trees in the swim center parking lot. I would still feel those comforting, all-embracing arms in dark nights, in dreams to come.

ᚺ

On September 25, 1987, a police officer rang our doorbell at three o'clock in the morning. "Do you have a son named Lorenzo Dow Patterson at UT?" he asked. I barely heard his next words for the deafening primal scream in my head. Ren had been killed in a car wreck, thrown out of the backseat of a Volkswagen convertible only a few blocks from the athletic dorm where he lived. We heard that his friends surrounded him in the street, screaming at him to stay alive. He had just turned nineteen.

We buried him in his UT swim sweats, with one purple sock and one orange one, a tradition of Hondo's. We used the pall I had made for another church to drape over his casket. Ren had helped me design it, as he did many of my art projects. A mariachi mass, six hundred people, the entire UT men's and women's swim teams, overflowed at St. George's Episcopal Church to standing room outside. A

friend sang "Let's Go Get the Sun," the words engraved on Ren's headstone. At the gravesite, nineteen balloons floated into the sparkling blue sky, while those present shouted "Hip, hip, hooray!"

As I was leaving the gravesite I heard singing. When I turned to look back, all of the swimmers, men and women, had gathered around his grave for their own private goodbye. They were singing, "The eyes of Texas are upon you, 'til Gabriel blows his horn." I will never hear that song the same again. Some knelt down and tied their swim medals onto the handles of the casket.

We would hear from the national swim world for the next year as those young people poured out their thoughts, grief, and condolences in letters, poems, and magazine and newspaper articles. Lady Bird Johnson sent a telegram: "My heart aches for you." When his team won nationals that year, Ren was posthumously awarded the NCAA Championship diamond ring. "He would have made the team," Coach Reese said kindly.

"Would have" haunts me. It will haunt me the rest of my life.

ᛋ

It was easier for me to forgive his friend, the drunk driver, than it was for me to forgive Ren for dying.

I made the mistake of stubbornly vowing that I'd get over this forty years after my death—in other words, never. I was resentful when I was in the craft store buying silk flowers for Ren's grave alongside mothers buying picture frames for their sons' photos and swimming medals. I was ashamed that I let pain destroy my marriage and that I left my good home and Sky in San Antonio. I was jealous that my husband Dow had several very real dreams of Ren, but I didn't. His first dream was ten minutes *before* the policeman rang our doorbell to tell us about Ren. In the dream, Ren tells Dow he's coming to say goodbye and wants to go see his room one last time. An angel accompanying Ren keeps saying, "Come on, Ren, we have to go now."

I'd prayed every day for a guardian angel to protect Ren. This was not what I meant.

The wildest news was of Ren visiting his best friend, Doug Gjertson, a world-class UT swimmer who was back home in Atlanta. We read about it in the sports section of the *Dallas Morning News*. The appearance of Ren's ghost for five nights in a row was so real that Doug never doubted it happened. Besides lengthy con-

versation, Ren had left physical evidence: dozens of Doug's swim trophies had been turned facing the wall on a shelf. "I used to turn Ren's wooden fish around in his room to let him know I'd been there," explained Doug. There were also Ren's unique signature doodles drawn on Doug's calendar at this desk, where Ren sat. "He was wearing his UT sweats," Doug told us, just as we had buried him.

Maybe the purpose of this apparition was an important message just for me, comforting information a mother needed to hear. Ren told him, "We went around a curve too fast. *It didn't hurt. Tell Becky and Dow I love them.*" (Doug didn't know Ren called us by our names.) "I wish I could tell them goodbye," he added. "The only thing I hate is having to leave everyone. I wish I could tell you how this is. And remember, I still have some of your CDs."

In love and sympathy, friends brought us food for an entire year. My friend Carolyn gave us a white crepe myrtle to plant. Pat Hammond brought the gift of words, A. E. Housman's "Ode to an Athlete Dying Young." Still in disbelief, Ren's high school swim friend Santos, then at Dartmouth, wrote a letter to Ren posthumously, addressing it and sending it to him at the athletic dorm at UT. At the 1988 Olympics, Doug wrote Ren's name on his fingernails when he swam, and then wrote "for Ren" on the back of his gold medal for the 800-meter free relay.

Kindness and words. They're all that matter in the end.

After my divorce in 1992, when I left the house on Prinz Street in San Antonio, all I wanted to take with me was a part of the kitchen wall, a four-inch-wide thin veneer panel on which we had kept a growth chart of everyone who entered, from cousins to high school swimmers and friends, and famous world-class swimmers. And there at a stopping point was a heavy mark with this note: "Ren, 6′2″, 1986." When framing pictures I discovered a piece of chipboard behind a picture in a frame. As a twelve-year-old, Ren loved to design game boards that had a path to follow, with advances and setbacks that eventually led to a destination. The drawing was never finished. It only had the beginnings of a path with just the word "start" on it. I framed that—Ren's game of life, as I saw it.

I keep this last fond image of Ren in my memory bank. Several weeks before his death, we were walking on the beach at a family reunion. Proudly, I looked back at my son, the one I had read to before he was born, with such high hopes. His body was tan, with streamlined muscles. His smile echoed his clear blue eyes. His sun-bleached mane was haloed by the orange sunset. The setting sun wrapped him in a golden-copper glow. With the wind blowing against him, he looked immortal.

I converted the workers' bunkhouse over the garage, where Shatzie once played and drew her chalk rooms on the floor, into a studio for me and my fabric. Sky later would use the garages below for his painting studio. I make large machine-appliquéd tapestries, design and create liturgical artwork.

I was so depressed that I took two years to rev back up and design the stained glass windows of the Beatitudes that my church, Saint Barnabas, had asked me to do three years earlier. It was hard to be holy after I lost my faith.

After Ren's death, the first place Mama took me was her beloved canyon here at the Home Ranch. We both just sat there on the side of a cliff, in silence, with blank stares. I was numb and blind to the beauty and comfort the canyon had once offered both of us. "Look at the curves of that walnut tree limb," she said. "Those tall elms would make good straight beams." I'd never noticed. "How does that shiny get on the grass?" she added. I could scarcely take in the beauty then. We heard a tinkling waterfall. "Listen to the quiet."

We picked ourselves up and walked, seeing iridescent flint chips on the caliche road. "Look! Here's snow-on-the-mountain, wedgewood, and verbena." She acknowledged flowers I'd never seen before. "Look at that yellow—pure color. Flower power!" she said of the masses of Mexican hat.

On our walk in the canyon, I salvaged a big rusty wreath of barbed wire discarded from fence repair. We came across a rare treasure of five blackberries. I climbed over a rickety fence juggling both items. "Look, Mama. I'm holding heavy spiky barbed wire in one hand and trying to protect these delicate berries in the other, while balancing on a wiggly fence!" Seeing the balancing act, she commented, "That's like life—we have to be both tough and tender."

On the walk up out of the canyon, Mama broke off a twig of tiny white blossoms and handed it to me. "The mock orange is so little and pitiful this year from the drought," she said. "But it survived!"

HS

The loneliness seemed magnified by the moaning wind encircling my house. In those lost days at times I wanted to just run away, leave the ranch. I would drive down to the gate, not knowing where to go or which way to turn, right or left. It didn't matter. Driving thirty miles an hour, I'd have to pull over to let someone pass. The driver would wave in thanks. I grabbed those waves from strangers like morsels of kindness to feast on. Sometimes they sustained me for a long time.

Mama thought she and Kerry should keep me company by living in the main house with me. One night I came home through the kitchen door without turning on the lights. Something hit me in the face. When I turned on the lights, I saw that Mama had hung her homemade venison jerky from broomsticks, at eye level, across the kitchen ceiling.

This would not work. I preferred to live alone with my loneliness.

But no one was lonelier than my brother Kerry. Rejection and negative stigma can put a mentally ill person in a world of loneliness we can't imagine.

Michael Nye told me a story of when Kerry was spending the night with him and Naomi in their King William neighborhood in San Antonio. Kerry was schizophrenic and insomniac. Michael thought that he had better check Kerry's bed to see if he was in it. He wasn't. Where Michael found him was out sitting in their chicken coop. He was smoking, a big fat hen sitting next to him. The hen also had a cigarette in its mouth.

⊢ς

I hung Ren's huaraches on my wall. They still held the shape of his feet. Like his handwriting could conjure up his voice, the feet-shaped huaraches conjured up his lively movement. I looked at them daily just to face the loss and pain for a determined moment. Then I could go on with my day. The constant worry I had for my kids—dead or alive—was now transferred into every living thing on the ranch.

Mama said one time, "You're never through with your kids." Exactly.

A newborn deer came into my life, picked up by someone who didn't know to leave well enough alone. Now I had him, unable to return to the wild with human scent. This baby deer was the most perfect and perfectly beautiful thing I'd ever seen. He had bigger than cartoon eyes, Audrey Hepburn eyelashes, delicate satellite-dish ears, paper thin, to detect a pin drop from miles away. Four pencil-thin stilts with tiny black hooves no bigger than your little fingernail miraculously held up his two pounds.

For the next six weeks I became his other mother. I let him suck on my ear. He made whiny squeaks that said, "Where are you? Feed me. Take care of me." Buckaroo, the baby buck, totally depended on me.

We called to each other in our own language.

I delighted in this tiny animal that could already run at lightning speed, streamlined with ears back, in the meadow of my backyard. He raced at least three laps around the big rock garden.

Already programmed into this tiny creature was a defense system. Besides his speed and spots, he took precaution not to expose himself to large openings. Following me on long walks, Buckaroo would run a few yards, then drop flat to the ground to "disappear" from predators. The presence of this fragile animal from the wild made me feel in love. I marveled at the strength to survive wrapped in this delicate, poetic, seemingly helpless form. His wobbly legs trembled at even the sight of a new potted plant. The day he disappeared from my backyard, my brain immediately shifted into stress gear. I couldn't concentrate on anything but his premature absence. It was almost sundown. Juan was still shredding, and I'm sure the noisy tractor bolted Buckaroo out into the fifteen hundred acres of our ranch. I walked almost that entire expanse, calling for him in my desperate deer dialect.

The thought bubble over my head read, "He can't survive on his own yet. When was his last meal? He can't find water. He's scared of his own shadow."

Comfort came from my son Kit, who said, "Look at it this way, Mom. Now you have something new to worry about."

That long dark sleepless night, I prayed to the saint of lost baby deer. The tentacles of my heart reached out to connect to Buckaroo's somewhere far away.

I arose in the middle of the night to continue my calls and search, trying to let go for the inevitable. There, waiting for me at my back door, was Buckaroo, skinned-up head and scrapes on his sculptural ears and legs, calling in his moanful little squeaks.

I called Mama to tell her the news.

"See," she calmly said, "you have a smart deer. The moral of this story, Becky, is you better enjoy today. You never know what tomorrow will bring."

"But I already want to jump to tomorrow and brace for the bad to worry about," I said, defending my right to ward off evil.

"You can't do that," she replied. "We are only given today."

In the first week of January 1997, an epic ice storm hit Stieler Hill with a vengeance and changed the landscape of the ranch. The timing was perfect, for a landscape was changing in me too. It paralleled my feelings of vulnerability, isolation, and loneliness. The storm also rendered me remote, with no road, electricity, phone, or water. I heard trees crashing at night like glass buildings shattering, falling in the frozen pasture. Silence, creak, crack, crash, thud, echo, hush, repeat. The sound of the wind was hell on wings, ripping, wrapping around the corners of the house, screaming, whining, blowing low notes like twin flutes.

Huddled by my fireplace, I wrote to myself and Ren. "Ren, I want to burn down the time between us. Time is my enemy. It fades your memory. Your death defines my life. I am trying to feel alive, present to myself, but then I remember you can't either. My heart still hurts. It stopped, frozen, encapsulated in eternal ice."

Morning light brought beauty, but also sadness, because I could see the changing landscape. It was a vision. Daylight revealed a glistening white shiny world of Swedish crystal that could only be sold at Tiffany's. Glass grass, Saran-wrapped everything, like in Dr. Zhivago's icy dacha. The most remarkable sight was "the burning bush," a single fiery ice tree backlit by the orange sunset. It glowed, shimmered, burned, radiated. "It's a miracle!" exclaimed Sky, searching for his camera.

I need a strong man, I thought, as my ax bounced off the thick ice on the horse trough. It was impossible to manipulate the frozen chains and open frozen gates welded shut with ice. At first this white wonderland was exciting, beautiful, an adventure and challenge for common sense. I honed my fire-building skills and balanced a little enamel coffeepot on the coals of my bedroom fireplace. But after three days it got old, then downright scary. I had no heat and was out of firewood, food, and water. A smidgen of self-pity set in. I needed a companion, a foreman, a helpmate, a man! I'm alone in this. Highway 87, silent and shut down, made me an island. After the thaw, the phone man said the storm had hit hardest on Stieler Hill. When the road opened back up, cars stopped on the highway to take pictures of the quaint awesome beauty, unaware of what I had gone through during the week.

Once again, Mama came to the rescue. She lived a mile down the caliche road in the Camp Shack, once a hunting cabin in the 1920s, now reclaimed as her home. She was in the same predicament. She carried water from a spring way down in the canyon, up a steep hill, in five-gallon containers. Besides water, she also brought me firewood and venison stew in a heavy iron Dutch oven. She's happiest, she says, when she has plenty of firewood and a freezer full of venison. I would return to the cozy functioning world again where so much is taken for granted. But for a few days the ice storm put things into perspective: back to the basics, discomfort, simplicity, survival. The trial showed the weak spots in me that made me doubt my self-reliance.

"Oh, this is nothing," Mama said as she rekindled my fire. "Just keep moving. I think of the *True Women* book. Those pioneers had it harder. They had no water, heat, food, and they still had to deal with this kind of weather."

Mama's courage and strength—I wish they would pass on to me.

In the backyard, the hammock trees and the boyfriend tree all made it through without losing limbs. The Mother's Day magnolia Mama had planted sixty years ago was down for the count, bowed but not broken. Eventually, with the thaw, it would slowly, gracefully raise its burdened branches but would never be the same again.

Mama came in with an ice cube in her hand. "Look at this brave violet!" she exulted. Then she handed me a delicate violet perfectly encased in thick ice, its suspended beauty waiting patiently for an escape.

While You're Resting, Pull Horehound

In 2005, I started visiting Raymond Kuhlmann, who was then eighty-eight years old, at the Live Oak Nursing Home to hear his stories of the Home Ranch. He had an incredible memory, and I wanted to get them all down while I could.

Raymond had been the foreman, the cowboy guru, of all our family ranches for half a century. Now here he was, no longer free to breathe the fresh air of thousands of acres with his animals. His big John Wayne–like body, crippled with arthritis, was not at the wheel of his old red truck anymore, but in a wheelchair in a small antiseptic room. But his make-do creativity was still at work. He used needle-nose pliers to button his shirt, made a hearing aid out of headphones from Radio Shack, and carried saddlebags on the arm of his chair that held tools for making crude leather purses.

With the ingenuity of all those years, he could fix anything and everything with baling wire, as when he once mended the malfunctioning accelerator pedal of a Jeep. He attached baling wire to the pedal, then, with a wooden handle, pulled and pushed the wire, lurching forward. The Jeep stopped abruptly, then jerked forward again. Raymond laughed all the way down the caliche road with this start-stop-jolting ride he'd invented.

In his booming Tex-German accent, Raymond started every story emphatically the same way: "I'll never forget!" That day he remembered in perfect detail a weather report of fifty years ago:

I'll never forget! On April 1, 1955, Henry Howell reported on the news, "scattered showers." That day it rained twenty-six inches. Hondo and I crossed the Big Sandy River at the Hicks Ranch on horseback. It was bone dry. We were thirsty. We dug in the sand for a drink. We used to build wooden squares to keep the sand out and make water troughs in the dry creek for the cattle to drink.

We were pushing cattle on four thousand acres. We got to the top of a hill and we saw clouds. We had late-sheared goats, so we sent Homer, Alex, and his boys back to the Block Creek to shed them. Hondo and I thought it'd blow over, so we stayed with the cattle. Here came a fast rollin' rain. When we crossed the Big Sandy again, we had to swim our horses across.

We had goats with sixty-two days of hair on. That's enough hair to not have to put them in a shed. But this wasn't normal weather, and you can go out of the goat business in one minute. If it rains and stops, they'll go home. But if it keeps on rainin' they'll chill down, can't walk. They'll get paralyzed, trip over just a twig. They'll die real quick if they get cold. You just have to let 'em die right there. Don't haul 'em to the barn. You save labor and everything. We lost 2,100 out of 29,500 that night.

Raymond told this story as if it had happened just yesterday—still with amazement and regret, still feeling the loss.

Raymond's anecdotes of the ranches and the workers are as insignificant as dead leaves that the wind blows by me, never to return again. They could pile up in a ditch and become compost. But the leaves become whispers, words, stories. Sometimes if I listen real hard I can hear laughter shaking the tree branches, jovial German drinking songs, plaintive Mexican corridos, a dog barking orders, goat bells alive with tinkling.

When I strain my ears to hear the wind's language, a limb scratching on the roof, a gate banging and creaking against an old rusted chain, or a single acorn dropping take on whole other meanings. The trees that produced these leaves have died, no longer exist. Out of the mouth of Raymond flew these leaves and their stories, kept for so long. I want to grab the leaves out of the air, keep them, and admire their colors.

At the artist's residency in Maine I painted seventeen paintings from his detailed stories. The day I returned to Texas—November 1, 2005—was the day of Raymond's

funeral. In the nick of time, I had captured his voice, his mind, his memories. We took his ashes on foot and by horseback up to his beloved lookout view, Thunder Mountain at the Block Creek Ranch in Sisterdale.

HS

Adolf found hired hands from the ends of the earth. Homeless, jobless wanderers would walk up Stieler Hill through the always-open gate, seeking a meal or employment during the Depression. Adolf never turned them down. He always fed them first. Even in 1950, I remember seeing many of these ragged down-and-outers sitting at the screen door on the steps with a plate piled high with slices of white bread, frijole beans, and roast beef.

Some of the "leaves that blew by" were loyal, rode for the brand. Some stayed, like Christian Breeman Shenle from Ohio, George "Honey" Koester from Washington, and George Wellington from Oklahoma. It took a lot of fatherly patience, character testing, and creativity on Adolf's part to put up with some of these characters. Some of the names you can't tell apart from dog names. "I learned trust and honesty from Daddy," Mama told me. "He trusted and helped everyone, reached out not only to transients but others' kids and family. But he gave them a workout, though."

Adolf stuck to his first rule, "Never hire a man with his hands in his pockets. It shows he's not ready to work." His other mantra they all knew: "While you're resting, pull horehound."

Emil Wieters, from Marion, Texas, walked up the highway in 1933. He was taken to the Old Stowers Ranch at Camp Bullis. They first stopped at the Prinz Store for a haircut, where Emil also wanted a gallon of wine. He kept Raymond and Joe Herrera up that night howling at the moon. Emil always wore blue overalls held up by one strap over his shoulder. He had a glass eye, which he removed when he cried or was drunk. In a fit of despair or rage he would pull out his eye and even throw it. One time at the Block Creek, he was mad at being teased about the horse he rode. So he said he was going to bed, left in a huff, stepped out the door, and landed four feet down. He simply remarked, "Now I'm outside."

Buck Pantemuel was kicked in the head by a horse and carried the permanent mark of the horseshoe nails on his head. At the Block Creek, in 1939, he was crossing a swollen creek on horseback. He had no idea of the floodwater's strength and depth or the entangled fence wire hidden below the muddy current. He was swept away and drowned in that crossing.

Runt Norman was a bull rider, fired because of laziness.

Paul Pankratz, a colorful Comfort local, was humorous, always joking. A very opinionated German, he blurted out odd sayings such as *"Wie die Alten singen, so zwitschern die Jungen"*—meaning, as the old birds sing, so the young ones chirp. He wasn't a stockman and never rode a horse; he was just a gofer and handyman. Paul wasn't even a very good handyman at that, but he was fun to keep around and livened things up by playing a push fiddle, which is what he called his accordion.

Frank Schultze was the temperamental but expert fence builder who built the cedar rail fence, now more than eighty years old, here at the Home Ranch entrance. He was a perfectionist who would blow up a fence with dynamite if it wasn't straight. He lived with his wife like a hermit in a cabin back in the pasture. When they divided up their things in divorce, they had six chickens and one rooster. So they agreed to kill and eat the rooster. Frank gloated that he got more because he could eat more than her.

Bartolo was a hand who lived at the Middle Windmill pasture at the Dreiss Flat Rock Ranch. He rode a black mare named Midnight. He didn't speak English. When thirteen sheep got out into the wrong field, he communicated the fact by throwing thirteen little rocks into the field.

August and John were two brothers who worked at the Sieben Eichen, or Seven Oaks, near Sisterdale. They lived in a log cabin and had only one good pair of clothes between them. When one of them went to town, he wore the good clothes. When August died, the undertaker asked John for some clothes in which to bury his brother. John grudgingly gave them up. But John hesitated more at having to give up a pair of underwear the funeral man insisted on. After the service, before the burial, Raymond heard John say in all sincerity to the funeral director, "August doesn't need that underwear anymore. I'd like them back."

Laramore once drove thirteen hundred head of cattle on foot through some unfortunate town. The cattle trampled the patches of collard greens planted there. When

Laramore returned, this time in a '34 Chevy pickup, he entertained himself by rop-ing some of the women on the street. He ended up in jail that day.

In the 1930s Poncho and Boots had the awful job at the Home Ranch of executing four hundred head of cattle stricken by hoof and mouth disease. They loaded the cattle in trucks from pens that would have been located where the entrance is now, then took them to the canyon, shot them, and dumped them over the rim.

Red Everett worked at many ranches. He regularly sharpened his ax the night before in preparation for heading out to work before daybreak. One icy winter morning at the Home Ranch he wanted to chop oak brush for the goats before they scattered. He accidentally chopped off three of his toes. The fourth one was left dangling, so he thought he might as well chop that one off too.

Homer Alexander worked at the Hicks Ranch near Llano. As a girl, Mama always went with Raymond to check on these places. She got used to camping out in the primitive shacks. Everything the Alexanders ate came out of tin cans, which they just tossed out the window into the backyard. When the mountain of tin cans was about as tall as the house, rather than clean up the mess, they just moved the house to another location, like nomads moving to a fresh campsite.

Mama was always fascinated with the little grave at the Hicks Ranch and the sad story that went with it. A man named Sagabiel once lived there. He took his wife and baby down to Crabapple Creek to wash clothes. Indians showed up, so he put his wife and baby on a horse and said, "Run!" His wife dropped the baby in her des-perate flight. When the neighbors went back, they found Sagabiel murdered and the baby pinned to a tree with an arrow.

Red Rees was the son of Ida Stieler, Adolf's sister, who died when Red was a teen-ager. Adolf sent his nephew to New Mexico Military Institute for a disciplined edu-cation. But Red preferred following his older brother on the racehorse gambling circuit all over the country and learned a whole new lifestyle. Red was a red-faced, fun-loving young man. But eventually he returned to his uncle for work. That's how Red knew where the racetracks were in New Orleans, a place where he and Raymond could unload a truckload of sheep to rest overnight on their long hauling trip to Fitzhugh, Alabama.

The hauling trip was for Mr. Lucas, who had given Adolf a mohair market tip. Adolf was able to pick up warehouse loads of mohair in Llano and San Saba when mohair was at a low price. He lucked out with his speculation and made good on the rising prices. To return the favor, Lucas wanted Adolf to hire his brother-in-law for eight hundred dollars a month and teach him to raise livestock. Adolf declined but sent twenty-four ewes and a buck sheep to him in Alabama.

Raymond and Red were assigned to deliver them in a 1940 Chevy double-decker truck. After unloading and loading them one by one at Red's familiar racetrack, they reached Alabama, where the Lucas family received them in grand style. They were served a candlelit five-course dinner. Raymond had always eaten off one plate, so he combined all his food in a soup bowl and stacked the rest as it came. The next day Red told Raymond that he had embarrassed him. Raymond replied, "Not as much as you embarrassed me by asking for sow belly instead of bacon!"

On their return home with Red at the wheel, he embarrassed Raymond again by driving drunk and reckless through New Orleans, outrunning the law, until Raymond could get in control of the truck.

Werner Roeder, Raymond's brother-in-law, and another hand had loaded two truckloads of cattle in the dark and rain. Werner had to pull off the side of the road to help the other truck. He heard a loud noise and commotion. Werner's truck had sunk so deep in the mud that it fell over. He had to knock out the back wood rails to let all the cows out into the road. On another trip, Werner was taking a load of cattle from the Moldenhauer lease up a steep hill on Number Nine Road at the Bat Cave. The cows shifted, tipping the trailer backward, causing the cab to stick straight up in midair.

Gene Stieler, Adolf's son, described his "job from hell" at age sixteen at the Home Ranch. He was assigned to man the buzzard trap in the Big Pasture at the border-line of the neighboring Hillingdon Ranch. Dozens of buzzards would gang up and peck the eyes out of the ewes and their newborn lambs. You can't eat the meat of a pregnant ewe, and it's too labor-intensive to try to save the wool from dead sheep. Their only resort was to shoot the blind sheep.

Buzzards created big losses. The buzzard trap was a big wire cage, big enough to walk a horse into. Gene would have to lead an old horse there and shoot it for bait. The buzzards were trapped as they entered through a wire tube. Gene would shoot the buzzards and remove them from the cage. At the Block Creek Ranch, dead armadillos were used for buzzard bait.

A South Texas truck driver was hauling a load of sheep for Adolf through Arizona when he was stopped for having an overweight load. The truck driver said to the sheriff, "I have to call my boss, Adolf Stieler." Moments later the sheriff received a call and said into the phone, repeatedly, "Yes, sir. Yes, sir." Then the sheriff politely said, "It's okay, you can go now. Do you need anything?" "No," answered the truck driver, amazed at his merciful change of tone. "But who were you talking to?" "Barry Goldwater," said the sheriff.

Adolf was always working on the bigger picture for wool and mohair. Although he was far away from the ranch on a trip to Salt Lake and San Francisco for the National Wool Growers Conventions, he was still the Boss. He was preoccupied with keeping the hands busy back at the ranch. He wrote to his son Gene,

We just arrived here on way to San Francisco. We are here to meet with the President and Secretary of the California Wool Growers Association. They are fine fellows. We had a big convention at Salt Lake and found out that we may have trouble to buy wool bags. Would advise you to buy about 200 or 300 bags from Schreiner's, maybe 100 from Ingram and tell Raymond to get 300 or 400 from Werner, which I have already bought. Take them all out right away, as these warehouses may not be able to get them out later. Also some sewing twine (no tying twine). You may tell Charlie Schreiner to let us have 100 sacks. Put them all in our wool house at home.

Tell Raymond to put goats out of Section into Shack Pasture if live oak gets short in there. If boys get time they may take wagon and haul fireplace wood to house which they cut in Section. . . . Nothing definite on wool ceiling yet. Keep Leandro busy on fence as much as possible.

HS

The accounts listed in the 1943–1946 ranch ledger recorded every penny paid to and spent by the hired hands. The neat handwriting of Adolf's bookkeeper Edith Saga-biel shows salaries ranging from $25 a month plus room and board for Albert Reck to $40 a month for Joaquin Longoria and $50 a month for Emil Wieters. Werner Roeder rose from $55 a month in 1944 to $100 a month in 1946. There's a note that George Koester earned $40 a month, but also that Adolf Stieler owed him $1,165 at 5 percent interest.

Poncho Aguilar earned $60 a month. He was paid $15 for breaking three horses. He paid $4.70 for Levis from Kallison's Western Store, but most of the hands were outfitted at Comfort's popular Fellbaum and Flach, which carried saddles, tack, clothes, and food. There were numerous entries from Handy Andy Community Store, Juenke and Schoenewolf, and Keidel Drug, where medicine never cost more than $1.25. Keidel Hospital charged Poncho $135 for surgery. He paid ninety cents for five gallons of gas, and his electrical bill was $4.61.

Paging through the ledger, I came across a 1944 three-cent-stamped envelope from Wallis Drug in Murray, Kentucky. It was addressed simply to "Adolf Stieler Goat King, Comfort, Texas."

HS

Two faithful lifelong workers who became as close as family were Raymond Kuhl-mann and Arthur Eickenloff. Both were hired as teenagers because they could count sheep. A ruined new pair of dress shoes caused a furious sixteen-year-old Raymond to leave home. He walked from Morris Ranch at Tivydale all the way to the Home Ranch at Comfort. "I arrived at the Home Ranch on the day of grandmother Emma Stieler's funeral," he said. He remembered meeting his sister Adelle and Werner Roeder at the gate. "I sat in the back of their pickup and waited at the funeral. It was March 15, 1933."

His beginning at the Home Ranch marked the ending of his first business deal. For weeding peanut fields, Raymond was paid with four turkey hens and a gobbler.

I was afoot, so I put two in a sack at a time, cut holes for the heads to stick out, and walked halfway, left them under a tree and went back for the others. Walked 'em home this way to Morris Ranch. They disappeared for a while, but one day they smelled water at the house and flew back. I fed them that evening. I had good luck with them.

Our family of sixteen kids then moved to Bankersmith, near Luckenbach. Gas was ten cents a gallon then. I paid Felix Kuhlmann $1.00 a load to move us and my turkeys in his bobtail truck. I sold my young turkeys for $150.00. It was the first money I ever made. I'd always worn hand-me-downs. So I purchased some pants, a shirt, and some new dress shoes. It was customary to oil all the shoes with neat's-foot oil to waterproof them. When I came in from plowing one day, I discovered Margaret and Roland had not only oiled my dress shoes I'd never worn, but filled them with oil. I blew my top and slapped the hell out of them. I got a good beatin', no questions asked. I sat on a hill and waited 'til after dark. I threw the shoes as far as I could throw them. I gave the rest of my money to Mama. I dressed up and left and that's when I arrived over yonder, at the Stieler Ranch.

The Boss, as everyone called Adolf, was counting sheep at the windmill gate behind the feed barn. He missed the count and yelled to Raymond to do it. Raymond got the count right, so the Boss said, "You want to work?" Raymond said yes. He started at fifty cents a day.

His first job was to mix the feed in the big barn, fill the big carbide cans with it, and let them down on a rope from the top floor of the barn. He fed the ewes and the lambs in the barn that came up from the silo field. By the time the pastures greened up, the ewes and lambs were turned out. In the fall he helped move the sheep to the stubble fields in Comfort. Right away, at sixteen, he was trusted to drive trucks full of lambs in a Model A truck. Buyers would come to the railroad pens at Comfort to weigh and load them into railroad cars. Even though Raymond only went to the third grade in school, his real genius was his incredible memory for numbers. The 1943 ledger says he earned up to $50 a month, then $85 by 1946. By 1949, at thirty, he was one of Adolf's partners.

Raymond married beautiful Maria Enriquez, an older woman who was already working to help Dora at the Home Ranch. Maria cooked for nearly twenty ranch hands, helped with the housework, and was a nanny to Shatzie. Her parents worked at the Hillingdon Ranch. Raymond and Maria raised four kids: Jimmy (Biggie), Mary Ellen (Dittie), Raymond (Buster), and Jackie. The Kuhlmanns were like a family to us for our entire lives. Maria lived to be ninety-two. Her ashes were put under a wisteria tree planted on a triangle of grass we call the State Park in the Camp Shack Pasture, Mama's favorite view, overlooking the canyon hills she loves so.

Ϧ

My sons weren't exposed to much ranch life. But my son Kit and his wife, Jill, did get to live at Arthur and Stella Eickenloff's ranch in Blanco for six months. They got to see a real worker in action, "built Ford tough," as Kit said. They watched consistent persistent Arthur in his eighties get up early, work hard, eat lunch, take a little nap, then get back to work again.

Arthur had lived with his parents in Sisterdale. In 1928, the Boss was over there counting sheep at one of his ranches. A young boy standing behind him was also counting. "How many did you get?" the Boss asked. "Three hundred fifty-five," answered Arthur. That matched the Boss's count, so at age fourteen, Adolf took him home with him right then and there, never to return.

Arthur's first duties were to help Adolf's wife, Dora, in the kitchen. He emptied the melted ice water from the icebox and dried dishes. He was rewarded with what he thought was the best, a glass of cold raw milk.

Arthur slept with the other seven hands in the bunkhouse over the garage, where my art studio is now. Arthur remembered a cold freezing night at about two in the morning when he heard big heavy footsteps coming up the stairs. "Oh, no," he thought, "the Boss is coming for me. He's gonna make me do it!" The dreaded job Arthur was asked to do was to spend the night in the cold goat shed with hundreds of smelly goats, to keep them from piling up on each other to keep warm, therefore suffocating themselves. He would have to lift up each goat that went down. He put hay out for them, saving himself a bale to sleep on. The smoke from the wood-burning tin heater inside the four-foot-tall shed almost suffocated him. As he was trying to sleep that miserable night, a goat licked his face in commiseration.

The ranch ledger reports that Arthur's total expenditures for 1943 were $1,349.70. The legendary boot maker T. M. Little made him a pair of boots for $18.50. Arthur began imitating the Boss, giving orders, taking command. Soon he became a manager. He was sent to work at the Wilson and Franklin ranches, 14,500 acres over in Blanco. Adolf leased the Franklin from 1936 to 1950. The actor Jimmy Stewart leased it for five years after that. Arthur's house was a tent big enough to cover him—except for his feet, which stuck out in the rain. Arthur endured hardships daily that would kill or discourage most of us. He lived in the saddle and ate hard biscuits and jerky. He worked like a machine for ninety-four years.

When a young woman, Stella Deckert, first invited him to dinner at her parents' ranch in Blanco, he was grateful to sit at a real table and eat real food. Stella conquered her future husband through food. Arthur remembered every dish of food on the table seventy years later—testimonial to that fact.

"On that first date," Arthur proudly told Kit, "I rode my personal horse to her ranch, not the company horse."

On November 8, 2008, the last Kuhlmann, Raymond's oldest son, Jim, left the Home Ranch in a Medevac helicopter that had to land on Highway 87. He left from the same gate his sixteen-year-old father had arrived at seventy-five years earlier with only his lace-up boots in a flour sack. Jimmy was in a coma. A few hours later he died of a brain hemorrhage. He was sixty-eight.

My mantra for the past eighteen years, the time I had again been living at the Home Ranch, had been, "Just ask Jimmy." Between Raymond and Jimmy I had asked where every buried pipe, valve, and main cutoff was. With them, I mapped out a huge ancient underground network of clay and iron pipes that mysteriously knitted together water tanks, pens, water troughs, several houses, and many hydrants.

A few weeks before Jimmy died, he casually mentioned to me, "Whenever I die, wait for a real windy day and throw my ashes down over the canyon. Don't want any markers that I existed." But I am left with physical reminders, evidence of the Kuhlmann kids having lived and played here with us. Everything leaves a story: the rock steps that lead to my front door are broken because Buster rolled down them in a fifty-five-gallon barrel. The remains of a flagstone patio at Raymond's house were Mary Ellen's effort at a 4-H project. In the well lot, Werner stuck a metal file straight into the ground, never to be retrieved.

With Jimmy's departure, the last drop of common sense fled the Home Ranch.

Not one bit of know-how, ingenuity, or survival skill remained. I was left with only the rotten, fallen-down stuff and the cruel and precarious laws of nature and gravity to watch over me. No one was in charge, and I felt it.

Ranches That Were

Adolf was never still.

Because of rising and falling prices of wool and livestock, droughts, and destructive weather, he shuffled his sheep, goats, and cattle around wherever he could find land. He was able to buy land and goats cheaply during the Depression—with the help of the bank, of course. He stayed broke most of the time. "It was nip and tuck," said Raymond.

It was said you could walk from the Home Ranch in Kerr County to the ranches in Blanco County and never be off Adolf Stieler's property. His son Gene said, "He didn't raise sheep and goats; he bought and sold them." Raymond said he was more of a sheep and goat gambler than a rancher. His land holdings were not especially large compared to some of Texas's big outfits, which have been written about so often, but Adolf ran more goats from the 1930s to the 1950s than anyone else since Angoras were brought to the United States in 1849.

Adolf's great quality was his perseverance. What made him outstanding in his field was that he was still standing. Through the hard times, he always bounced back with the deliberate determination of nature itself, no matter what disaster derailed him. He did it with risk, philanthropic generosity, a jovial attitude, a relentless work ethic, and resilience to tragedy. "People once called me the Goat King," he said. "Later they called me goat stieler. And now they just call me the old goat. If I had to do it all over again, I'd go into the goat business."

It is considered bad taste to ask a rancher how big his spread is. But these are some of the ranches I heard about, owned or leased, from 1920 to 1970. They served a purpose, the ranches being connected one to the other. Adolf could practically walk across Texas herding his goats on foot. Collectively, these large or small pieces made up the ranch that was us.

Home Ranch (Kerr and Kendall Counties)	5,160 acres
YO–Weaver (Mountain Home, Edward County)	17,000 acres
Block Creek (Sisterdale, Kendall County)	3,000 acres
Stowers #1 (Kerr and Edwards Counties)	11,888 acres
Stowers #2 (San Antonio, Bexar County)	10,000 acres
Manchaca (Blanco and Kendall Counties)	2,100 acres
Wenzel (Blanco County)	1,800 acres
Franklin (Blanco County)	9,500 acres
Three Twenty (Blanco County)	320 acres
Leroy Brammer (Blanco County)	750 acres
Delaware (Blanco County)	950 acres
Wilson (Johnson City, Blanco County)	5,000 acres
Dreiss Flat Rock (Kendall County)	2,000 acres
Hobbs (Blanco County)	320 acres
Sieben Eichen (Sisterdale, Kendall County)	700 acres
Schladoer (Blanco County)	600 acres
Sykes (Kendall County)	1,500 acres
Land/Borchers (Kendall County)	2,000 acres
Uecker (Kendall and Blanco Counties)	1,600 acres
Esperanza (South Bexar County)	2,670 acres
Sultemeier (Kendall County)	160 acres
Elmendorf (South Bexar County)	3,800 acres
Little Bit (Kendall County)	200 acres
Cotulla (La Salle County)	3,000 acres
The Herman Kohte (Cherry Springs, Gillespie County)	500 acres
Moldenhauer (Kendall County)	500 acres
Hicks (Llano County)	5,500 acres
Crocket Morrison (Uvalde County)	5,000 acres
The Hohman (Llano County)	1,200 acres
Kickapoo (Real County)	1,500 acres

Fryer (Leakey, Real County)	2,000 acres
Black Bull (South Fork of Guadalupe River, Kerr and Real Counties)	55,000 acres
O'Keefe Ranch (Sierra Blanca, Hudspeth County)	118,000 acres

From 1938 to 1960, Adolf leased the Stowers Ranches from the owners of the Stowers furniture stores. Stowers #1 was an 11,800-acre ranch in Kerr and Edwards Counties. An ex–bull rider, Tom Sperger, and his wife, Margie, ran the ranch. I remember as a girl hunting arrowheads in a field of plowed dirt and coming across a treasure—a killdeer nest on the ground made entirely of flint chips. My eyes sifted out a perfect bird-point arrowhead and drill.

"Adolf ran six or seven thousand goats there," Raymond said. "We'd chop oak trees down for them to eat for the winter. The cedar was so thick there you couldn't blow smoke through it."

"I started riding for my dad when I was seven," Raymond's son Jimmy told me. "There were many rattlesnakes at the Stowers. I was riding horseback with Dad and Tom. We saw a huge rattlesnake scurry by and watched it crawl under a big four-foot boulder. Dad told me to rope the big rock and lift it up. We saw about fifty rattlers crawling around under there." Raymond claimed to have witnessed this phenomenon: a mother rattlesnake, sensing danger, swallowed her fourteen babies to protect them. "Put the rock back down!" ordered Raymond. They waited there while Tom went back for a gallon of gasoline, then set fire to the nest. The large numbers of sheep and goats back then were easy prey for coyotes, buzzard, eagles, and wild dogs. Thousands were lost. The rattlesnake was a threat not only to livestock but to humans, dogs, and horses as well.

Stowers #2 was a ten-thousand-acre ranch where Military Highway and 1604 now are located in San Antonio. It adjoined Camp Bullis. During World War I, the US Army leased the ranch for maneuvers, which explained the unexploded cannon shells lying around.

One pasture was four thousand acres. The windmill man who lived on the place named the pastures: East Mill, Broke Down Mill, Bull's Mill, Pump Jack Mill. The army had shot at all the windmills. The windmill man knew everything there was to know about windmills and wells, but he didn't want a phone. He wanted people to find and come to him. Neither did Red Rees want a phone. He was Adolf's nephew's hired hand, living on the place in the two-story white house with thirteen rooms. But there was one time when Red did need a phone.

Raymond's nephew Alfred Kuhlmann slept up at the bunkhouse over the garage at the Home Ranch. "At four one morning," Alfred said, "Adolf came and woke up three of us. He handed each of us shotguns and boxes of shells." "Raymond is taking you over to the Stowers," Adolf said. "The pack of wild dogs is out of control killing sheep, and Red can't handle it by himself." "We were left there for four days and nights," Alfred said. "Just that first night we killed fifty-six dogs. Boy, my shoulder hurt for days after that!"

In the 1960s, Hondo and Raymond were partners at Stowers #2. They would bring back fifty-five-gallon drums of food scraps from Camp Bullis Army Post to feed the hogs they'd gathered at the Hicks Ranch. From that they salvaged a five-gallon bucket full of knives and forks that had been thrown away with the slop. "US" stamped on the flatware marked it as government property.

At the other Stowers Ranch near Hunt, Hondo had noticed Tom and Margie's monogrammed towels saying "His" and "Hers." "That sure is a lot of togetherness," Hondo jealously commented to Raymond. "But we have 'US' written on our silverware!"

Adolf leased the YO–Weaver, a seventeen-thousand-acre ranch, from Walter Schreiner's widow, Myrtle, from 1942 to 1952. In those days, the leasers made all the improvements on land they didn't own. Adolf drilled wells, built windmills, and improved fences. Adolf was dating Myrtle at the time and had marriage in mind. But both were headstrong and hotheaded, and it ended in a standoff.

"We had five thousand goats up there," Raymond remembered. "Don't remember how many sheep. The Reyna family, Leandro Longoria, Charlie Everett, and Walter Wehmeyer worked up there. Shatzie went along to cook on a gas stove for everyone during shearing time."

Gene and his wife, Odette, lived at the Weaver and managed it for ten years. Gene went to the Sierra Blanca Ranch when that lease was up. Gene told me that Leandro Longoria rode a gray mare named Brigham.

We would get up at four a.m., with our lunch tied to the saddle horn. We began our seven-mile ride to check wormies in a ten-thousand-acre pasture. If we got there too late, the sheep were already scattered, looking for shade under the brush. It was hot out there.

We killed hundreds of rattlesnakes on that ranch. One time the goats wouldn't go into a pen to the shed. They made a wide circle away from the gatepost because a rattlesnake was coiled up there. The goats had forced it up and held it at the post. Walter Wehmeyer reached down, grabbed it fast, threw it down to the ground real hard, and stomped on it!

Gene grinned, a tough twinkle gleaming in his eyes. "That's when a man was a man!"

$$\vdash_\smallsmile$$

The O'Keefe Ranch at Sierra Blanca was the biggest ranch Adolf owned. Comprising more than 180 sections, or about 118,000 acres, it was originally state land near El Paso. Almost pure desert, brush, thorns, and ditches, it was surrounded by the blue Sierra Blanca Mountains. Gene ranched 26,000 acres, and Adolf shared ownership of 92,000 acres north of Gene with Comfort banker Albert Faltin. They bought it in 1947 for six dollars an acre, when land was forty dollars an acre in the Hill Country.

I lived there with Mama, Hondo, and my brother Juan for a year in 1950, when I was five. Gene was the main operator for ten years. I had a pet crow that ate grapes out of my hand. The sheriff, Joe Carson, gave me a Shetland pony that I named Smokey Joe Carson and rode in the Fourth of July Parade in Sierra Blanca. As girls, my cousin Sandra Stieler and I freely galloped horses over the plains. They rolled with us in the water tanks, leaving us to slip and slide in the muddy saddles at top run as we hung on for dear life. Our playmates were prairie dogs. It was at this ranch that Mama made her brother Gene a birthday cake out of a dried cow patty, decorated with delicious-looking pink icing that we kids danced by, swiping it with our fingers. When he cut into it for his first bite, it wasn't as dried as we'd thought.

There were dead coyotes, wild dogs, and rattlesnakes hanging like trophies or warnings on miles of fences. Sheep, goats, and cattle were raised there. "It was not good for goats," said Gene. "We lost hundreds and hundreds due to malnutrition and predators." Adolf sold it in 1964.

For a cattle roundup on that vast open space Raymond, Gene, and Werner and Owen Roberts and their horses were hauled in a trailer truck to the back of a twenty-section pasture before daybreak. "We unloaded our horses, and it took until two thirty p.m. to arrive at the house. We were five cows short. Owen Roberts lost five cows, so we put him on pipeline duty instead of the fence line."

Water and the pipeline were definitely the most difficult priorities on that ranch. The most important thing Adolf did for the town of Sierra Blanca was to bring it water, which had previously been trucked in. The ranch was watered by pump jacks, which looked like oil-well pumps.

"If it rained as far away as New Mexico," Raymond said, "then our dirt tank here in West Texas filled up with water. We put a little windmill there and ran water through every seven miles of pipe to a pump that continued on to more pumps, pipeline, and troughs." Raymond had never seen such a huge water tank, made out of a hundred-thousand-gallon oil tank. It collected water from forty-two miles of pipeline buried in the sand. It was labor-intensive to hire someone to weld all the cracks caused by sun, ice, wind, and sand erosion.

"At times when there was little or no water in that huge tank, there was still enough water in the forty-two miles of pipe to last three months for the house," Raymond had calculated. After Adolf's hard work, and the expense and maintenance involved in bringing water to his ranch and to the town of Sierra Blanca, he was angry when the city sent him a water bill.

H)

A colorful member of the family, and the most influential mentor to Adolf, was his uncle Robert Real. Adolf's mother, Emma Real Stieler, was Robert's sister. From him, Adolf learned the art of raising and trading livestock. Robert, one of eight children of Caspar and Emilie Schreiner Real, was the nephew of Captain Charles Schreiner. He had been in charge of the Schreiner empire of ranches since 1880, some six hundred thousand acres in Kerr, Kimble, and Edwards Counties known as the YO.

YO stood for "y otros" ("and others" in Spanish), or so I was told by a descendant of the Taylor family. The Taylor-Clement Ranch, originally from Goliad County under the YO brand, moved to the Harper area, and Captain Schreiner bought it in the late 1870s. He kept the existing brand on the longhorn cattle.

Uncle Robert's expertise was in sheep and goats, which he learned from his father Caspar Real, another leading sheep raiser who, in 1879, was Kerr County's first sheep inspector. Now his son Robert was in charge of his uncle Schreiner's huge flock of forty thousand head of sheep. In 1913, Charles Schreiner wrote to Robert on the stationery of the St. Anthony Hotel, where he kept a permanent residence when in San Antonio. Robert's scope of responsibility was vast.

Dear Robert: . . . I am afraid we will have a low tariff [tax on imported wool]. . . . If the tariff on wool is very much reduced a few meat sheep no doubt will go down. . . . We better feed a thousand with cracked cake. We have plenty on hand and it wouldn't cost us so very much. We ought to sell nearly as many sheep as we raise . . . and if necessary order a lot of cake and go feed 2,000 to 2,500 head. . . . We want to plant milo maize and kaffin corn. I believe we can easily raise all the feed we need on the different ranches. . . . Please notify the other ranch hands also. . . . With best wishes, your uncle, Chas. Schreiner

Uncle Robert's headquarters was the 64,000-acre YO–Live Oak, from which he sent out instructions to all other ranches. He was authoritative, shrewd, and a tough taskmaster in getting work done—and done right.

A stocky man with a big white Teddy Roosevelt mustache, he was known for his strict, arrogant demand for respect, especially from his workers. The Live Oak was actually a little town in itself, with a school, a store, about a dozen houses, and a jail, which Robert himself built to keep any unruly workers in line. Any worker who approached his fenced-in cabin and didn't take his hat off out of respect faced the possibility of being shot. In fact, Robert did shoot someone once who crossed over the stile with his hat on, and he got away with it.

Robert always slept with a pistol and a bottle of whiskey by his bed. My cousin Felix Real told me that when Robert was in the hospital in San Antonio, a nurse said, "You can't have that liquor in this room." Pointing his pistol at the nurse, he said, "This says I can."

My cousin Albert Keidel went with his father, Dr. Victor Keidel, on many house calls to see Uncle Robert. His unpainted house was up on stilts, with hound dogs lying underneath. Children who came there had to stay in the kitchen with Robert's common-law Mexican wife, Lulu, who could often be found there hacking up a kid goat to fry like a chicken. Albert was finicky about drinking whiskey with him because Uncle Robert would take a glass off the mantle, wipe out the tobacco spit with his finger, and pour him a drink. Likewise, Albert was finicky about eating Tante Hedwig Stieler's lettuce, cream, and sugar sandwiches because he knew she poured the "night water" from the chamber pot onto her lettuce garden.

Robert liked it out there in that lonely country. There were ten miles of rocky road between Robert's headquarters and the county road. "Why don't you ever fix your road?" my grandmother Dora would ask. Robert replied that his real friends would still come, and the others he didn't care about anyway. A chauffeur drove Robert around in a Model T touring car, since he never learned to drive. My grandparents Adolf and Dora always picked him up to go to San Angelo for the Sheep and Goat Raisers Convention. When he met them at his gate, Dora asked, "Where's your suitcase?" "Here," he said, holding a rolled-up paper bag containing a change of underwear, his gun, and a bottle of whiskey.

Uncle Robert inherited 10,000 acres of the 64,000-acre YO–Live Oak from Captain Charles Schreiner. He and Lulu had one daughter, Elvira, who married Ernest Love. They had a son, Robert Love.

In 1937, when Robert Real died, Adolf bought his nine thousand sheep. Twenty-year-old Raymond was in charge of rounding them up in a ten-thousand-acre pasture. As usual, he amazed me by remembering the details sixty-eight years later. Slim Ely, Robert Lott, Herman Whitney, Manuel Ayala, Jim Heffner, and George and Ace Tomlin helped out.

I'll never forget. It was on a Sunday in the hot summer. Starting at two a.m., we heard the chickens squawking in the trees. That was the Boss, Adolf, who wanted us to start early. He'd called in thirteen double-deck trailer trucks to haul the sheep to Fort Worth and other places.

We made a big roundup in the ten-thousand-acre pasture called Double Wells, and we pushed the sheep into an eighty-five-acre field. We hobbled our horses and ate our lunch. That evening we counted and were missing 123 sheep. It rained that night and there was water all over the ranch. We rode again on Monday, Tuesday, Wednesday, Thursday, and were still short, so we quit. Friday we found the rest.

I don't know what was harder, rounding up nine thousand sheep in the hot sun and rain in a ten-thousand-acre pasture, or lifting each of them by hand to the upper decks of thirteen trucks.

HS

The Best People on Earth Are Dogs and Horses

"I never use a rope on an animal," I heard my grandfather say. "That means you can't control it." Adolf got in the pens with his one and only arm holding his wooden stock cane—his shepherd's crook—to catch the hind leg or neck of a sheep or goat. But the most indispensable tool, the one no stockman could do without, was a good border collie sheepdog, which in German we called a *Schäferhund*. Not many people are closely in tune with animals anymore. But when I see those who are, that lost art of the unspoken understanding between human and animal always amazes me.

Raymond recalled how tuned in his dog was to him. As a boy, he trekked all over the countryside barefooted, with his dog following close behind. If he got a sticker, he just lifted his foot and the dog pulled the sticker out with his teeth; Raymond didn't even have to look back.

Raymond trained more sheepdogs in his eighty-eight years than anyone I know. There were Old Gyp, Lucy, Tippie, Lil, Freckles, Banjo, Fiddle, and Dean. Queenie was a shorthaired hunting dog. "Rascal was the best dog I ever had," Raymond said. "Someone backed over him and he was crippled.

"Then there was Sport. One time Sport came scratching and whining at the kitchen door. They followed her back behind the barn, where they found old man Roland, a hired hand, crying, with a board with a nail stuck in his foot."

And then there was Nettie. "Nettie was great in the pens, but she wasn't good in the pasture. She'd quit the sheep to run a deer," Raymond said. "She'd look up in the trees for varmints. She'd see a squirrel and beat it to the tree."

The really smart ones he didn't have to train. Bozo was one of those dogs. "Pretty smart, pretty smart," Adolf said about Bozo, and he was right. Raymond agreed, saying, "A very good dog. If I put my saddle on a horse, no one else better dare go untie my horse. Bozo protected my property with fierce loyalty and would growl anyone away who came near my horse."

Once, at the Home Ranch in the 1930s, Raymond saw some wild pigs in the twelve-hundred-acre Big Pasture, across the highway in the canyon that joins the Alfred Giles Hillingdon Ranch. Adolf had gotten very good hounds from Jess Johnson in Llano. But after weeks of trying to get those sows with Johnson's hounds, Adolf and his brother Fritz gave up. "They could only pester them so far from their bedding grounds. Then they'd scatter like birds," Raymond said. "No luck."

"I'll never forget," Raymond continued. "One day I was shedding goats in the goat shed in the Big Pasture. I had all of the pens open. I heard Bozo bark, but it was a different bark, a different tone of voice. So I said, to heck with the goats, he has something. He's smart. I saw Bozo with those wild pigs. He held the pigs by running circles around and around and around them. Then he'd dash in and nip a sow, stay a distance, look over his shoulder but run towards the house. Then he'd take after 'em again, but run 'em towards the house. Again and again he'd circle 'em, nip at one, run towards the house until finally, they rallied at the gate. Bozo took off down the fence line. He entered a hole he knew about in the fence, dashed in, and nipped a sow. She followed him in with all the others, and I shut the gate. There were six sows and forty-two pigs. I loaded those pigs in the bobtail and put 'em in Werner's Lot. Fed 'em, let 'em grow out. At that time we had as many as seventy to eighty out there."

$$\vdash\varsigma$$

"Coke was a beautiful chestnut sorrel," Raymond once told me. "He worked with me and Bozo. He wasn't a good stock horse, but he was wonderful to ride. He was a show horse we bought from old man Keller for fifteen dollars. Coke would lie down to be shod. And when he was saddled, Coke would lie down and you could walk on him. He would rear up on his hind legs, and I could hold his front feet in my hands. Coke would lean against the barn while I put a fifty-pound sack of corn

in the saddle. From the saddle, I'd open the gate, strike a lope, pull the string on the sack of corn, and let it spill out around the oak tree in Werner's Lot. That's how I threw out nine hundred pounds of corn a day to those eighty pigs."

If you had common sense and one good dog, many problems could be solved. There was the time at the Elmendorf farm south of San Antonio when a cow was hanging around an irrigation pipe that went under a county road. The cow kept bawling for her lost calf. Raymond's first thought was that maybe it was stolen. A lot of rustling went on down there. Then he deduced that the calf had fallen into the siphon pipe filled with standing water, where there could be deadly gas pockets. How to get the calf out of either opening was the challenge. He pitched his dog Jet into the pipe, which went straight down. When Raymond called, Jet would bark, scaring the calf out of the other end, where Raymond waited with a loop on a rope. He then lifted Jet out by a chain.

"Jet had thirteen pups that a neighbor killed with 1080 rat poison," Raymond said. "She carried all thirteen dead pups to the screen door and laid them there so as to ask for help. Jet worked a lot of ranches. She was at the Block Creek during the floods. In '69 she was getting old, and she was run over at the Elmendorf."

Dogs were also used to reunite the cows with their calves when they got separated. Cows didn't always pair up with their calves after they were worked or moved. Raymond would push the cows out into a field and tie the dogs near the calves, which were in another pen. When he'd call the tethered dogs, they'd bark, and the mamas would come running to their babies.

"In later years I switched from border collies to kelpies. Deacon was one of 'em," Raymond said. "They were shorthairs, and they had to sit in the front seat with me muddy. I didn't have to clean 'em much—just rub 'em off with a gunnysack."

Mama's two personal dogs were Hero and Tiny. Hero was a huge black Newfoundland given to her by her uncle, Dr. Victor Keidel, to be her guardian. As a young girl, she was free to roam that big ranch down to the canyon, playing in the springs or in some pasture. Hero was faithfully by her side, so no one worried about her safety or whereabouts. "The happiest day of Hero's life," Mama remembered, "was when it hailed and the pond behind Werner's house froze over. Hero played, ran, slipped, and slid on that ice all day long, as if he knew he was finally the cold-weather dog he was bred to be."

Then there was Tiny, a little fox terrier. The saddest day of Tiny's life was December 3, 1947. Mama, still living at the Home Ranch, gave birth to Juan on the front seat of the pickup truck on the way to town. She was hospitalized for two weeks, as was customary then. Back at the ranch, after smelling her blood in the truck, Tiny ran and ran and ran around that truck, going crazy with grief, until she just keeled over and died.

The horses of the Home Ranch were as memorable as the people who worked there. During the 1930s, besides Coke, there was Cricket, a paint mare whose eye was stricken with cancer and had to be removed. Mable was another paint. Punk was an all-around big strong short-backed horse that was used to break colts to a hackamore by ponying them alongside. When the colt sat down, Punk dragged it. It only took once, and the colt didn't throw down after that.

Mama's girlhood horse was a big bay thoroughbred mare named Mocky, given to her by her uncle, Dr. Victor Keidel. Mocky's bloodline was from the famous racehorse Man o' War. At twelve, when Mama was sent off to St. Mary's Hall school in San Antonio, Mocky went with her. She took riding and hunter-jumper lessons at Brackenridge Stables. Whenever Mama came home to the ranch with her thoroughbred and English saddle, the ranch hands teased her. She was embarrassed that her horse was not one of the more "useful" stock horses and even hid her English saddle.

Her favorite place to ride Mocky was in the Blackjack and Post Oak pastures across the highway at night to hunt raccoons. There would be a full moon when she rode with her Uncle Victor. Sometimes they'd have to smoke the coons out of their hollow in the trees by building little fires in them. Her horse just followed the dogs. At two or three in the morning, Mocky would carry her home asleep in the saddle.

In San Antonio recently, at Huebner and Fredericksburg Road, Mama looked over from the I-10 freeway at the concrete jungle full of buildings, parking lots, skyscrapers, and asphalt. "I remember riding there! For miles, the western part of San Antonio used to be all open country then, and Mocky and I ran and ran and ran. Once a week I rode with my boyfriend Peon, a Cuban from Peacock Military School, who was the best rider and captain of his drill company. He chose me for his partner. As a group, we rode wild, jumping ditches and fallen trees, free and open. What a thrill! He was a good dancer at our little dorm dance nights. He was proud and respectful, and he wanted me to come to Havana in the summer to meet his parents. Boy! I kept that secret from Daddy."

Her memory mirage of open prairies and princes quickly vanished in the smog. Looking over at the sea of choking development, it was hard to imagine a time when one could run fast and free as the wind on horseback there.

Smokey, named after the writer Will James's horse, was one of the best horses that ever came to the Home Ranch. Stolen horses from Mexico were hot items in the early 1920s because Mexicans had the most expensive, highest-quality horses. Our friend, Texas Ranger Charlie Miller, brought that horse to the ranch as stolen property disguised as a gift, and no one ever knew. It was never known which side of the law Ranger Charlie was on. But a stream of stolen horses from Mexico came through here, and the game warden and Charlie were involved somehow—chasing, hiding, or finding.

Because Smokey the beautiful stallion was a hot item, he was sent out of sight to the Franklin Ranch. He became the horse of Arthur Eickenloff, who was living the bachelor life there in a tent. But some local Mexicans knew about Smokey and wanted him for themselves. They tracked Arthur down at the Pflugrath dance hall near Blanco, beat him up, and threatened to kill him, but they never got Smokey from him.

Raymond's names for horses revealed their personalities. Politician took one step forward and then two sideways. High Pockets was tall. Enchilada took his name from his saucy red color. Rocket Lady and Dunny, rough-riding but with great endurance, were the only form of transportation that could navigate up Thunder Mountain and the rough hills at the Block Creek Ranch where no vehicle could go.

Rocket Lady and Dunny belonged to Juan. "I bonded with Dunny like no other horse. Horse and man," Juan confessed. "He was a big Spanish dun, wore a size two horseshoe. He was raised on the Block Creek, so his feet knew rocks and hills. If you approached a creek, you better hang on, 'cause he was gonna jump it. I could ride on him backwards, bareback, down a hill."

Before Juan went off to Vietnam, he had worked most of his young life with Raymond, Hondo, or Adolf. "You can have sheep packed tight in a pen," Juan recalled. "Open a gate, and for some reason they won't cross that invisible line to go out of it. Once they were packed in there so tight it was impassible by human, dog, or horse. So Raymond threw a dog on top of those sheep, and it ran across their backs to the gate. The dog pushed one or two through, then they all followed. It was like, you know, breaking the surface tension on a bubble of water and all the water flows through," Juan said, making a scientific comparison, as was his custom. "When I was little," he continued, "I could scamper across those woolly backs full of stickers like a monkey and do the same as the dog."

Once he saw what he called "the darndest thing." Said Juan, "I was pushing sheep through a pen and they were stopped, crammed, wouldn't budge to go through an open gate. I was on Dunny. Dunny stamped his feet, and they still didn't move. Finally, Dunny picked up a sheep with his teeth and threw it forward. He threw several. It caused the whole group to move. No one ever knew how I became one with that horse."

$$\vdash \!\! S$$

"You want a 'What are you gonna do now' story, Becky?" Juan asked me recently as we sat around a table at Luckenbach eating fried catfish. His daredevil eyes twinkled in front of many memories packed in his head, and I was baited. Juan's latest hunting dog, Tula, rubbed up against all of us under the picnic table.

"We were taking a nap after a hard morning of work at the Elmendorf in South Texas. It was hotter 'n hell inside those thick adobe walls of the ruins that were attached to the shabby frame house. Dogs woke us up barkin'. I thought, there's another bored, hyper border collie with nothing to do but run the horses around in a pen in the 103-degree heat. All of a sudden the bark turned into a loud wailing and yelping. Raymond and I ran out there to see what happened."

They soon learned that a horse had kicked the dog in the face. "It was a brutal kick that looked like it'd smashed its face in. We'd never seen such a gruesome sight. The dog ran over to Raymond, still crying. When it opened its mouth, the teeth were still clenched, but the roof of its mouth was separated from the top of its head. We were shocked to see inside the head, sinuses and all, jaws still shut. In a panic I said, 'What're we gonna do now, Raymond?' Raymond grabbed the hysterical dog and had to wrestle it to hold it firmly between his legs. He clamped down on the dog's mouth, holding it together as hard as he could. He held it tight for what seemed like a long time—maybe two or more minutes," Juan remembered. "When he let go of him, the roof of the mouth stuck to the top of the head. That dog lived to work many more days."

$$\vdash \!\! S$$

One dog can do more work than you can, or it can cause more work for you. Juan and Raymond were working sheep at the Wenzel one hot July day. The wire fence that encircled the house kept in twelve chickens—and one bored sheepdog with nothing to do. The dog, used to working every moving thing in sight, didn't spare the chickens. He had cornered them where they couldn't escape through the V-wire fence, and he took his time nipping at them until there was barely a feather left on them. No blood, no nicks, no bites, but just about every feather had been skillfully plucked from twelve chickens by one dog.

"What are we gonna do now?" Juan asked Raymond when they faced this surprise discovery. "Wring necks, Juan. Let's get busy. Without feathers, they won't last long in this heat," Raymond said. "I learned how to ring necks, gut chickens, and painstakingly pick off every remaining feather," Juan said. "It took hours. I'd rather have been working sheep."

ᚼ

"I can still hear her breathing. Everywhere I look on this ranch I can see her," Juan said of his great love. "She was beautiful to look at. Sitting in the front seat of my truck, she held her regal head like Queen Nefertiti. When my wife left, she took everything—my son, my furniture, my dishes, my dog Mietze. Now this loyal creature is all I have. She ran around like she owned this three-thousand-acre ranch. I lived with her for four years. She only left me once—rode off in Benji Frantzen's van one night at Luckenbach. But she returned, to be at my side, comfort me. She was someone to come home to at night. And I loved her more than anything."

"She," the great love of Juan's life, was Pepper, a sleek black hunting dog who died by Juan's own truck tire at nine thirty on the night of May 22, 2000. She had been running alongside the truck as usual. But it was Juan's history of bad luck to keep losing dogs, trucks, and women. This would be an especially painful loss.

"Those mute animals can say more with their eyes than we humans can with our mouths," Juan said. "Call it body language or horse whispering. It is a silent communication. Whether I'd be arguing with someone or kissing someone," Juan confessed, "Pepper'd get right in between us to referee or join in."

Juan recalled that on the last day of Pepper's life, she "dove into a cactus patch to catch a big raccoon. She wrestled with it, killed it, and proudly brought it to me, head held high. She was patient and brave as many an hour I'd pull porcupine quills out of her tongue and face. Cactus thorns, too."

Juan added, "She always knew what to kill and what to rescue. One time I was sitting on a stump, feeling low, and Pepper came up with something hidden in her mouth—a surprise. She nudged my hands open and put a tiny baby rabbit in them, alive and unharmed."

Sock was a big powerful sorrel gelding that came to the ranch as a stud named Woody. Woody put in his work years with Raymond on several ranches. Then, when no one was interested in him anymore, Woody was put out to pasture and ignored for ten years.

With a passion for Civil War history, my son Sky, at fifteen, announced that he would like to be in a Confederate cavalry reenactment group. After locating such a rare thing, Terry's Texas Rangers in Dripping Springs, all he lacked was a horse. Sky knew nothing about horses, but he found the huge sorrel gelding in the highway pasture at Hondo's ranch. He jumped on him bareback and rode up the hill out of sight, where he was promptly bucked off. Sky named him Sock for his one white foot. After Sock passed the gunfire test, not shying from an overhead shot made by a loud black powder pistol, Sky became the youngest inductee into this wild outfit.

Throughout the years, Sock seemed to be one of the few constants in our lives. He was the only steady family member for Sky after the time of my divorce and move from San Antonio to the Home Ranch. With Sock, we all experienced some of the happiest, most wonderful moments of our lives.

Sock's greatest purpose in life was to be Sky's mount for the next three years in great and glorious battle campaigns of the Old South. In field drills and high battle, Sock galloped, oblivious to revolvers and sawed-off shotguns blasting in his ears, the flapping of waving flags, rebel yells, or the slash and clank of drawn sabers. He was the only horse to behave on a picket line all night long. One time, on a practice weekend with his rebel ruffians, Sky ducked his head to ride Sock into a bar without hesitation when all the other horses had balked. There was barely room for the big horse to turn around among the chairs and the customers in the bar. He didn't even flinch with everyone's rowdy cheers.

Sock and Sky participated in a campaign at Corinth, Mississippi, in the retreat from Shiloh. It was a real endurance test, for they slept in the rain and lived in the saddle for three nights and days. Sock carried everything they needed—food for horse and man and extra horseshoes.

One of those lifetime experiences came several years later, when I rode Sock with my second husband, Oscar Barrales, and his group, the San Antonio Charros, in the prestigious and colorful Battle of Flowers Parade during Fiesta in San Antonio. The charros are the most elegant, heart-stopping vision in the parade, with their sombreros and custom-made trajes, twirling maguey ropes. Perched on my sidesaddle throne alongside high-stepping horses and nervous prancing stallions, I proudly rode my big, steady, calm ranch gelding, whose head hung low. He could have been walking asleep, for all I knew. Sock plodded over empty bottles, not flinching at the confusion of noise, balloons, confetti. As he carried me through the downtown streets of San Antonio among thousands of spectators, I felt as if I were in a dream, an elegant, proud woman of Seville.

Oscar once used Sock in a horse-training experiment to teach an oversexed stallion a lesson. This big palomino stallion wanted to get at everything in sight, from mares to geldings. He would even undo latches, knots, and fences to try. But Oscar summoned old Sock, who was even bigger. Oscar tied them together four inches apart, cheek to cheek, and forced them to run around in a round pen. The training trick eventually cured the palomino.

Eventually Sock was getting old and crippled. It was harder and harder for him to walk. Sock's last assignment was carried out with humility and shame: the mighty warhorse was offered up for pony rides on my granddaughter Emmalyne's fifth birthday. Sock stood patiently as we snaked hot pink vet wrap around his legs, tied pink ribbons and flowers into his long, rusty mane and tail, and threw a velvet pink blanket over his saddle. Sock limped along slowly, painfully, but planting in every eager kid a memory of thrill and elation, over and over.

A cool purple glow simmered on the eastern horizon, about to give birth to January 29, 2007. I rushed to the barns as usual to check on Sock, who was lying down paralyzed on the cold ground. We'd brought Sock and pasture mate Brownie in from the Hundred Acres for shelter from the ice and snow storms. I summoned Sky to help me roll Sock to his feet. Sock belonged to Sky and Sky belonged to Sock, a thirteen-year relationship. Both were twenty-eight years old. With his last burst of energy, Sock struggled to his feet. It was a huge effort that raised him up, teetering on trembling legs that were frozen stiff.

"We have to be realistic, Sky. Sock isn't having fun living anymore," I gently hinted. "Are you with me?" Sky mumbled, "I get it." My head knew before my heart agreed that today I had to do something. Weakness gently pushed me to be strong. I tried to get courage talking to the vet's secretary. Dr. Pat O'Neil would come at four p.m. She suggested a horse gravedigger, Abel Cantú, whose family lived at Luckenbach. We wanted to do the most honorable for Sock—no buzzard bait, no brush pile, no bullet.

Abel's backhoe hit rock on a grassy clearing on the 1950 airplane landing strip after we'd tried several other even rockier places. But Abel's machine dug, roared, banged, shook, and chopped through to make a gaping hole eight feet cubed, big enough for a septic tank.

Throughout the day, Sock had goodbye visitors. Neighbor Michael Malone had bonded with the horse when he rode arthritic Sock at full gallop in a movie filmed on the ranch. Sky and friend brought Sock a last snack. I picked ticks off his warm shiny red coat, which glistened copper in the sun. We rubbed his sad watery eyes, caressed his scarred white blaze on his tired worn face and blistered nose. We talked to him, appreciated his faithfulness. How he'd tolerated our whims. All of the wonderful varied memories ran like a movie film through our minds.

Now, at four p.m., I went back up to the barn with dread. I haltered Brownie first. Sock followed close behind, wanting to be with people too. Sky haltered Sock in a new rainbow-bright halter and lead rope. With Sky leading limping Sock and his friend leading Brownie, they started the long slow march to the plot in the Hundred Acres, proceeding as slowly as possible. At this point, we were all shifting into robot gear.

Michael met them halfway. The procession stopped. When Michael cut some souvenir horsehair from Sock's mane and tail to use in making memorial hatbands later, a sense of reality finally brought tears to Sky. "I'd made up my mind to be tough and not cry," Sky admitted later. "Shatzie handed me something like a handkerchief out of her purse in case I did cry. I stuffed it in my pocket without looking at it."

Doctor Pat approached the tearful group with a somber demeanor. In a gentle low voice, he encouraged Sky. "Sky, I can tell you're doing the right thing," he said as he quickly surveyed Sock. "Sock deserves dignity, not to die suffering on a cold ground."

Brownie and Copie, a border collie, kept a fixed eye on Sock. The ancient landing strip offered an expansive clearing of grass, met by a gray sky that seemed taller than usual. We felt small. We huddled close and gathered near, but not too near, the deep rock pit. Sky lingered and hesitated, letting Sock munch dry grass from his familiar pasture, which would leave remnants of that homeland taste in his mouth. Totally oblivious to what was about to happen next, Sock eagerly grazed along.

Finally, Doctor Pat coaxed Sky and told him to prepare to hold Sock's head up with the lead rope so as not to let it hit the ground. Time was suspended in slow motion, the anticipation of life meeting death in the blink of an eye. I yelled, "Viva Dixie, Sock!" With the first injection Sock seemed to perk up, took two deep breaths, and fell flat over on his side. After the second shot, Sky kneeled down and caressed his neck. Mama broke the dramatic silence with "That's how we should all go!"

"Sky, I want you to take off his halter," suggested Pat. It was a touching final detail, a rite of relinquishment.

Walking back home, Sky pulled from his pocket the handkerchief that Shatzie had given him. It looked like the oldest red bandanna in the world, paper thin and faded almost pink. Upon closer look, it had a name written on it, like laundry markings from a nursing home. It said "Kuhlman," a misspelling of Raymond's surname.

"When I realized it was Raymond Kuhlmann's bandanna," Sky said, "I really did want to cry. Holding his bandanna in my hand gave me support, not for my tears, but emotional support that Raymond's spirit was looking down on Sock and the rest of us. The great ranch foreman and the great ranch gelding gave me an instant burst of strength that said, 'All is well.' I don't think Shatzie realized what the bandanna did for me. She was just wiping up a snot-nose kid as usual. I still have the bandanna, and when I see it I think of that difficult moment with a sad love."

$$\vdash S$$

Herding Goats on Foot

"It's unbelievable what you can do with a dog," Raymond said. "If you live with them, they get to know your motions, understand your movements." Sometimes they would drive as many as two thousand angora goats on foot down the highways with a single dog for help. The goats stretched from fence line to fence line, making the already white caliche roads even whiter. The longest such trip was from Kickapoo Springs, just below Rocksprings at the head of the Nueces River, all the way down to the Block Creek Ranch at Sisterdale. It took seventeen days to walk the distance.

Between 1937 and 1941, Adolf was buying thousands of goats for fifty cents a head. At that time there weren't many trucks for hauling, and besides, the goats could graze along the roads, which were then gravel or dirt. Adolf and his team knew enough ranchers along the way that when night fell they could ask for pens and water. If night came and they knew no one, they helped themselves, cut the fences, and spent the night anyway on someone else's property.

But let Raymond tell the story:

It was fairly safe then. A horse was just in the way. We had a flagman ahead, a holdup man to keep the goats from traveling too fast, a pushup man at the rear, a flagman behind him, and sometimes a truck driver. I fixed a pickup with a double-deck tarp. We had all our eats and bedding on top, and the bottom was left for played-out goats that couldn't make it. They needed a ride for a while. We didn't go but two and a half miles per hour, but still there'd be weak ones in there. We picked up Arthur Eickenloff, Buck Biedermuhl, Hilmer Fullman, George Koester, and Joaquin Longoria. I left my dog Bozo for them to use at the Home Ranch and took her pup, Bozo Junior. Every night I put a molasses can of beans on the coals, and Junior slept right by me.

When I'd see a car approaching us, I'd take Junior with me. I jumped the fence, went to meet the car, and came back, Junior following me. Finally, I got Junior to do this by himself. I'd holler to the guy in the car, "I'll set him over the fence and he'll lead you through the goats." He did. He was just a little pup, but he learned fast to part the white sea of goats.

One time I heard a car comin', and boy, she was burnin' up the highway. The lady stopped her Cadillac and yelled, "How in the hell am I supposed to get through all this mess?!" I said, "Lady, there's a detour sign ten miles back. You didn't see it?" Then she really got mad. I laughed and said there's no detour sign. I said, "Lady, I'm tellin' you I'm sendin' that dog through those goats, the goats are scared of the dog, he'll part the goats, and you'll drive through."

So she did, and when she got through she was so impressed she stopped and spent the rest of the evening with me. I'd already fixed a place for the night. Supper was on. I was cooking beans, potatoes, and bacon and eggs on an open fire. Before the lady left she said, "I'll give you ten dollars for that dog." I said, "Lady, please leave before I bounce a god apple off your head." "What's a *god apple*?" she asked. "One of them flint rocks over there . . . 'cause we have so many."

The first night we camped at Camp Wood at Sheriff Jung's house. Then we came down to old man Hughes. He owned the land on the other side of Dietert School. There was a pen there, and I went to ask him if we could stay. He said yes, but you won't have any water. I said there's nothing we can do about that. We'll find some somewhere tomorrow. We put the goats in the pen. They were crowded but there's nothing we could do 'bout it. I parked the truck and everyone slept on the same tarp.

I woke up and it was lightning. Joaquin was with us. Someone had spilled half a gallon of Karo syrup, and Joaquin's bedding got most of it. "*Chingada mala hacha!*" he hollered. We laughed and laughed. Then it started raining. I thought, boy, I better see if I can get out of here. I was already stuck. It'd rained

enough that I couldn't get out. There wasn't enough room for all of us to sleep in the truck, so we just set up all night in the rain. No light.

The next morning I went to ask old man Hughes if he had a tractor. There was high water everywhere, everywhere! Old man George Koester, who was with us, had a lot of syrup spilled on the inside of his coat, so he wore it inside out. He was a frightful sight, an unshaven raggedy man with his funny hat and lining hanging out. When we walked through Hughes's gate, here came three dogs, scared, bristled up. They passed me and went right for George. Hughes called his dogs off and yes, he'd get his tractor.

Adolf never checked on them. He trusted them, and anyway, he was probably out buying more goats. A man who came to my ranch recently told me how he used to deliver goats to this ranch for Adolf after they were purchased at the auction.

"Are the pastures filled up to the fences with goats yet?" Adolf asked him. He answered no. "Then go buy more and bring more!" Adolf commanded.

Raymond continued,

We made it down and turned into Dr. Winchak. He had bitterweed on his place. The whole countryside was polluted with that. We fed the goats salt and Noxvarmin everyday to make them immune. We got to the Medina River and counted 'em in. A guy rode up and said, "Don't drink that water, it'll kill you!" There was bitterweed hanging down in it. Buck Biedermuhl was thirsty and said, "Well, I don't see how the hell you could be any deader from wantin' of water as from drinkin' it!" He stuck his head way down deep as to not drink off the top and took a couple of swallows. "Hell, that's good water," he said, and went further down and drank more. We left Buck there for two weeks to take care of the goats. We'd come back for him later. He had his clothes, saddle, but no horse.

One morning he called and said, "It's not workin'. Every morning I find fifteen or twenty dead. They curl up asleep and don't wake up again. The bitterweed's killin' 'em." We had to go up and get him and the goats.

From there we turned off at Garvens Store and went down to the Guadalupe River and arrived at the highway at Rodolf Smith's and the old Cliff Lodge. The old pens and old road were still left. We slept there. Next day we came through with the goats up to Tivy, hit Cypress Creek Road, then brought them on to Sisterdale from there.

One time they were herding sixteen hundred goats between Castille and Brady and reached a town called Pontotoc. A cold norther blew in on a Sunday. Raymond remembered, "It was windy and wet, and we helped a hundred-year-old lady into a church." It started raining hard, and they went on down the road seeking shelter or a pen for the goats. At the first house they were met with "We don't want any goats in here! And don't stay at the next two places either. They're my brothers and they'll refuse you too!" At the fourth house Raymond found the family all dressed for church. But the landowner took off his Sunday clothes and helped them. "They built us a fire, cleaned us up, and had dinner for us."

Driving nine hundred sheep from Marble Falls through Blanco to Sisterdale, they came to a bridge. The sheep refused to cross it, having never seen a bridge before. So they were driven along the banks of the Pedernales River, where they all picked up cockleburs in their wool. The trip was delayed for days while the men removed each bur by hand. That took work—it's no coincidence that the inventor of Velcro got the idea for it from the strong grabbing tenacity of burdock, the Swiss equivalent of the cocklebur.

Home at last from another one of those great goat drives, thousands of angoras were penned up at Adolf's brother Fritz Stieler's ranch, the original homestead, just two miles below the Home Ranch. Fritz's daughter Lillian Real, nicknamed "Pluppy," remembered waking up to the tinkling of all the goat bells. Looking out her upstairs window and seeing nothing but white, she thought it had snowed.

They sometimes drove cattle on foot, too. On one trip, Raymond said, when they hit the little town of Mason the cows went crazy, chomping up everyone's yards and gardens. Women were swatting cows out of their flowers with brooms. Some cows saw their reflections in store windows and crashed through them, thinking they were following the herd. "We weren't too welcome back there anymore," Raymond said.

The last cattle drive on foot was in 1942, when Adolf bought 280 cows and calves in Rocksprings to pasture in Blanco County. On horseback and afoot, Adolf and crew herded the cattle as they slowly grazed the highway right of way. They arrived in better shape weeks later than when they were purchased.

Raymond told me, "By the late '40s, traffic got too bad to herd shipments of angora goats up and down highways on foot. When horns honked, goats scattered. Flagmen were ignored, and brakes were unreliable. That's how 150 Stieler goats were killed on a bridge." Texas highways were changing, speeding up. But from the 1920s to the 1940s you could still happen upon roads solid white with goats, still see horsemen, herders, and dogs all traveling afoot, driving their sheep and cattle.

Shearing Time

When I arrived for one of my visits to the nursing home, Raymond quickly removed his cap and put his big, almost bald, square head down for my inspection. "What do you notice?" he asked with enthusiasm. I saw a buzz haircut. "I got a haircut nine days ago, and look how it's already growing out! That's how we sheared the goats. When there's a decrease of the moon, goat hair grows slower. We sheared them when the moon was increasing so their hair grew faster."

Shearing time was high excitement at the ranches. The first burst of activity was rounding up and bringing in all the sheep and goats. "We rode horses out in the pasture using nothing more on the horse than a bosal noseband," Raymond said. "In cooler weather we rounded up on foot." There were two shearings a year, one in spring and one in fall. The goats were sheared first, then the sheep. Raymond spent six weeks in the shearing pens. They'd shear four days at the Wilson, five days at the Franklin, then the Block Creek at Sisterdale, and then the Home Ranch, where it took two weeks to shear the fifteen thousand or so sheep and goats there.

One time Raymond was passing through the tiny town of Hye with a trailer-load of goats from the Wilson Ranch. Old man Fritz Deike extended his hospitality, saying, "Bring 'em into the dance hall to shear. We have electricity!" Raymond took him up on it.

Although it was exhausting work, it was a happy time. The team of Mexican shearers made it so. They sang everywhere, all the time. Their singing could be

heard even over the deafening popping, roaring, and whirring of the shearing machines and the chorus of goat bleatings. They sang up their work, making it fly by easier:

> Soy mexicano del norte,
> Donde se canta el corrido.
> Si quieren que yo les cante
> No mas que no me hagan ruido.

> I am a Mexican from the north,
> Where one sings songs about true stories.
> If you want me to sing them,
> Then don't make any noise.

One truck held a four-drop machine, that is, with four shearing blades, but the bigger truck held an eight-drop machine. Joe Herrera had the biggest, an eighteen-drop shearing outfit. He could shear two thousand sheep in one day. The shearers, because of their faithful, invaluable work, became legendary names to me. There were Manuel Ayala from Kerrville, Benito Rios from Comfort, and Vicente Garcia, Joe Herrera, and Enrique Rubio from Fredericksburg. Today, almost anyone who drives up my lane for various jobs says he remembers shearing here or knew someone who sheared here.

They'd catch a goat by the leg, shear the legs first, then tie the legs up with a shoestring to finish. An oilcan was kept nearby so that the clippers could be kept in working condition, and the oil was used often. If you were skilled at it, the white fleece peeled off in one blanket. The goats screamed blood-curdling yells, but a heavy knee on their necks kept them helpless. The creamy white bundles were turned inside out—the dirty part was folded in—and tied with wool bag string. This made it easier for the wool buyers to inspect the quality, length, and kemp of the hair or wool. A young boy was sent around to gather up the bundles and sweep up the clippings. He threw them into a huge ten-foot-long wool bag, and a "bag tramper" stomped the bundles down. As young girls, both my mother and I enjoyed this job. Our feet and hands became soft because of the lanolin. To this day, that rank pungent ammonia from goat urine and the oily lanolin is the smell of home to me.

The shearers kept track of how many goats they sheared by counting metal washers, or marking numbers on the shearing barn wall with chalk. In September 1939, a total of 29,500 goats were sheared at the Home Ranch, Raymond recalled. The shearers earned four cents a head then. The annual angora clip for the Stieler ranches was 200,000 pounds.

The shearers and their families were given two goats a week to butcher, cook, and eat at their campgrounds near the barn. It was a thrill for me, then age five, to go to their cook fires, where there was always a pot of beans simmering and all the fresh flour tortillas you could eat.

It was here that love of the ranchero songs was planted in my heart. My dad, Hondo, sang with them around the campfires with his guitar at night. It gave birth to a custom within our family. That Mexican music still connects me to eternity today:

Pues yo me paso contento,
tomando mucho sotol.
De noche ni sueño siento,
Pero vuelvo con el sol.

I go around happy,
drinking a lot of sotol alcohol.
At night I'm not sleepy,
but I return with the sun.

The registered Stieler brand for sheep was a painted red circle. This brand came from Adolf's maternal grandfather, Caspar Real. The ewes got a paint brand on the shoulder, the muttons on the hip. When Adolf lost ground financially, which was often, he became partners with banker Albert Faltin. Faltin loaned Adolf money all the time, at 20 percent interest in those days. For collateral, muttons were branded with double O, one on the shoulder, one on the hip. Adolf was able to pay off his debt with double O muttons.

Likewise, the registered Stieler brand for goats was a right horn painted green. If both horns were painted green, that too meant bank collateral. "Sometimes it was almost all double green horns and double O for 'the company' of Adolf and Albert," said Raymond. The painted wool from branding amounted to a mountain of waste. It had to be picked out by hand and sometimes thrown away. Some companies bought it for saddle blankets, but not for clothes. Eventually, Raymond and Hondo quit paint branding because of the waste.

The cattle were branded with an HS for Adolf's father, Hermann Stieler. Every animal on the ranch—sheep, goats, cows—also wore a Stieler brand on the right ear. The mark was two cuts on the right ear with a sharp pocketknife, a crop and an undercrop. The left ear, notched twice with a swallow fork and an underbit, showed that the animal had been "worked"—bobbed, castrated, vaccinated.

Adolf depended on the financial security banker Albert Faltin offered because huge losses were usually inevitable. Shearing in the spring, from late February to May, was risky in Texas. Freak floods or freezes were deadly to hairless goats. In 1945, twenty-five hundred goats were lost at the Block Creek Ranch in Sisterdale. Seven hundred were lost on Thunder Mountain alone. "Max didn't shed them," Raymond said. He still felt the regret. "And neighbor Kurt Kramer lost every goat."

When Raymond told the Boss how many were lost, Adolf's response to Raymond was "*Sag nichts!*" (Don't say anything). He didn't have to explain that the bank owned the goats. Adolf was quoted in the *Livestock Weekly* in 1953 as saying, "It's a matter of record that goats can break a man faster than any other class of livestock, but they can also be your profit some years."

Angora goats, more than sheep or cattle, were Adolf's true love, and he stuck with them through thick and thin. "Where do you want us to put these goats, Adolf?" a Comfort man overheard the auction manager ask. Adolf had just bought some quality angoras at a livestock show. "Oh, just put 'em over there in my Cadillac. The goats bought it, so they should ride in it!"

The Adolf Stieler sign at my entrance gate caused a passerby to turn around and come up my driveway. Evidently the mere sight of that sign brought a story to mind that still lived in this man with burning detail after fifty years. He got out and stood in my driveway long enough to tell me this story, then he left.

His father was Energy Lanier, a sheep and goat rancher from Llano. During the drought of 1957, his dad and Adolf Stieler had bought all of the mohair in Texas to send to England to be milled. They bought kid hair for $1.65 a pound and older goat hair for 95 cents a pound. Then, along with the stock market, the mohair prices fell to 95 cents and 35 cents. "Dad cried, 'Sink the ship!'"

I stood there listening, this tragic news just now reaching my ears. In April 1955, way over the hill from our hills, he continued, Energy Lanier was also shearing fifty thousand goats at the same time, on different ranches. They were high up on Llano's Riley Mountain, shearing some four thousand goats, when Lanier's son saw a dark cloud coming. "Look, Dad! Stop the shearing!" he yelled. It had reached 81 degrees that day, but by two o'clock that afternoon it was sleeting. They lost nearly four thousand goats, even though they had a cave for shelter on the ranch. Billies were worth fifty dollars apiece, so it was a huge loss.

REGISTERED BRANDS

FIRE BRAND
FOR CATTLE

PAINT BRAND
FOR SHEEP
EWES - SHOULDER
MUTTONS - HIP

PAINT BRAND
FOR GOATS

RIGHT EAR
REGISTERED MARK

CROP

UNDER HALF
CROP

EAR MARKS
FOR SHEEP, GOATS, CATTLE

SWALLOW FORK   LEFT EAR
MARK FOR BEING MARKED

UNDERBIT

In the bigger national picture, Texans were able to produce more volume of wool and mohair in the early days because they knew how to fight the eagles, coyotes, and wolves. Two features characterized the success of the Texas sheepmen. They were effective in the wool warehouse system. Second, they were successful in blending the best features of the Spanish, Mexican, German, and English techniques and traditions. But the Mexican sheepherders on foot proved to be the most effective and the most patient, and the sheepmen relied heavily on them. By the 1940s, Texas produced 40 percent of the nation's wool and 90 percent of the nation's mohair, the bulk of which is grown on the Edwards Plateau in Southwest Texas.

It was the pioneering wool and mohair industry that did much to civilize and develop the new land of Texas with woolen mills, highways, trucks, and, most important, banks. Before 1880 the West Texas wool clip was hauled by wagon to San Antonio. The principal wool merchant in San Antonio was T. C. Frost, who operated until 1892. The Frost Mercantile handled sheepmen's supplies and operated in connection with the wool warehouse. In one corner of the store was a small room, its one window topped by a "Bank" sign, where growers deposited the money from their clips. This enterprise formed the nucleus of the present-day Frost National Bank of San Antonio.

Another warehouse pioneer was Captain Charles Schreiner, known as the "Father of Kerrville." Schreiner built a warehouse by the railroad in Kerrville in the 1870s after he organized a store and bank in 1869. He partnered up with August Faltin, whose son Albert was Adolf's partner. The store/bank they started financed local ranchers. For a mortgage on wool, for example, the lender advanced money to the rancher after the wool was in the warehouse, stipulating that it must be sold by the warehouse making the loan. Schreiner also insisted on livestock diversification and required borrowers to use part of the money borrowed on buying sheep.

$$\vdash\varsigma$$

Captain Schreiner was Adolf's great-uncle, and his advice and lending enabled Adolf to achieve the success he did. When Adolf was a young man, Schreiner financed him in buying and selling cattle. Then, when the price of mohair was low, Adolf asked Schreiner to back him in switching from cattle to goats. Since goats were selling cheap, Adolf bought thousands, leasing and buying ranches where

available. He drew on his Schreiner account until he owned thirty thousand goats, and then he could pay off all his debts.

Adolf was also a pioneer in developing the industry in the Hill Country. He, Louis Stieler, Dan Hoerster, and Walter Wallendorf bought the old railroad pens in Comfort where the railroad used to pass by in 1942. They used them as trading pens for an auction in Fredericksburg. The Geistweidts later bought the auction, which is now known as the Gillespie County Livestock Auction.

Adolf and Bob Sieker of Kerrville bought the warehouse in Comfort from Ida Holekamp. Adolf also leased one from Schwethelm and then one from Peter Ingenhuett. The old railroad tracks ran between the two buildings. As a kid, it was a great joy to me to leap from one of the hundreds of wool bags to another in the Comfort Wool and Mohair Warehouse as if I were a mountain goat.

"In the 1940s and '50s, mohair brought $1.35 a pound," Raymond concluded. "The Stieler Ranch made enough money on the goats to take care of the sick cows. From 1960 to 1968 mohair fell to just twenty-two cents a pound. Many goat raisers begged Adolf to take thousands of goats off their hands for free because they couldn't afford to feed them." A Central Texas livestock dealer said that whenever he found a choice bunch of mutton goats, he called up Adolf Stieler because he always seemed to have a home for more animals. He did. By the 1970s, mohair was up to eight dollars a pound. But by then it was too expensive to raise the goats.

Although the price of mohair was low in the 1960s, the Texas Angora Goat Raisers Association was still alive and well enough to continue its long tradition of having an ambassadress to promote its "diamond fiber." In 1964 I was elected Miss Mohair of Texas in a glamorous contest in Brownwood. This contest paralleled the national and state Miss Wool competition held in San Angelo, which my grandfather Adolf and his second wife, Tops, organized.

I was nineteen, a freshman at Texas. From Littlefield Dorm in Austin every weekend I launched out with my custom-made mohair wardrobe on trips for appearances, speeches, fashion shows, and parades. Miss Wool, Linda Allen from Sterling City, and Miss Texas, Jeanie Amacker, a sorority sister, often accompanied me. Mama drove me all over Texas and back in the sweltering heat in an un-air-conditioned station wagon from which I was supposed to step out fresh, fashionable, and unrumpled.

From the George Washington Parade held in Acuña, Mexico, to the streets of New York, I experienced a fun and glamorous time that launched a modeling career for me over the next ten years. On one of my trips as Miss Mohair I met singer Eddie Fisher in an airport. He asked me if mohair came from an animal called a mo. Today, as I'm going down the highway at seventy miles an hour, I might spot out of the corner of my eye a goat whose horns are caught in the fence. I stop, back up, free its horns, and give it my blessing: "I'm still your queen, you know."

⊢⟨

On July 4, 2008, my cousin Allen Stieler, Adolf's nephew, and his wife Karen, who are still persevering as sheep and goat raisers, invited me to an Angora goat shearing contest they were organizing in Rocksprings at the fairgrounds. Rocksprings, known as the Angora Capital of Texas, is on the edge of West Texas, where it's hot and rocky. Shearers also came from Ozona, Camp Wood, Sonora, and San Angelo. Some of the prizes donated for the winners were a Zapotec-woven rug of their own mohair from Robin and Carol Giles, and some beautiful luxurious men's jackets by Dolores, a designer of wool and mohair fashions. In a hot, crowded tin barn we watched three contestants whirring away, each shearing three goats against the clock. Besides speed, the judges noted skill, nicks, and double cuts. I wanted to see the lost art again, smell the old familiar smells, hear the whir of the machines and helpless yells of the goats.

Allen Stieler got into the goat business in the 1970s. He recalled his Uncle Adolf, then in his seventies, saying, "You need to buy some goats, boy!" "Where would I put them, Uncle Adolf?" "Well, you buy them first, then you find a place," advised Adolf. Allen recently reduced his flock to twenty-five hundred goats and two hundred sheep. "We can't raise a very big lamb crop of more than three hundred anymore, because of the bobcats and wild hogs," Karen said. "Mohair now brings $2.25 a pound for older goats and $3.00 on up for younger goat hair," said Allen. "Ninety-nine percent of the mohair in Texas now goes to South Africa. There it's washed and spun into top, looking like an umbilical cord. From there it follows cheap labor, Peru or India, to be blended with other fibers and woven into different fabrics. The coarsest grade ends up in saddle tack and carpet, the finest for knitting yarns and blankets."

"Allen works too hard at this," Karen added. "But it's in his blood. He'd rather die out there than quit. It's just too much work for too little return."

Allen's son Justin Stieler travels all over the world as president of the Mohair Council of America. Justin's kids show Angoras at shows, and two granddaughters are judges of mohair at 4H contests. These are the only family members still involved in the Angora business.

I looked for the old maestro shearer, Eddie Franco of Rocksprings, who said he taught all of his four sons the trade. "You can get $1.75 a head shearing goats now," he said, "and $3.00 a head for sheep; they're bigger and stronger." Two of his sons were now winning prelims, semifinals, and finals. His son Steven Franco ended up winning second place. Oscar Arredondo of Camp Wood took home a $500 prize with first place. Franco told me, "No one wants to learn to shear anymore—or even raise goats. It's too backbreaking, too labor-intensive. They'd rather work for wages, like at McDonald's."

Now Whatta Ya Gonna Do

You are out in the middle of nowhere stretching fence, and you have to sink a metal T-post into a solid-rock dried creek bed. There are no jackhammers or drill bits out here. Whatta ya gonna do? Raymond told me of this slow, persistent method. He would heat the rock with a prickly pear burner. Then he'd bang at it with a heavy tamper, drizzle water over it, and repeat the process until the rock began to shatter, thus making a shallow hole for the T-post.

A water tank is so full of moss you could practically walk across it. Whatta ya gonna do? Raymond would fertilize the moss in the spring, shocking it to grow so fast it choked itself out and died. Then he could clean it out. One of Raymond's remedies for a dirt tank that wouldn't hold water was to pile a lot of brush in it and burn it. The ashes would create lime and seal the bottom like cement.

When you have to castrate and mark thousands of sheep and you're alone, with only your two hands, whatta ya gonna do? Raymond had invented a castrating contraption out of plywood and a screen door that stood up like a wall. The sheep was strapped down on its back and held with four spring-loaded girth rings that pinned its legs down.

In those early days there were no modern medicines, tools, or available veterinarians to work those thousands of animals on so many ranches. All you were armed with were self-taught survival skills, common sense, a sharp pocketknife, crude homemade remedies, and the sense to know when to persist and when to give up.

Many times, when you were birthing a calf, one of its legs would come out with the head. Then you had to push the head and foot back. Every time you pushed back, the cow pushed out, and eventually your arms would cramp up. Said Raymond:

Once you get the calf headed in the right direction, you can pull 'em out with an obstacle chain. But if the calf gets hung up on the stifle joint, the cow's hip, you can drag that calf all over the country and it'll never come out. To unhook the cow's hip you gotta take the cow by the tail, put your foot on the calf's back, pull the tail, push the calf, pull and push until you unhook the hip.

Back then we just had creosote dip. I sloshed it on my arms to disinfect. But you had to be careful. If you had one sore on your hand it could give you blood poisoning. I've seen a cow get paralyzed from the pelvis pinching a nerve. The cow can't get up or walk. The last resort is to shoot her. But if we could, we used to put 'em in a big sling and work their legs. If you can get 'em home to the barn, just let 'em alone.

I'll never forget. We had one at the Block Creek like this. The calf had already choked to death. Urine had burned and blistered the cow's hide off layin' there. Hondo said to shoot her. I said, "No, I'm gonna show you she'll walk." Every day I'd roll her over back and forth onto her other side. Fed and watered her. One day Chuy, the boy, ran up and said, "The cow she's got up!" We took her to Elmendorf, and she raised many a calf.

"Down at the Esperanza we had bloated cows who ate too much clover or fresh alfalfa," Raymond said. "The cows are in pain, aggressive, can charge at you. I didn't have the regular tool, a trocar, which is used to stab a hole in their stomach to release pressure. So I used my pocketknife. You stick 'em high on the side, hoping to stab one of their five stomachs, or *books*." What's hard, Raymond said, is that you have to hold your finger over the hole on this wild crazed cow and release the air slowly. If it spews out too fast, like a geyser of green cornflakes, the cow could have a heart attack because the blood rushes back too fast from the head to the heart.

Sometimes he was a keen diagnostician, as when he deduced that eating mistletoe was causing cows to miscarry at the Hicks Ranch. Other times he was a coroner. Raymond continued:

We lost cows heavily one year from bud disease. It's a certain time of year you have to watch mold form on leaves when they first come out. Shin oak always got the blame for bud disease, but the cattle at the Block Creek always got sick on Spanish oak. Bob Faust the vet said to always keep plenty of linseed oil on hand. Get it down their throats, wait a week and do it again.

You can tell a cow has bud disease because they stand funny. The acid from the leaf mold kills them. Their nose and mouth are peeling and fever dries the mouth. One cow drug along like this for eighteen months, so I shot her. I'd had enough of that. I'm teaching myself. I got a bucket of water, an ax, and a knife. I cut the ribs open to get to the stomach, which has four leaves, or books, one short, one long, one short, one long. They were red and swollen, stopped up and hard from ingested oak leaves. That cow had been living on one small opening in the stomach.

There were no injections for pain or tranquilizers, and to castrate a horse without it was no easy job. Whatta ya gonna do? He told me he'd put a long double rope around the horse's neck and run it between the front and hind legs. Each rope went around the shoulder. One fellow holds one rope, another fellow the other. The hind legs get pulled up to the shoulders, and the ropes get wrapped and tied.

Lying down, the horse is turned on its back. "I make an incision, take the 'seed' out," Raymond said. "You never cut the cords. I cut deep so the cut can drain. I put a hot burnished knife blade on the wound to help it heal up; shake the knife, put it in my mouth to hold it, then bathe the cut in creosote dip."

He concluded, "Juan used to transport water buffalo by helicopter in Vietnam. That information was useful to him when he came home to the Block Creek and had to tie up Dunny to castrate him."

$$\vdash\mathsf{S}$$

Dipping goats in concrete trench troughs full of poison for scab, lice, and fever ticks was a crazy, labor-intensive time. Thousands of goats were forced to jump into a stinky vat of poison made of sulfur, lye, and lime made from burned limestone rock. Their heads had to be pushed under and quickly lifted, or they'd drown. The animals could easily die—or the hair could burn off of goats and cows alike if your recipe was wrong.

"From the Home Ranch," Raymond said, "the Stieler cattle were driven down the highway two miles to the homestead ranch of Adolf's brother Fritz. Neighbors gathered to help, and then you were obligated to repay the favor. The process had to be repeated all too often. Nowadays they use sprayers for this job."

One of Adolf's hands was a nephew who had a mind of his own. Bernard Stieler used to work for him in the summers. "He called me Spatz, which means 'sparrow' in German," Bernard said.

I was sickly and didn't grow very fast as a child. In the 1920s, during the tick eradication program for cattle, they had to be dipped in vats every six weeks. Well, Adolf had a pasture that was eight thousand acres. The other hands and I had to leave the ranch at three or four in the morning, and it would take a normal full day's ride just to get to the far side to drive the cattle in. Boy, we could get sore, staying twelve to sixteen hours in the saddle. In the middle of the day, Uncle Adolf would come riding out in a car, looking immaculate as ever, asking why we weren't driving them faster. Talk about seeing red. I remember once I was so angry I just turned and rode home.

Screwworm was one of a rancher's biggest nightmares until the late 1950s and early 1960s, when the Agriculture Department came up with the outrageous idea, everyone thought, of dropping sterilized blowflies from an airplane over the ranches. The project worked, and the flies stopped reproducing. But before that miracle, flies attacked any cut or opening—navel, bobbed tails, ears—on an animal.

"Ticks were so thick around the horns that the cow, sheep, or goat would rub them raw on a tree. Then the blowflies would attack and make worms. We bought many a five-gallon can of Cooper's Cattle Dip," recounted Raymond, now far removed from the unending labors he'd once had. "It was strong enough to kill the ticks but left the skin raw and open. We doctored worms once a week, riding before dawn to get to them before it got too hot. The brush we chopped for the goats to eat ended up being for their crematory piles."

"If you saw a sheep or goat standing kinda humpback, skinny and with diarrhea, you knew it had stomach worms," said Raymond.

You had to hold 'em just right to put Phenothyazine in their throat with a hand syringe, being careful not to get it into their lungs. Phenothyazine was eventually put into their salt blocks, but it became useless. They became immune to it.

In the 1930s, the Mormons came out with a drench, but you had to hire a Mormon to administer it. They could never get there fast enough. They gave Adolf five hundred dollars to advertise their drench in a magazine. I told the boss that drench wasn't worth three whoops in hell! I was mad. There was no improvement. You may as well give 'em water. It's worthless! Later the Mormons came back and apologized that it was indeed worthless.

Then a newer medicine came out in a long tube of liquid called Trimasol. I built a chute, put on chaps to protect me from stickers in the wool, and strapped a container on my back to give it to the adult and kid animals. I could drench three hundred an hour. They kept improving that stuff. Today, they just give one shot for everything.

When my grandmother Dora lived here, from 1920 to 1936, she presided over what she called her "Kitchen Cabinet." It was actually a huge wood box that supplied wood for the iron stove in the small but busy kitchen. Visitors would sit there. From here she and Maria, Raymond's wife, prepared meals for at least sixteen people a day—workers, family, drop-ins. Food was even delivered to workers at close-by ranches. Someone was always sitting on that wood box talking to her. She was an educated, cultured woman on a remote ranch. She was interested in everything, and these people brought the outside world to her and kept her company. One of the members of her kitchen cabinet was Bruda Ingenhuett, a friend and rancher from Comfort who took care of a sixteen-thousand-acre ranch. He was also a piano player for Guy Lombardo's band. His stories enchanted her.

Another wood-box regular was Bob Faust, a veterinarian from Comfort, who came so often that he was part of the family. He taught Raymond and Arthur Eickenloff and other hands what he could, because he couldn't be everywhere.

Bob Faust made his own sore mouth vaccine on the ranch. An ice tray held a few tools: a whetstone to sharpen the pocketknife, a plastic pipe, sore mouth vaccine, and a watercolor brush. Using Raymond's sheep-castrating contraption, he would make an incision in the sheep's groin and dab the vaccine on with the paintbrush. It would scab over within twenty-four hours, and then he removed the scabs to make more vaccine. You had to be careful removing the scabs or you could get sore mouth, too, if you had an open cut.

Һ
)

People who worked with so many animals were always trying to think of time-savers. Bob Faust invented a self-loading paint-branding iron to brand the sheep, but the idea didn't get past the front gate. Then sheep and wool prices fell and no one wanted paint on wool anymore. The story that Bob Faust branded on my mind was not about him saving animals. He saved my uncle Gene Stieler's life. The tragedy took place at a ranch owned by Adolf's brother Walter, two ranches down the hill, where the Falling Water subdivision is now. Every ranch had a trench silo for cane. Uncle Walter's silo was extra deep, and one day a Mexican worker and his son were trying to drain the water out that had seeped in. The father was filling the buckets when his son saw him gasping. The boy jumped in the sloshy silo mess to save his father, but they both died. Then Uncle Walter jumped in to save them, and he died too.

Tante Hedwig, Walter's wife, was working in the kitchen and sensed that things had come to a standstill. When she arrived at the silo, the three bodies were floating on top, face down. Gene, a teenager then, already had a rope around his waist to jump in next. Bob Faust happened to drive up at that moment and saw a frantic, bewildered Tante Hedwig on the tractor with a rope, her husband already dead before her eyes. Faust told Gene not to go in and explained that a deadly gas, phosgene, had formed under the water and had been disturbed by one of the buckets. No one knew this until three tragedies too late.

Һ
)

In the 1960s, a friend of Raymond's named Deffinger called him from Elmendorf. It was a last desperate call for help. "My sheep are dying—two or three a day! Help me!" Raymond answered the call. "He didn't know anything about drenching,"

Raymond said. So when one sheep died, Raymond again performed his self-exploratory autopsy from the tailgate of his pickup. "When I opened up the stomach, there were so many worms," Raymond told me, "I could scoop 'em out with my hands." He drenched five or six hundred ewes a day. "In twenty-one days you have to do it again," Raymond told Deffinger. "Have at it, then, Raymond," Deffinger said.

"It was the first time in my life I made fifty dollars a day," Raymond said proudly. "I used to make five dollars a day, or fifty cents an hour. Mexican workers used to get ten cents an hour. At the end of my efforts at Deffinger's, only one sheep lived. Now what am I gonna do?" he asked. Raymond told Deffinger, "I can't do this. Sell your sheep and forget about it!"

"After all the trouble I had," Raymond said, looking back over the years of ranching, "I'm lucky I still made money on sheep."

I am living on this same old ranch that has seen so much suffering on the part of animals. Back then you had to be practical, callous to their pain and value. When a chimney swift nest fell down from the inside of the fireplace in my bedroom, I was kept awake all night by the baby birds' frantic squeaks for help. I gathered them up and drove a round trip of a hundred miles to the Cibolo Nature Reserve near Kendalia. Mama said, "Why didn't you just feed them to your cat?"

I spotted a pregnant ewe in trouble, half dead, unable to give birth. I called the land leaser. I got old-school practicality. "Just ignore it, Becky," she said. "That sheep's only worth thirty dollars, and it would cost more than that to call a vet."

But worth is measured in tender mercy. Last month I paid $450 to a vet to pull four baby teeth from my slobbering donkey, Bean Dip, whose job is merely decoration.

One day I might have to be a devil, but the next day I can be Saint Francis.

201 out of 250 kid goats were killed and hung from trees by the Mexican Eagle

two weeks in May, 1969   Block Creek Ranch   Sisterdale, Texas

Two Hundred One   Becky Patterson '05

On Top of Thunder Mountain

Sisterdale, south of Luckenbach on FM 1376, has always held a nostalgic enchantment for me. It impresses me that the "Freethinker" Germans, the members of the Freier Verein, settled there in 1848, before Comfort. It became known as a sanitarium for the sick, who were healed by the freshwater cures that Dr. Kapp promoted. How worldly it was for its founder, civil engineer Nicholas Zink, to have built roads in Greece from 1821 to 1829 before coming to Texas. How interesting that curious classics students trek to the cemetery, where they can read headstones in Latin, which the intellectual Germans spoke and read there.

At Sisterdale, my grandfather Adolf worked sheep, goats, and cattle on his Block Creek Ranch after 1929. My brother Juan now lives there. Hondo and Raymond Kuhlmann were Adolf's working partners. Adolf leased or owned all the neighboring ranches, from Sisterdale all the way to Blanco—the Wenzel, the Manchaca, the Section, the Three-twenty, the Franklin, the Esperanza.

In 2004, Sister Creek Ranch became a new neighbor to the Block Creek Ranch. Beth and Bruce Johnson from Dallas celebrated the grand opening of their dream horse center. At two thirty that afternoon we all gathered around the arena to see the Guadalupe County True Women's Drill Team. I spotted eighty-five-year-old Raymond Kuhlmann observing from his wheeled walker perch. My mother had brought him from the nursing home for this event. After all, this brand-new stuff was on land he knew like the backs of his arthritic hands.

From where Raymond sat we could see, off to the south, Thunder Mountain. Located on the Block Creek Ranch, it is the highest elevation in the whole area. It held much magic and nostalgia for both Juan and Raymond.

We feasted on catfish and hush puppies at tables spread under shady trees. Sitting at our table was Lee Roy Kneupper, an eighty-five-year-old Sisterdale native. I asked him when he had last plowed his fields with horses. He said 1946. Raymond said they put up telephone lines at the Block Creek in 1955. But every time there was lightning and thunder, the lines died. I enjoyed talking to these old-timers, who got to know every acre around here.

We talked about fighting the predators ranchers had to deal with—eagles, coyotes, screwworm, and slick lawyers. Although we were surrounded by easygoing luxury, all things new and clean, Raymond's eerie story of the Mexican golden eagle haunted me.

It was in the late 1960s at the Block Creek. Raymond had just marked 250 kid goats, castrating them and cutting notches in their ears. Days later, crossing the divide, he saw from a distance an eagle swoop down and come up with a kid goat. At about two hundred feet up, the eagle would drop the goat to kill it and dive down to retrieve it. Raymond followed it, and when he got to the pens he counted only forty-nine kids. On opening a gap, he smelled something. He followed his nose in four directions but couldn't find anything—until he looked up. Draped in the bare limbs of the live oaks were 201 of his 250 kid goats with their eyes and entrails torn out, all killed by one eagle.

"They only come in May, and then they return to Mexico," Raymond said. I asked him if he'd ever killed any eagles. Only that one, he said. He watched every night where it would land on a point, a bluff, or a ridge between canyons.

I waited until midnight, took a dog and a gun. It was a clear night, and you can see a form in a leafless tree. They won't leave their tree at night. That's the only way you can approach one. The eagles are still there, but they don't flock to one place anymore due to lack of large herds of sheep and goats. They feed on rabbits now. From horseback, I almost knocked a jackrabbit outa the claws of a heavy-laden eagle with my hand, but he dropped it right by my horse, dead.

Well watered and fed, the two hundred guests were asked to move over to the Sister Creek Ranch bar, where the Cosmic Dust Devils were stirring up some stormy music. Raymond rolled his walker over and sat stoically, his hearing aid on overload. Thunder Mountain loomed in the silent distance under the quiet haze and moonlight over at the Block Creek. When I looked over at Raymond, I thought of the line of a Willie Nelson song: "Still is still movin' for me."

"I don't want my ashes put on Thunder Mountain anymore," Raymond confided. "Too much commotion. I carry my memories with me. I could get up the east side of Thunder Mountain with a four-wheel-drive. But I like the south side. It's hard to get up it even on a horse." Raymond concluded, "I'd top Thunder Mountain at five thirty a.m. I could see the whole world from up there. All the neighbors—Hubert Smith, Eucker, Bill Whitworth, the Manchacas. Since you don't talk to your neighbors much, about all I could do to check on them was to see when they got moving in the morning by watching when the smoke came outa their chimneys. Everyone cooked with wood back then."

HS

Dora's Door

On New Year's Eve, 1998, I was a dinner guest of Lady Bird Johnson's at the LBJ Ranch in Stonewall. After dinner, the small group of neighbors and friends gathered in the living room to enjoy the fire, coffee, sherry, and small talk. "Let's go around to everyone," Lady Bird suggested, "and mention the one item in your house that is most dear to you, that most represents you." With this parlor game challenge, I immediately thought of the carved door at the Home Ranch.

My grandmother Dora designed the door in 1936. Its aesthetic construction was overseen by her twenty-six-year-old nephew and architect Albert Keidel. It was carved by master woodsmith Mr. Schultze from San Antonio. Inspiration came from the doors at the Spanish Governor's Palace in San Antonio. The symbols in the panels tell the story of our family's origin, our forebears' land and work.

Starting with the center panel, I told the story of the door to Lady Bird and her guests. Our ancestors (a bas-relief face) came across the ocean (a shell) from Germany to Comfort, Texas. They made friends (broken arrow) with the Comanche (Indian with buffalo headdress). Horizontal panels in the middle represent the land's use: a beautifully carved longhorn head and Texas cattlemen's brands, including Hermann Stieler's HS, a sheep and goat, hand clippers, and a spinning wheel. We sheared the Delaine and Angora, spun and wove their wool into cloth. The L-shaped panels identify the indigenous Hill Country flora and fauna: turkey, deer, bluebonnet, cactus, pecan, oak, peach, wild cherry, and Mustang grape. The bottom L-shaped panels show that we were ranchers (lariat, saddle, six-shooter) and farmers (plow) who raised grain (maize).

"I would very much like to see your door, Becky," Lady Bird said to me several times. But neither Lady Bird nor Dora ever got to see the door. Dora never saw her idea finished. She was cut down in the active, high-hopes prime of her life, dying at the age of forty, in 1936, in a car wreck. At the time of her death, the addition on her Spanish-style dream house was in full-tilt construction. But the door, her plans, her thoughtful intentions remained.

I never met my Oma Dora. I know her only from the books she read, the garden she kept, her creative ideas and cultured values, the stories of her genteel manner. Because I have so few clues to her life, I am propelled now by the momentum she lost. I found the biggest clue to her life in her own handwriting. In yearning, I looked at her handwriting as if it was her voice to me. It was a quote from her favorite German poet and philosopher, Johann Wolfgang von Goethe:

Egal was du machst oder träumst, dass du machen könntest, fang an.
Kühnheit hat eine Schöpferkraft, eine Macht, und dabei auch Zauberkraft.

Whatever you do, or dream you can do, *begin.*
Boldness has a genius, power, and magic to it.

Dora, born in 1896, was one of the youngest of Clara Rosenthal and William Neunhoffer's nine children. Already highly educated at sixteen, William came from Künzelsau, in the state of Baden-Württemberg, Germany, in 1868 by way of New York, with not much more than a trunk full of Goethe books. He was working on a dangerous surveying job for the Union Pacific Transcontinental Railroad in Kansas. All America remembered when Plains Indians attacked the train. The Indians forced their captives to march to their camp in the dead of winter, with no shoes and no blankets.

What brought William to Texas was frozen feet. The exposure caused permanent bad health, so he moved to the South and worked in a firm in Galveston. In 1880, at twenty-eight, he bought the Cypress Creek property in Comfort. With his flowery command of language, he became the orator at Comfort's lay funerals. Because of his education and his good and fair business judgment, he was elected Kerr County Commissioner in 1886.

"Even though I never knew my grandfather personally," Mama said, "his generation that came from Germany gave me some answers—who and why. He was part of the philosophical group that was genteel, showed compassion for all classes, and appreciated beauty. They were all literary, musical, idealistic, dreamers. When he took Clara Rosenthal to the symphony in San Antonio, that romantic date sealed the deal."

William died suddenly in 1903, at the age of fifty-one, of bad health. He left frail Clara and nine children with no means of support. The Kerrville paper reported, "The funeral procession was the largest that ever entered the gates of the Comfort Cemetery. The funeral was conducted by the Order of the Woodmen of the World, of which he was a member." His three boys left home and became well educated: Bill was a lawyer, Oscar served as a postmaster in San Antonio, and Al worked for Shell Oil in Venezuela. But Dora and her sisters—Anna, Ida, Bertha, Emma (Mietze), and Hilda (Talla)—went only as far as the fourth grade and then stayed home to help Clara with her backbreaking work, tilling the fields for her small truck-farm business. Cypress Creek provided eels, too, a delicacy that they sold along with their produce.

Dora was the only girl to further her education. She graduated from San Antonio's only high school, Fox, which had eleven grades. Her sister Mietze sent five dollars from butter sales and Oscar and Bill sent five dollars each to pay for her room and board. Before Dora married, she taught school at Sisterdale. Dora had a giant tenacious spirit for such a small, delicate frame. She was rather homely and had that big Neunhoffer nose. But Mama always told me your smile and voice are your looks, so she thought her mother was the most beautiful in the world.

$\vdash\varsigma$

Dora and Adolf met at the Sisterdale dances. Both had vivacious, witty, fun-loving personalities that lit up any room. On February 25, 1917, they married. Dora wore white wool and carried an armful of red roses. They lived on the Hermann Stieler homestead with brother Fritz Stieler and his wife, Lillian. Neither Dora nor Lillian was cut out to be a ranch wife, but they soon learned the ropes.

On the first hog killing, chaos broke out. A big black hog got out of the pen.

Someone fired a shot that put a hole in the big *Messingkessel*, or brass pot, of hot water on the fire used for scalding pigs. Dora's job was to prepare the intestines for sausage stuffing, running warm water through them, then salting, wrapping, and folding them. When they called for her to bring the casings down, here she came, tray teetering in one hand, the other holding a Goethe poetry book she was reading. *"Was haben Sie?"* grumbled her brother-in-law. "What did we marry?" Dora put her head and book down in shame.

"You have twins!" shouted Dr. Keidel, Adolf's brother-in-law, as he ran out to find Adolf working on a fence. A shocked Adolf ran to see the two bundles he was holding, only to notice that one was just a rolled-up towel. Practical jokes are still a tradition in our family. Their son Eugene was born in 1918. After three years at the homestead, those living arrangements soon came to a halt when Eugene started putting beans up the nose of Lillian's two-year-old daughter Roberta and feeding her slop that had been set aside for the pigs. Lillian strongly suggested it was time to move on. So Adolf moved to the northernmost part of Hermann's ranch, the rougher country, two miles up on the divide. To make the move, they had to go around the back on Bear Creek Road, since there was no highway yet. Going up a steep hill on Hasenwinkle Road, a barrel of Dora's good dishes rolled out of the wagon. She burst into tears because it was all she had. She never let Adolf forget it.

The new family built a little three-room shack, later known as Werner's house, to live in while a bigger four-room wood frame house was being built. In 1924, on a cold January morning, Dora and Adolf's only daughter, Helen Ruth, was born in the new house. She was affectionately called Shatzie, from the German *Schatzie*, meaning "treasure," "sweetheart." Out of the six girls, Dora was the only one to have children. This was because she did not do as much of that hard fieldwork, or so the other sisters surmised.

$$\vdash\mathsf{S}$$

Right away a huge three-acre garden was made between the two houses. Teenage Raymond's first job was to help Dora in the garden. There were rows and rows of vegetables intermixed with rows of flowers. Pinto beans were the largest crop. Dora canned the corn that came out of the field. There were tomatoes, okra, different lettuces, kohlrabi, both green and white onions, asparagus, dill, parsley, and cabbage for sauerkraut. Traditional in any German garden were phlox, larkspur, marigolds, and zinnias. But Dora was proudest of the popular flowers of the day, the iris and the dahlia.

One of Shatzie's chores as a little girl was to oversee the water as it ran down the long rows and, if the ditches broke loose, to go fix them. She sat under a peach tree in the little Mexican rocking chair that Tante Talla had given her, proudly reading her important mail, the *Weekly Reader*, her dog Hero by her side.

"Sometimes my sweet small grandmother Clara sat quietly by me," Mama said, "patient and loving, winding the cotton string saved from the feedsacks into little balls. Nothing was thrown away. The string was used to crochet everything for the house, from dishrags to doilies. The sugar sacks, when sewn together and ironed, made the softest sheets. Maria slept with me on them. Other feedsacks were used in making cheese, like *Stinkkäse* (stinky cheese), dishtowels, and even dresses. The finer ones were used for hanging clabber on the clothesline."

Recently, when I was at Pluppy Stieler Real's eighty-fifth birthday party, the older women were laughing and talking about feedsacks, recalling how they had to iron their brothers' feedsack underwear and discussing which ones made the best sheets. This is when someone was finally brave enough to tell about the time Tante Anna went to see her brother-in-law, Dr. Victor Keidel. She was a very large woman and was wearing underwear made out of Guenther Flour Mill sacks. "Old man Guenther's face was printed on the front, and his beard was in a very appropriate place!" We all laughed. "I heard that Dr. Keidel kept a sober face, though." Another commented, "I loved slipping into bed with old man Guenther's face on the sheets!"

Even with Maria and Adelle Roeder's help, Dora's job was huge. There was endless canning, baking, and butchering. Butchering was a special time for family and neighbors to come help. "Butchering one or two calves and several hogs," Mama remembered, "was a necessity, a ritual of toil, but also of great family camaraderie and bonding. Uncle Fritz was in charge. All the aunts showed up—Tante Anna, Tante Mietze, Tante Bertha. It was always jolly, a lot of laughter and making *Spass* [fun]. There was always plenty of food, drinking, and singing." Nothing of the pig was thrown away but its squeal and tail. "*Dreck macht Speck*," or dirt makes bacon, as they said. *Panus*, a concoction of cornmeal and meat scraps, was stirred with a big paddle in a cooking pot outside. They made *Schwarte* (hog's head cheese), putting the meat with gelatin into a washed cow's stomach, and *Blutwurst* (blood and liver sausage). Shatzie loved to help Werner clean out the cow, sheep, or goat carcasses that hung from the butchering tree by the goat sheds. "I knew how to pull out the innards," she said, "and I reveled in rubbing my hands in the warm blood inside the body."

Dora had become the flexible mix of the true Texas ranch wife, tough and tender, brazen yet refined. Although she lived on a remote ranch, she kept up with world news and cultural events.

⊢S

One day Dora turned her hen and chicks loose in the front yard to scratch and peck. Suddenly Dora screamed, ran in the house, and came out with Adolf's big heavy shotgun. A big chicken snake was winding its way toward the hen and her brood. The gun was so heavy that Dora had to lie on the ground to shoot. She aimed the gun at the snake, and all of a sudden there was a big bang. When the huge cloud of dust, grass, and smoke settled, the snake was found hanging from a tree branch. Little Shatzie couldn't believe her eyes.

⊢S

Shatzie's world at the Home Ranch while Dora was there was a safe, happy, enchanted life where imagination ruled. She did not lack for playmates. She matched up with a little Mexican boy, Joaquin Longoria, son of Victor, a good ranch hand. They shared his mama's good tortillas, covered the immediate home area both dressed in striped denim overalls, and rode on make-believe horses made of wooden boards in the barn. Another playmate was Bob Sherman, the Comfort Methodist preacher's son. They'd play hide and seek in the mountains of hay bales or sweep the floor upstairs in the big barn for roller-skating. The fun ended when Bob tried to kiss Shatzie. Another friend, Putsy Karger, lived on a truck farm on Cypress Creek. Her dad irrigated the fields of vegetables from a large rectangular tank where Shatzie swam with classmates from Comfort. "A good birthday was when we played Red Rover!" she remembered. "Simple fun." Fun to Shatzie was cutting grass in the rock walks, pulling weeds, or helping with the wash in the separate washhouse. One time she turned down an invitation to a birthday party so that she could go top corn at the Albert Land Ranch with their five kids. Whenever the hired hands were gone for the day, Shatzie was allowed to go upstairs into the big bunkhouse over the garage and "play house" by drawing rooms on the floor with chalk.

Although the ranch was a huge world, it felt intimate, especially with Maria, Shatzie's nanny. Maria would take Shatzie on the back of Old Dunn across the Big Pasture four miles to visit her parents, Felix Enriquez and his wife, who worked at the Giles's Hillingdon Ranch. "The Big Pasture was big country," Mama remembered. "Coming over the last hill was a grand sight. It looked down into a picturesque valley onto a whitewashed log house banked by hollyhocks and other flowers. The welcome was always warm—gentle greetings, warm tortillas, warm wood cookstove, good smells. Maria's sister Angelita taught me to play with paper dolls cut out of catalogs and to make dollhouses in shoeboxes with Sears & Roebuck furniture. The quiet loving atmosphere was a memory of security all my life."

Another example of security and family for Mama was at the dinner table of her great-uncle, Felix Real Sr., brother of her grandmother, Emma Real Stieler. Shatzie's dancing lessons in Kerrville connected her to the Reals—cousins Beepsie and Francis, the "stars" of the class, and sisters Hulda, Ella, and brother Felix, the cousin who would later marry Shatzie's other cousin, Pluppy Stieler. "It was an image of the perfect family," Mama remembered. "There was no playing until the chores were done. All seated around the big table, everyone was orderly and respectful. Papa Felix was in charge as the food was passed around. There was always a big pot of beans. I felt privileged to sit at that table and admired the family unity."

For Shatzie, Dora's special trips to San Antonio were like going to New York City. On the highway to San Antonio, now called Fredericksburg Road, Dora drove her new Willis Knight, a big heavy luxury car that always got a flat tire on the curve going through Leon Springs. Piercing San Antonio's tropical sky was the sparse skyline of palm trees and the tallest building, Atlee B. Ayres's Transit Tower. Downtown, Shatzie and Dora would eat lunch at Woolworth's for fifty cents. At Kress's, Dora bought Shatzie her last china dinner set for her and her dolls for three dollars. It was in San Antonio that Dora was inspired to go home and build a tennis court after seeing one at Arthur Real's house.

Several times Dora took Shatzie and her cousin May Louise Neunhoffer to the City Auditorium for concerts or ballet performances. She could afford only two tickets, so she sat out in the lobby waiting for the girls until it was over. On one of these special events, Shatzie was awestruck by the black opera singer Marian Anderson, who filled the auditorium to overflowing but couldn't even get a room across the street at the St. Anthony Hotel because of her race.

Back home at the ranch there was no other world like Shatzie's magical canyon. She felt safe going anywhere on the ranch with her big black Newfoundland dog Hero at her side. Down in the canyon south of the house she found her make-believe friends she read about in Raggedy Ann and Andy stories. "It was here the fairies floated in their big sycamore leaf boats. It was an enchanted place where North Creek and springs ran through the tall canyon walls. When I close my eyes," Mama reflected, "I remember the beauty all around me, being lost in the wonder of the big rocky bluffs, pools of water and the big rock boulders covered with wild violets, columbine, and maidenhair fern. The canyon could shut out the other world. I never knew about fear. Hero was at my side."

$$\vdash\!\!\!\big)$$

Dora was forever taking care of someone, whether it was the stragglers wandering in off the road or someone staying to sober up, and she did it with grace, wit, humor, and tact. Her feeling for social work ran deep. She had a special interest in orphanages. Whenever Dora took Shatzie to have a dress made by seamstress Mrs. Sherman, she always bought material enough for two dresses. The second was for Shatzie's "sister," a pen pal who lived at the Methodist Orphanage in Waco. "I always knew someone else had a dress like mine," Mama said.

Shatzie grew up witnessing her aunts and Dora taking care of the two old grandmothers, Clara Neunhoffer and Emma Stieler, with such gentleness and kindness. They visited, fed, bathed, and read to them with patience and compassion and no complaints. She had also heard Tante Mietze tell about the era in the late 1800s, when thousands sick with tuberculosis came to the better climate of Comfort to heal. As a young girl, Tante Mietze carried buckets of blood to sell to the tent city patients to drink.

After World War II, the care from the Neunhoffer aunts continued. They sent care packages. The Neunhoffer family still over there in Germany lacked common necessities. The most appreciated items sent were baby clothes, undergarments, and cloth diapers to replace the newspapers they used. Then there was coffee, sugar, canned corn, venison sausage packed in lard, and canned lard. The best lard rendered, the type with the smoothest texture, was from the deer. So thrilled with it were the recipients that they spread it on their bread like butter, and so grateful were the Neunhoffers that they sent us their family banquet cloth, with hand-threaded trim and the monogram HN, for Hilda Neunhoffer.

Another highlight for me," Mama said, "was to help out at Camp Laf-A-Lot, a camp in Comfort for underprivileged children. Every two weeks they would arrive by train. Aunt Bertha and I gave our time cooking and serving. At sixteen, my cousin Francis Real and I helped out at Camp Idlewilde cooking and teaching horseback."

Mama reflected years later, "Why did I cherish playing with the underprivileged? I didn't want to show off. I always felt more comfortable with the kids who were regular, down to earth, and real. In the community of Comfort there was a real bond, happy camaraderie! All the varied opportunities and exposure provided for me there were not fully appreciated until I went off to boarding school. In San Antonio everything was regimented and scheduled. Everyone was a stranger with their own cliques."

It wasn't unusual for Shatzie to visit the girls at the Protestant Orphanage on the west side of San Antonio. On Sundays she was given permission to leave St. Mary's Hall by taxi. "I would just sit on their bed and talk to them all day; both of us wanted friends. We just made girl talk, happy talk—no bragging or preaching, just talking and listening."

Twice, severe accidents caused Dora and Maria to have to drive little Shatzie through the twenty-three gates to Fredericksburg. When Shatzie was three, the tip of her nose was cut off on a lard can and had to be sewn back on. At four, she was severely burned all over her body by scalding hot bathwater. With Shatzie's pained body wrapped in a sheet, they made another trip through the same twenty-three gates. For three months she stayed at Aunt Clara and Uncle Victor Keidel's house in Fredericksburg, at the mercy of others. Lifted on sheets, she was bathed in baking soda twice a day, wrapped in Unguentine, gauze, and sheets. This service to her from family and caretakers—Maria Kuhlmann, Laura Franzen, Uncle Victor, Aunt Clara, and Dora—left an indelible impression of gratitude that would forever define and deepen her own compassion for others in need. Finally, after new tissue had grown back, she was happy to return to the ranch and the adventure of the magical canyon where her animals awaited.

$$\vdash\!\!\mathsf{S}$$

The members of Dora's circle of friends were active in dancing, gardening, reading, and bridge clubs. It was a lively and genteel group. There were Miss Saban from Cypress Creek; Vera Flach; Mrs. George Karger, who organized the Episcopal Church; and "Aunt" Grace Martin, the switchboard operator. These Texas German women hungered for intellectual stimulation, what they called *Wissbegier*; it was as essential to them as rain and sun were for their gardens. The reading clubs provided this need for camaraderie and self-improvement, and the Cypress Creek reading club was held strictly in German.

Dora was one of the first members of the Comfort Literary Social Club, started in 1907. She was president from 1926 to 1928. Their study of drama, music, and literature was serious. They studied William Shakespeare's *Othello* for a year. Since most of the members were ranch women, often a special guest such as a Texas Ranger or the famous sharpshooter Plinky Toeperwein gave demonstrations and lessons in shooting guns. Nothing fancier than homemade bread and butter, tea, and coffee were served. Members were fined twenty-five cents for being tardy, a rule still in use today.

Vera Flach and Dora, who both lived on remote ranches, started a little after-school reading club for their daughters. Shatzie, her cousin Pluppy Stieler, and shy Jean Flach went to Vera's house in town. Refreshments of goat's milk and bread topped with butter and sugar were served as Vera read to them. Vera Flach also directed theatrical productions; one of these, for Comfort's fourth grade, was *Alice in Wonderland*. Shatzie's Tante Bertha had just made her an Alice dress and pinafore. With that dress and her long blonde braids, she thought, surely she would be chosen to be Alice. But she got a shock: Vera's daughter Jean was assigned the part. Shatzie played the part of the dormouse in the teapot instead.

After my Uncle Gene's death in 2007, I found the group of books Dora had chosen for him as a boy. Among the books on Dora's reading list for her son were classics and books about heroes, like those written by Charles Lindbergh, Zane Grey, and Will James. There were also *Julius Caesar*, by William Shakespeare; *Strange Adventures of the Sea*, by J. G. Lockhart; *Adventures of Robinson Crusoe*, by Daniel Defoe; *The Woman Who Commanded 500,000,000 Men*, by Charles Pettit; and *Lust for Life*, by Irving Stone, about Vincent van Gogh. The book Gene was reading at the time of his mother's death was *Vinegaroon: The Saga of Judge Roy Bean*, "dedicated to the sheriffs and rangers of Texas."

To look at the shelves of Mama's collection of Texana, I realize how Dora instilled in her the love of books. "I am a witness. I become one of the characters among them, too, getting to know the people, to live their events. With books I'm never lonely. Books are some of my best friends. The books I read as a young girl defined my life," Mama told me. "Especially *Rebecca of Sunnybrook Farm* and *Pollyanna*. It was from these books that I got my positive outlook. Pollyanna was so optimistic and good she was a joke. But she always made something good out of everything. I was never alone in the country because I always had my books."

HS

The Home Ranch, with its open gate, was always receiving passersby and a lot of uninvited company. Before there was an auction in town, ranchers came to buy, sell, and trade with Adolf. Dora, with her southern hospitality, had to supply food and drink. She became the supreme hostess. In the Big Pasture during Prohibition, the hunters built a huge hunting lodge out of old utility poles. "It was party heaven," Mama recalled. "There were big parties, dancing and drinking, long tables full of food. Everyone knew about it, and if parties didn't take place in cleared-out barns, then they came here. There were always plenty of women. A wilder time could not be described. You could do anything on private property. It burned down in the 1950s when Isaac, Mama Club, and their brood lived there. She had left her iron on."

At the Home Ranch, Dora was always busy getting rid of guests who'd worn out their welcome or had drunk too much. "One night when our small house was full of loud company," Mama recalled, "she came into my room to comfort me and brought me the hot lid off the iron stove, wrapped in newspaper then a towel, to warm my feet. I still think of it today as a comforting memory when I'm trying to get to sleep."

"Don't worry, little sweetheart," Dora whispered to her once. "There's a man out there who sells pianos, and we're gonna get one!" The piano started Shatzie's cultural life. At first Dora took her for piano lessons with Miss Holekamp in Comfort and dance lessons with Miss McMannis in Kerrville. Later Dora took Shatzie to dance and music lessons in San Antonio.

Mama particularly remembered a pageant she was in at Mission San José amphitheater. The ballet told the mission story of the drought-stricken Indians dying. Shatzie entered, leading the group of raindrops dressed in their dazzling costumes of long blue strips of cellophane. She tripped over one of the dead Indians and fell with a thud, changing the mood of the climax from pitter-patter shower to thunder. "At my first ballet solo with a costume, my knee wore a huge bandage from Gene rolling me down the gravel road in a barrel," she confessed. "But it was all right. I imagined that I was beautiful."

HS

The piano wasn't the only thing acquired from company. The hunters brought Dora the treasured gift of a new blue and cream enamel wood-burning cookstove. It came with a special accessory, a container on the side providing constant hot water. Dora immediately put the new stove to use. She was known for making grand, beautiful wedding cakes. Shatzie remembered Dora's nonchalant make-do attitude when one cake fell and broke. She just stuffed the hole with homemade bread and slapped icing over the patch. The Neunhoffer women traditionally filled the centers of their angel food cakes with a little nosegay of frilly yellow Lady Banks roses, tiny pink sweetheart roses, or velvety wintertime pansies. But the cake Dora made for Shatzie's sixth birthday would forever be remembered as her most creative.

Mama's last existing doll, a crackled-faced Patsy Ann doll, wears her old tarnished bracelet and a new calico smocked dress. She is eighty years old. She now stands on the dresser in Mama's log cabin and stares wide-eyed across the bedroom among the other few treasured keepsakes. Patsy Ann attended Mama's sixth birthday. It was on a cold January day in 1930. The bad weather, the lack of roads, and the overall remoteness prohibited Shatzie from having any friends at her birthday party. But when Shatzie came home from school that day and entered the living room, it was a sight to behold. Seated around the dining table were all of her many dolls. On top of the lace tablecloth were place settings of formal china in front of each guest. In the center of the table was one of Dora's famous angel food cakes. Ribbons sprouted out of the center and led to the hand of every doll. Tied to each doll's hand was the gift offering of one penny.

$$\vdash\!\varsigma$$

Shatzie and Dora were at the Ingenhuett General Store in Comfort, sitting on stools waiting for their groceries to be bagged. Muckle Ingenhuett marched directly over to Dora and let out a stream of awful language that shocked little Shatzie's ears. In the Neunhoffer family, loud language and harsh conflict were never heard. The clan surrounded itself with a strong but calm, gentle aura. In a discussion they could express themselves without having to win a battle.

Muckle was cussing like a sailor, accusing Dora of winning a bridge game by cheating. Dora sat quietly on the stool, not saying a word. She took Shatzie by the hand and walked out of the store. On the way to the car she simply said to Shatzie, "We have people like that in our lives to remind us how *not* to be."

"Aristocracy," Dora added, "does not mean the class of people they think they are. Aristocracy differentiates one from the other by the quality of thoughts one keeps. And another thing, *mein kleine Schatzie*. Remember, when you're down, never lose your sense of humor."

When One Door Closes

Dora's world at the Home Ranch was a heavy burden for her narrow frail shoulders. There was the constant stream of people—hunters, ranchers, guests—and the feeding of dozens of workers. Adolf was generous, gregarious, always inviting everyone. In 1929, one of these invited hunting guests and Adolf were climbing over a fence when Adolf's gun accidentally discharged, shooting the guest in her heel. All of Comfort supported Adolf when she sued him for a large amount of money. She didn't win. But there were other allegations and problems from Adolf's womanizing. That, the lawsuit, and the workload were all too much for Dora, and she had a nervous breakdown.

In those days, trips were recommended as a remedy for depression. Over time, Dora would take three trips for recuperation, one to Colorado, another to Europe, and a third to Chicago. After the lawsuit scandal, Adolf sent Dora, Shatzie, and the wife of his cousin and lawyer Henry Stieler to Brook Forrest, a posh dude ranch in Colorado Springs, to smooth things out. Shatzie's uncle, Dr. Victor Keidel, suggested an even bigger trip for Dora in 1930: a Mediterranean cruise. Dora and her best friend, Jessie Alberger, went to Morocco, Spain, Palestine, and Egypt, and Dora detoured to Germany to meet relatives.

Another R&R trip to get off the ranch was to the 1933 World's Fair in Chicago. Dora's main desire was to see Marcel Duchamp's cubist painting *Nude Descending a Staircase* and James McNeill Whistler's *Arrangement in Grey and Black*, the famous portrait of his mother. Her sister-in-law Lillian Stieler had a new 1933 Ford. Crammed into the car were Lillian's daughters Pluppy and Roberta, along with Shatzie and cousin Wilbert Stieler, eighteen, who drove most of the way. But when Lillian took the wheel, she hit a tree and had to leave the bumper in Oklahoma. "Those wild Texas women drivers!" grumbled the mechanic. They had to wait two weeks for new parts and were forced to stay in the only available room—at a mortuary. Shatzie and Pluppy loved playing hide-and-seek among the caskets.

In Chicago they stayed in a boardinghouse to be frugal. More impressive to Shatzie than the fair was the Murphy bed and elevator in the rooming house. A highlight was buying a doll at Marshall Fields and eating in their tearoom. Of course Dora had to see the important Chicago sights, among them a meatpacking plant and Jane Addams's Hull House, a health center and shelter for young women. When asking the policeman for directions to the plant, he just said, "Turn left here and follow your nose!"

The mementos that Dora brought back from trips taken to heal and restore bring me greetings and comfort today, eighty years later. I feel the soft fragile embroidered black-and-white silk Spanish shawl with its tangled white fringe. I can wind up and release the song held captive in the carved wooden German music bowl, and ring the sweet tinkle of the brass Egyptian camel bells in my ear. I wonder about the source of the evaporated tears that were once collected in the little glass tear bottle from Jerusalem's Wailing Wall.

I found another message from Dora when I opened her 1900 book *German Watchman Songs*. Among the pages was a yellowed note in her handwriting, another Goethe quote:

Greisst nur hinein ins volle Menschenleben.
Ein jeder lebt's, nicht vielen ist's bekannt,
und wo ihr's packt, da ist es interessant.

Reach into the fullness of life!
Everyone lives, but not many know how to live.
And wherever you touch that life,
you will find it interesting.

On June 5, 1936, just after the new Highway 87 had been completed, Dora was taking Shatzie to her tap dance recital in Comfort in her brand-new four-door Chevrolet. Bill Austin, who was living in a tent at Werner's house while veneering rock on the ranch house, was cleaning the windshield. "What are you cleaning the windshield for?" Raymond asked. Austin answered, "I want to get the dust off. It's gonna get dark before we get to Comfort." Maria and Bill Austin went along, riding in the back seat, Shatzie in her dance tutu in the front seat.

On the outskirts of Comfort, about where the Dairy Queen is now, there was a slow-moving horse-drawn wagon piled high with a household of belongings. Attached to it was a two-wheeled trailer carrying a milk cow and colt. There were no flags, no lights. Dora ran right up into them with a terrible impact. The cow flew out of the trailer and hit the hood; the impact dented the hood deeply and decapitated the cow. Blood and hair hung on the car where the cow had hit. Austin's head crashed into the dome light and was skinned up. Maria had a broken arm. Shatzie had glass shards in her face. Dora's chest was crushed, impaled by a pipe. She was taken to Dr. Jones's clinic in his house.

Dr. Keidel and Aunt Clara came down immediately. "It's too sad, but she doesn't have a chance," he pronounced. Dora stayed alive for twenty-four awful hours. Gene would never forget watching his mother's face turn black. Shatzie sat outside on the porch of the clinic in her tutu, her face still bloody with glass shards, confused and uninformed. As visitors passed by she heard them say, "Poor thing."

At the funeral, the only words Shatzie remembered hearing from the preacher were "It was God's will." She would live her life doing good, but it would be years later that she would come around to acknowledge God, and then only in nature and in the spirits of people and animals.

Back at the ranch after the funeral, where hordes of people gathered, Shatzie overheard a man talking to her father. "Adolf, now what are you going to do with her?" Those, too, were chilling, life-changing words to Shatzie's young ears. A bolt of lightning shot up her spine, stiffened it, enraged it. They struck into this little girl a tough and independent attitude. She no longer felt safe and secure in her happy fantasy wonderland ranch. "From this day on," she told herself, "I never want to be trouble or a burden to anyone. I will be independent and need no one's help." She tried to adjust to the private school she was sent to, but deep down inside she was saying to herself, "I should've never left the ranch!"

The Home Ranch was never the same again. Dora's spirit of vitality and fun, her level of class, kindness, and care, her interests in all kinds of people, high and low, left a vacuum. After Dora's death, the plans for the Spanish-style ranch stopped. There would be no rock barns or outbuildings now, only tin and wood. Her unfinished dream tennis court was the first thing to go, giving way to weeds and grazing animals. The only thing finished was the grand and beautiful great-room addition to the house, designed by Albert Keidel.

Within, huge cottonwood and post oak beams from the ranch held up the twenty-foot-tall cathedral ceiling. Mission San José, in San Antonio, was the inspiration for the plaster shell niches. Dora had designed wrought iron Spanish-style fireplace screens. The screen's windows and bronze doors came from England. There was a walkabout deck and sun garden up on the red Spanish tile roof. The rocks and buckets of cement for it were lifted up by a pulley anchored to the saddle horn of good ol' ranch horse Punk, acting as leverage below. "The luxury Dora had been looking forward to most," Raymond said, "was her butane-run refrigerator and carbide lights." He added, "We got sand from a creek at Old #9 Road." Ernst Shark, from Germany, did the rockwork. Dora knew about but never got to see his work and the huge stone steps up to the sunroof. Albert had found hand-chiseled stone posts and lintels from old houses for the steps. "I could stand up on that deck and see the hills of the Block Creek Ranch at Sisterdale. And from up on the windmill at the Block Creek I could see the new shiny roof of the ranch house, if I looked through a scope!" exclaimed Raymond, the memorizer of landscapes.

Albert canceled the heavy dark Spanish furniture Dora had ordered from Stowers Furniture and replaced it with W. R. Dallas ranch style and mission style from California, with rawhide woven chair seats and toile folk painting. Albert always added an indigenous touch. In this case, the long burnt-orange drapes were made from the ranch's own wool and mohair, milled at Eldorado Woolen Mills. They hung high from the wrought iron curtain rods made by Voss Ironworks.

Gene would miss his mother, his only ally and defender. There was the time when this rebel teen and another accomplice "borrowed" one of Bernard Stieler's new cars from his sales lot for midnight joyrides. On another spree, they tore through Comfort and threw beer bottles into the schoolyard. When the boys got back to the ranch, Dora was waiting for them with a calm cool head. "Looks like you boys are trying to be heroes again. The sheriff called and is on his way up here. I suggest you saddle up some horses and ride off in the pasture as far and as fast as you can!"

Raymond would also miss his ally. "Dora was a wonderful person," Raymond recalled. "One time she saved me from the Boss's reprimand when I delivered some angoras to the Robert Real YO–Live Oak Ranch instead of Julius Real's at Turtle Creek. I didn't know the Reals from Hitler. But on the way back I felt I'd made a mistake."

"Stay here and wait for Adolf," Dora told Raymond. Then little Dora faced the big Boss. "See here, Adolf! You are to blame more than this kid; you didn't direct him right. Now leave him alone, don't pick on him!"

Gene, sixteen, was sent off to schools, Schreiner in Kerrville and Texas Military Institute in San Antonio, but he was not fluent in English, and the crossover from German would always give him problems. The German nickname Dora had given him, DoDo, was from the often-sung song "*Du, du liegst mir im Herzen*" (You lie in my heart). Later, a Mexican hand would change it to Duro, meaning hard or endurance. "He became an angry problem kid," said Raymond, "who would never get along with his father. He didn't stay at the Home Ranch, and eventually went to the Franklin Ranch to live and work with Stella and Arthur Eickenloff." Shatzie spent one more year in school at Comfort, and then she was sent off to St. Mary's Hall.

Ironically, Dora was the first fatality on the new highway her husband had helped build. The death of his wife was a hard blow to Adolf. In only six more years he would be at the peak of his career and fame as the "Goat King." The ranch, however, became even more of an entertaining center and a bachelor pad for Adolf and his son Gene for the next fifteen years. Shatzie came home to her beloved ranch on weekends from St. Mary's Hall and helped Maria cook and serve as hostess the way she'd seen her mother do.

Ruth McCaley, who named her house in Comfort Blue Haven, knew everybody. She was always sending people to the Stieler ranch, an interesting highlight for the Hill Country. One of those guests was world-famous violinist Jascha Heifetz. Teenage Shatzie was nervous making dinner rolls in the woodstove. "I showed off, though," she said, "making flaming cherries jubilee for dessert." Her father embarrassed her when he boisterously commanded, "Get out your fiddle and play something!"

After Dora's death, Shatzie would beg her father to go to church with her. One Easter he finally gave in. It would be the first and last time. To Adolf's surprise, the man passing the collection plate was the same man he had caught stealing his goats the week before.

When at St. Mary's Hall, Shatzie continued her ballet studies that Dora had started with strict and prominent teacher Ruth Matlock, who demanded perfection by tapping her cane on the floor. Miss Matlock told Shatzie she was to be her star solo dancer for the big city ballet performance. "I was a stubborn spoiled brat and told her no," Mama recalled. "She kept begging me, and I still turned down this privileged opportunity. If Mama were alive," she said with regret, "she would never have let me get away with that! Overall, I will remember Ruth Matlock as one of my mentors I idolized. Through her strict old-school standards she taught me I could do anything through hard work."

⊢⟩

"When one door closes, another opens," Mama always said. "You just have to jump over the threshold through it." When Dora's door closed, it was Shatzie's many aunts who took over. On the Neunhoffer side, Aunts Bertha, Mietze, and Talla rose to the occasion and helped out. But there was one particularly helpful aunt on the Stieler side: Aunt Clara, Adolf's sister, whom Shatzie also came to idolize. She was the refined but tough wife of Dr. Victor Keidel, a busy country doctor, whose innovative work gave him the distinction of performing the first blood transfusion in Texas. Aunt Clara started the first library in Fredericksburg, which was merely a collection of her own books. She also started the Gillespie County Historical Society. Like the Felix Reals, the Keidels gave Shatzie the definition of a genuine family. Six-foot-tall stalwart Clara at the helm was an image to Shatzie of another strong, caring pioneer-style woman.

"Without a lot of fuss she accomplished a wide range of affairs daily," Mama remembered. "I spent days at a time in her home, once as a patient, but also as a playmate and helper to her daughter Ruthie, who was badly crippled with polio and always recovering from surgeries."

Aunt Clara was a real ranch woman. When her country doctor husband went out to their ranch in Kerr County, he would mainly play with the dogs or hunt. Clara was the one in charge. Shatzie was at her side, a ready helpmate, as Clara would oversee the help and check to see if a gate was open, fences were up, or lambs left out. She took feed and, with her brothers Fritz and Adolf, helped drench cattle and deworm sheep. Back in town she ran a household, often used as an infirmary, with efficiency and formality, and held the fanciest tea parties in town.

"She was a fantastic cook. Aunt Clara's icebox was always stocked with beef broth, chicken bouillon, fresh cream, butter, and clabber and cheese made from her cows' milk," Mama said.

Harvesting asparagus and cutting lettuce in her garden was an adventure. They butchered their own beef, hogs, and sheep right there in town. Since girlhood she maintained her own flock of chickens. She never forgot that her pet hen was sacrificed as a rattlesnake bite remedy for her two-year-old brother Adolf. If you've ever cleaned a chicken, you'll notice the caustic effect the insides have on your hands. Years later, the venom from that first bite made Adolf immune to a second bite in adulthood. Uncle Victor's office was only three blocks away, so the table was always set at noon and filled with family, friends, and relatives regularly. It was a close-knit group; agreeing or disagreeing, there was always support for one another.

Uncle Victor's doctor office was the same one used by his father, Albert, and his grandfather William, Fredericksburg's first doctor and judge in 1846. Both were educated as doctors in Germany. "On the transom of that little rock house," Mama reminded me, "you can still see the wooden arrows carved by artist Herman Lungkwist, which were meant to show the town's friendship toward the Indians. So when times changed and the Fredericksburg area needed a larger better hospital, it became a big family project. They converted the two-story old rock Priess hardware store next door." Victor's son Albert was the architect, combining his classic tastes with Old World charm for the Spanish tile floors, ponds and fountains, and wrought iron balconies.

"After the hospital was completed," Mama said, "I helped with daily chores, Clara and I cooking in the kitchen and cleaning rooms. It was a rigid strict training in cleanliness. On occasion Uncle Victor let me don a nurse's gown and watch in the operating room. There were two memorable occasions that were fascinating: a massive skin graft on a woman badly burned, and a Caesarian. Following Aunt Clara helped me choose home economics as a major at the University of Texas."

HS

"I should've never left the ranch" was to be Shatzie's mantra for the rest of her life. She didn't cry over her mother's death, never felt sorry for herself. It wasn't until sixty years later, in her seventies, that Mama finally found the tears for Dora's life. She was driving along in the truck one day, and the heavens just opened up with a flood of inconsolable tears, painful grief, and sadness. The last glass shard had finally been removed.

At age eighty-five she was down at the Shack, where Sky now lives, cleaning out all the heavy old cotton sheets she'd collected. She ran across a stash of her mother's books that had missed being thrown out. With her hands dirty from weed pulling, she tenderly clutched a small book, bound in soft leather with gold embossing. It was Charles Dickens's *Bleak House*, inscribed by Dora to her mother: "To Clara Neunhoffer from Dolly." Dolly was Dora's nickname. Mama said, "I looked at the small print, big words, fancy long-winded writing style with no pictures. I wondered if any kid nowadays would ever sit still to read or listen to this book."

In the blink of an eye, Shatzie was twelve again. "This was the book Mama and I were reading when she died. I'd sit on the couch and she'd read to me. I'm now going to finish it!"

God's Love

In 1856, my great-great-grandfather Gottlieb Stieler arrived with his wife, Wilhelmine Urban, in Comfort, having come from Oranienbaum, Germany, where he had been a government forester. They bought sixty-five acres, Lot 93, near North Creek and Cypress Creek. The Gottlieb Stielers were one of Comfort's original fifty families. Forty of those families still live in Comfort today—some, like the Stielers, in the same houses. They had six children: my great-grandfather Hermann, Heinrich, Wilhelmine, Emilie, Ernst, and Adolf, my grandfather's uncle and namesake.

Comfort was still virtually a wilderness, and life there was hard on Wilhelmine Urban Stieler. She had lived in comfort in Germany, but never would she live that way in Comfort, Texas. She had no idea what was in store for her family only six years later. For Gottlieb and his family to arrive in Texas in the mid-1850s was the worst time to escape their own problems. There were the Indian and slave problems, yes—but the Anglos would do more harm to the Germans than anyone else would. To understand the ideals of the German "Freethinkers" in Comfort is to understand the trouble and danger they were in at that time in history.

In 1854, when Comfort was just becoming a town, its founders planned it to be the perfect utopian social democracy. "Freethinking" meant free education for women and all races. It meant prohibiting slavery and welcoming runaway slaves. No lawyers were allowed, because they were peace killers, and no churches, either, since the Germans were escaping religious persecution. They said, "Go to New

Braunfels if you want a church." In fact, there wasn't a church in Comfort for fifty years. At funerals, orators spoke. No one could ever even recite the Lord's Prayer. It wasn't until the train wouldn't stop at a town without a church that Comfort allowed one.

The Germans' religion was culture. They brought with them books, paintings, and musical instruments and conducted meetings in Latin. German West Texas was to be a separate state, taking up a big part of Texas. Everyone was harmonious, cheerful, easygoing, *gemütlich*—that last word coming from *Gemütlichkeit*, which means coziness or, even better, comfort.

The Germans worked, played, and organized hard. Their social activities—the reading, shooting, singing, and exercise clubs—eventually formed the center of their Unionist movement. It was at a state singing festival in San Antonio that they started the first political talk of revolution against the Confederacy. In June 1861, Sisterdale's Eduard Degener formed the Freier Verein, or Free Club. Its members wrote a constitution for German West Texas that pledged to remain "true to the Union," loyal to their first government.

In 1861, Texas secession turned to war. The Germans thought they could quietly stick to their ideals of freedom of speech, ignore the war, be treated as conscientious objectors. But Unionists and abolitionists were considered spies and traitors. Eduard Degener's Loyal Union League did not want to create friction between Unionists and Confederates, but it would allow them to bear arms to protect their families from Indians. However, it was really to avoid service and harassment by the Confederates. This was another dangerous move. Gottlieb was mustered into Comfort's militia on February 19, 1862. Their constitution eventually would lead to the Battle of the Nueces. The lines were drawn. The Germans had no idea what kind of danger they were creating.

$$\vdash\!\!\big)$$

In his book *A Hundred Years of Comfort in Texas*, Guido E. Ransleben sets the stage for how the tragic event of the Nueces Massacre came about during the Bürgerlicher Krieg, the Civil War. In August 1861, Jefferson Davis proclaimed that all male citizens of the United States age fourteen and upward within the Confederate States would be allowed to leave peacefully within thirty days, after which they would be "treated like alien enemies." In April 1862, the Conscript Act required military service of all males over age sixteen, demanding that they register for the draft, in part in order to identify all disloyal persons. The Hill Country Germans never accepted this reality. Their intellectual attitude made them adamantly independent.

A malicious man named Captain James Duff was appointed by Governor Ed Clark to oversee martial law in the Hill Country and to demand loyalty oaths. Not even Sam Houston took one. Neither did many Germans, even when threatened. Comfort's founder, Ernst Hermann Altgelt, ran off to Germany during the war and left his wife in charge.

Eighty Germans, none over thirty-five, from the Luckenbach, Grapetown, Sisterdale, Comfort, Fredericksburg, and Kerrville areas gathered at Turtle Creek near Kerrville on August 1, 1862. Sixty-four decided to leave Texas, peacefully, by way of Mexico to join the Union Army. The group included Degener's two sons—twenty-one-year-old Hilmar and twenty-year-old Hugo—along with Emil Schreiner, A. Luckenbach, Gottlieb's sixteen-year-old son Heinrich Stieler, and Heinrich's eighteen-year-old friend Theodor Bruckish. Most were equipped with old German muzzle-loading rifles and six-shooters. Some were without guns. Some had only musical instruments. Fritz Tegener was the leader of this group in exodus.

Since these men were allowed to leave peacefully, they had no fear that Duff would follow them. They took their time, hunting, traveling slowly, giving patriotic speeches, and singing German folksongs along the way. A traitor named Bergman led Duff to where they were camped along the Nueces River, twenty-five miles from Fort Clark and fifty miles from the Rio Grande. On August 10, at four in the morning, Duff's men, one hundred strong, attacked. The Germans had no cover and were outnumbered by men with better guns. Tegener was immediately wounded twice. Young Emil Schreiner took over. Just before his own death, he cried boldly, "*Lässt uns unser Leben so teuer wie möglich verkaufen!*"—Let us sell our lives as dearly as we can!

The Germans fought valiantly for one hour. After three separate attacks, nineteen were killed, including the two Degener boys. Some fled between attacks. Duff's men executed the nine wounded Germans in cold blood, with shots to the back of their heads. Heinrich and his friend Theodor had escaped.

The *Henkerzeit*, or hanging time, of 1862 terrorized the Hill Country. In Fredericksburg, just like the Missouri-based terrorist William Quantrill, James P. Waldrip and his vigilante *Hangerbande*, or hanging gang, were striking fear into everyone. Over in Comfort, Captain Duff had a list of Tegener's men. Those who were not killed at the Nueces were hunted down, shot, or hanged. Some were even found and killed as far as the Mexican border. According to Fritz Schellhase's journal, dictated on his deathbed to A. D. Stork around 1913, Heinrich and his friend Theodor survived the massacre, hiding in the brush. On their walk home they argued about which way to go at a fork in the river and separated.

"Stieler knew he was right," Schellhase recounted,

and went along the North Fork of the Guadalupe. He went down the river until he got to Kerrville Road. One mile west of Kerrville he went to Rees's house. He wanted a furlough. German men were not allowed to travel without one. Stieler was too young to have one, not eighteen yet, but Rees knew him and gave him one. Then Stieler went to Kerrville and stopped at Mrs. Degener. At that time a man named Lowrance, along with Theodor Bruckish, came in, and at the same time some Confederate soldiers came in too. Lowrance turned Bruckish over to them. The soldiers asked Bruckish if Heinrich was in the war also. Best friend turned traitor, he said that he was. The soldiers took Bruckish and Stieler prisoners.

Heinrich was hanged, along with Theodor Bruckish and others, near where Highway 16 is now. Their bodies were mutilated. They had signs around their necks reading "Spy." Heinrich would always be referred to in the community as "that murdered boy."

Word was sent to Gottlieb and Wilhelmine that their son had been murdered. Since men weren't allowed to travel, Heinrich's brave sister Wilhelmine and their mother hitched up two horses to a wagon and traveled miles, braving Confederate soldiers along the way, inquiring about the location of the dead men. They took Heinrich's disgraced body down and buried him on the Stieler farm in Comfort, and little Wilhelmine was hailed as a heroine.

After that tragic time, Heinrich's mother went insane with grief. In her mind, no one was safe anymore. Terrible things could happen. Whenever anyone came to the house she would run and hide. Reality was lost in her traumatized heart and soul.

Treue
der
Union

Gefangen genommen
und ermordet
Heinrich Stieler

GOTTLIEB
STIELER
GEB.
AUG. 22. 1817.
GEST.
AUG. 26. 1893

Als Gatte als Vater als Freund
Ruht hier von vielen beweint
Ein Mann der Tugend stets übte
Und Treue und Rechtlichkeit
liebte

WILHELMINE
STIELER
GEB.
17. FEB. 1823
GEST.
19. NOV. 1897

STIELER

She was sent to a state mental hospital in Austin for ten months but was sent back home as incurable.

Gottlieb was forty-three, Wilhelmine thirty-eight, sister Wilhelmine fifteen, and brother Hermann twelve when they lost Heinrich. The next year, sister Wilhelmine married Heinrich Heinen. They had a son, Hubert Heinen, who became the best-known, best-loved, and most influential teacher in Comfort from 1895 to 1935.

Family members of those slain at the Nueces were prevented from going to the site, now called Bushwhacker's Creek, to gather up the bones. But in 1865, after the war was over, a group of twenty-four men, including Gottlieb, went there. They found a pile of bleached bones and eighteen skulls surrounded by rocks and brush. In

1866, the bones were interred in a cypress box made by cabinetmaker Mr. Serger and buried in Comfort under an obelisk with the inscription *Treue der Union*, "True to the Union." Heinrich's name is included on the north side of the obelisk, along with eight other Unionists honored, with the inscription (in German), "Captured, taken, and murdered." It is very rare to see a monument dedicated to the Union dead in a Confederate state.

The massacre was one of the most shameful acts in the history of the Confederacy. The only fault of these citizens was that they were too idealistic. Eduard Degener of Sisterdale, who had lofty ideas about American liberty, imparted these convictions to his sons, two of whom were killed at the Nueces and another imprisoned. He said that although his sons lacked good education here in this new land, above all he wanted to teach them to work hard for their own sustenance and to have "minds free from prejudice, and spirits which would sustain their individual conclusions without a thought of consequences."

HS

The war killed off any idealistic fantasies among the Germans. There would be no more attempts for a cooperative or a perfect community. Comfort didn't grow for years afterward because of the loss of so many young men.

To this day, Comfort remains unincorporated. Its people don't want government interference, a mayor, a council, police, or a sales tax. Until recently, everyone chipped in four dollars each to bury whoever died. Until recently, German was the main language spoken. Recently, Gregory Krauter, owner of Ingenhuett Store, refused to conform to a state mandate to change his address to make his place easier for emergency services to find. Comfort's people are still as individualistic as ever.

HS

The German Americans were always treated with suspicion. Although firmly loyal to the Union during the Civil War, the Germans were considered beholden to a foreign regime, the one they had left behind. In 1916, Shatzie's uncles Bill and Albert Neunhoffer worked as American spies in Mexico for the agency that evolved into the FBI. Their covert activities led to the arrests of dangerous terrorist German spies who were working on behalf of Kaiser Wilhelm.

Roland Stieler also brought national fame and honor to Comfort. He was the son of Uncle Walter Stieler, the one who died face down in the poisonous grain silo. Roland left these landlocked hills to become the captain of the battleship USS *Lexington* during the end of World War II, bringing it from wartime status to peacetime status after the war. Along with another German Texan, Admiral Chester Nimitz of Fredericksburg, the commander of the Pacific fleet in World War II, Roland became a seafaring hero.

On the fiftieth anniversary of the Nueces Massacre, in 1912, the main speaker was Henry Stieler, Heinrich's namesake and our cousin from San Antonio. To this day, every year, loving family and friends gather at the Treue der Union monument to remember. There are speeches and singing in English and German, and mounds of fresh flowers and evergreens are laid down. The Fort Sam Houston brass band plays.

But it is only God's love—which is what the German word *Gottlieb* means—that allows us to forgive our enemy. James P. Newcomb's speech on the twenty-fifth anniversary of the massacre emphasized just that: "Whatever bitterness of the strife remaining, let us bury it here. Let us encourage a healthy sentiment of loyalty . . . with malice toward none. Let us leave this spot with grateful hearts over a restored Union, inspired by the noble examples of the dead."

Wilhelmine and Gottlieb have their own obelisk side by side at the Comfort Cemetery. Chiseled in German on Gottlieb's white granite monument are these sentiments: "As a husband, father, friend, here rests a heroic man, mourned by many, who loved righteousness and loyalty. *Ruhe in Frieden*." Rest in peace. Finally.

Captain Hermann Stieler

At the Institute of Texan Cultures in San Antonio, I was surprised to find the name of my great-grandfather, Hermann Stieler, on a storyboard on the wall in the German immigrant section. He was noted in particular for having been a prominent wool grower who established one of the largest cattle and sheep ranching operations in the area. Born in 1849 in Germany, he was six when he immigrated with his parents, Gottlieb and Wilhelmine, to Comfort.

Hermann's first business venture as a teenager was the establishment of the first freight line between Kerrville, Comfort, and Camp Verde in 1867. The country was still untamed, and Indians were a constant threat to the families living on farms and ranches. One of the last Indian raids in the area was on eighteen-year-old Hermann himself while he was out on one of his freight trips. His father had lost sixteen-year-old son Heinrich six years before, and he almost lost another then. Gottlieb reported the skirmish to the German newspaper *Freie Presse für Texas*:

Last Friday, July 31, 1868, my son Hermann, 18, while driving a wagon with one yoke of oxen on his return from Camp Verde, was suddenly attacked by five Indians on horseback near Mrs. Denton's farm on the road between Comfort and Kerrville. The Indians advanced toward the wagon yelling horribly. My son, however, did not lose his nerve. He stopped the oxen, jumped from the wagon, and opened fire immediately, wounding one who crawled into the brush. The others retreated temporarily. This gave Hermann time to reload.

The Indians then charged at him at full speed 150 yards away. They tied their horses and attacked my son on foot from both sides, jumping, not standing still. Three Indians fired with six-shooters; one used a bow and arrow. My son defended himself with his rifle and six-shooter, keeping cover under his wagon. The Indians emptied their six-shooters and used bow and arrows. When my son only had two bullets left, he retreated into the brush to reload. Meanwhile the Indians stole everything in the wagon—a wagon sheet, two blankets, a pair of shoes and a provision box. My son, having reloaded, returned to the wagon and drove home, fortunate to still have a scalp.

Our family Indian stories were about fighting off Indians, who were just trying to survive as well. But survival is a gamble. The paradoxes of cruelty and kindness, murder and mercy, are separated by a moment's decision of destiny. My maternal great-great-grandfather, Adolf Rosenthal, and Louis Strohaecker were neighbors in Comfort. One night the Indians were in the process of taking horses from Strohaecker when Rosenthal came walking home around midnight. An Indian arrow hit him—or, rather, hit a cane that he was carrying over his shoulder. The lucky cane was a gift to him from Sam Houston, for whom he'd done survey work. The arrow split the cane and made only a small wound in his chest. A second arrow hit the other hand as he was feeling his chest. By then he had figured out what was happening, and he ran home as fast as he could.

Gottlieb Stieler's son Ernst married Louis Strohaecker's daughter Anna. On another occasion, Indians stole some of the horses that Louis had sold to the army. Louis and his partner tracked the Indians all the way from San Antonio to the Lubbock area. They caught up with the Indians, who were moving with their wives. An Indian killed Strohaecker's horse and shot him in the right ankle. He and his partner killed the Indian. When the Indian realized he was dying, he took a butcher knife and cut his wife's belly open. But before she died, she told Strohaecker where to find water.

HS

After the freight line business, Hermann worked with and under Captain Charles Schreiner, one of the most astute men in early Texas, and acquired valuable training. Hermann became an accomplished stonemason at the age of eighteen. He worked for Captain Schreiner, building his stately mansion. That historic landmark is located at 223 Earl Garrett in Kerrville, next to the Kerr Arts and Cultural Center. The house, presumably designed by Alfred Giles in 1879, took eighteen years to complete. You can still see Hermann's meticulous work on the side closest to the art center and in the back. The work is classic, clean, smooth, simple—so typical of the German style. Hermann worked on this building long enough to meet his future wife, Emma Real, Schreiner's niece, the daughter of Caspar Real and Emilie Schreiner. On weekends he would borrow a dun mule from Schreiner and visit Emma at Turtle Creek.

Hermann married Emma in 1878. They also had nine children, like the Neunhoffers, but instead of six girls there were six boys—Walter, Emil, Alfred, Fritz, Adolf, and Gus—and three girls—Clara, Ida, and Alma. In 1892, Hermann finished his own home for his family on North Creek, six miles north of Comfort, still visible from Highway 87. The house shows his fine expert rockwork. They made their own burned lime in the kilns there on the ranch. Burning wood for seventy-two hours produced twelve barrels of lime. Mixed with sand and water, it made a crumbly mortar.

Following Schreiner's advice, Hermann quit being a stonemason and acquired land and livestock for ranching and farming. With the money he made from masonry work on the mansion, he bought three thousand acres, where this ranch is now, from the state of Texas. His name is still on the county survey maps today. Hermann traded land for livestock, and he became known as a good sheep man, raising fine wool Delaines.

Hermann became successful, with land holdings of twenty-five sections stretching from Bear Creek down to North Creek (where the Reserve and Falling Water are now), and as far across as from Sisterdale to Kerrville. Hermann put his sons Fritz and Adolf in charge of the most northern part up on the divide, known as Stieler Hill. Hermann passed his knack for trading livestock on to his son Adolf, for whom trading would become a way of life.

Up on the windswept divide at Stieler Hill Adolf lived with Tomás, the Mexican sheepherder who worked for Hermann. From herding sheep barefooted with Tomás to hunting wolves with Fritz, Adolf grew to love his father's land, that hilly, rugged, rocky country. Before the days of fences, primitive corrals were made of brush for the sheep, which were impervious to the black timber wolves. The sheep required more attention than cattle, and a black wolf would tear an animal apart even when people were present. The wolves got many sheep. On Hermann's spread, ten shepherds were needed to guard them. Only years later did Walter Real, son of Caspar and brother-in-law of Hermann, introduce a breed of dog, the running walker, that was effective in controlling wolves.

All that remains of Tomás's presence today is the stoic stone chimney from his burned-down cabin, located next to the cabin in the Camp Shack pasture. When Tomás died, he was buried under a walnut tree at the foot of the canyon. His replacement couldn't bear to stay there, claiming he heard Tomás's ghost wailing in the wind. The chimney stands lonely now at the brink of the canyon, a monument to the first guardian of the first flock. It still listens every night to the groaning wind and the howling coyotes on Stieler Hill, just as it did a hundred years ago.

In 1917, while still living with his parents at the homestead, Adolf had an opportunity to go into the goat business. Mohair was selling at a new high of sixty cents a pound, and goats were in short supply. So he bought seven hundred goats from a man named Davenport in Uvalde at $5.50

a head. This was to become the starter flock that would develop into the nation's largest herd of Angora goats. Hermann had given Adolf some land, but he didn't stipulate that it should only be used for sheep and cattle. He regarded goats as loathsome, "fit only for crummy backyards."

The forty-mile drive home on foot from Uvalde, with one borrowed herder and his dog, took five days. Knowing his father's dislike of goats, Adolf timed the arrival at nighttime. He herded them as quietly as possible past the house, penning them in a rock pen made for sheep. By the middle of the night, all seven hundred had climbed over the rock fence and headed back toward Uvalde. Adolf (in a Model T Ford), the herder, and the dog took after them and, by daylight, turned them around and got them back to another part of the ranch. Adolf then goat-proofed the thousand acres he had bought from Alfred Giles on Stieler Hill. Not until the project was a success did Hermann learn about what he'd done. When Hermann heard that Paul Ingenhuett had financed the deal, he told Paul not to bother coming to him about it if his son didn't pay the debt.

Hermann retired in 1916, leaving his ranch interests to his sons Adolf, Fritz, Gus, and Walter. Besides, they wouldn't have to go fight in World War I if they had ranching responsibilities. In 1918, Adolf entered the ranching business on his own and took over some eight and a half sections of his father's land.

Hermann was a handsome, distinguished-looking man who, as Shatzie remembered, always wore a black suit. He was strict and conservative, stuck to old-fashioned principles, and trusted the old ways. After the first cars came out, he was still the only one driving a horse-drawn hack. Hermann died on November 11, 1928, at the age of seventy-nine, leaving a reputation as one of the best-loved, most respected pioneers of the Hill Country. After the will was read, Adolf's mother Emma sold Adolf the 3,713 acres he had been in charge of for the sum of one dollar.

$$HS$$

When Hermann Stieler married Emma Real, he married into a dynamic pioneer family. Emma's mother, Emilie Schreiner, went from being born and raised in a castle to living with her husband Caspar Real in a log cabin. Born in 1836, my great-great-grandmother Emilie Schreiner lived in her family's beautiful Castle Bouxhof Reichenstein, in Riguewihr in the Vosges Mountains of Upper Alsace, France. Her father, Dr. Gustave Adolph Schreiner, a dentist, was also born there in 1800. His wife, Charlotte Bippert, was born at Riguewihr in 1809. Besides Emilie, they had four boys: Gustave Adolph Jr., Fritz, Aime, and Charles Armand (of Kerrville fame). Going back another generation, Dr. Gustave Adolph's Swedish father, also named Gustave Adolph, married an Austrian of noble blood, Marie Louise von Boux. The Castle Bouxhof is named after her.

From Comfort, Emilie Schreiner, at seventy-eight, wrote in German about her long trip to America:

In the year 1852, at sixteen, I immigrated to San Antonio, Texas, with my parents and four brothers. We traveled via Strasbourg to Paris, visited our kinfolks and took in all the sights. Then we went to Le Havre, where we had to wait three weeks for our ship, which took us to New Orleans. From there we went by steamer to Galveston, and then to Indianola. We went by mule team to San Antonio, where we arrived September 23, 1852, after a weary trip. A month later, our father, Gustave Adolph, died from a rattlesnake bite. Our mother died five years later, leaving us orphaned in a new country and on our own.

Caspar Real, twenty-five, came to San Antonio from Düsseldorf, Germany, in 1849 with his mother, Sabina Krey Real, and his brother Adolph. Right away he learned the new language. He met and married Emilie Schreiner in San Antonio soon after. A drought caused him to look for land and water farther north with the help of a famous pioneer scout, José Rodriguez. He bought land from the state of Texas for sixty cents an acre six miles from Kerrville, at Turtle Creek.

Caspar brought the first flock of sheep to Kerr County. Besides the nine hundred fine wool Delaine sheep, there were several hundred hogs and cattle. His cattle, a mix of Hereford with Durham bulls, were the first improved breed over the usual Texas longhorns. Caspar, Emilie, their kids, his brother Adolph, and his mother all lived in the tiny two-room log cabin. He later helped move his brother-in-law Charles Schreiner to Turtle Creek. In spite of numerous Indian raids, Caspar endured until his high-quality flock grew to four thousand. Caspar Real set an example to his children as a servant and leader to his community. He and Emilie produced eight children: Walter, Emma (Stieler), Albert, Arthur, Julius, Robert, Mathilde (Ingenhuett), and Charles (Karl), who followed their father as contributors to the Hill Country.

Generals, doctors, well-educated women, knights, the Bouxhof castle, and

Riguewihr in the Alsatian mountains all seem a fairyland away, but Emma was a culmination of all her roots. She had a sweet, quiet, genteel demeanor with a generous hospitality. But with her imposing large size, she was also firm in demanding order and respect from her sons and later, as Shatzie remembers, her grandchildren. Emma often reminded Hermann that everything he ever learned about sheep he learned from her brothers and father Caspar. His answer was always "*Ja, Mama. Es hat mich nicht lang gebraucht das zu lernen!*" Yes, but it didn't take me long to learn!

ⱶ)

In 1920 Adolf moved up the hill from the homestead. It was extremely remote, the highest elevation in four counties, at 2,001 feet above sea level. It was rocky but rich in stands of oaks, cherry, and tall post oaks, with deep canyons and springs. He memorized the fifty-two hundred acres of landscape. Every inch was walked over, every pasture named. On the east side there was the James Section, the Blackjack, the Five Hundred (Turkey Hollow), the Big Pasture, and the Three-twenty. On the west side, where the house is, there was the Camp Shack, the Six Hundred Section, the Horse Trap, the Well Lot, Werner's Lot, the West Field, the Cilo Field, the Windmill, and the Salt Lick.

The only road from Comfort to Fredericksburg was a narrow unpaved one that went from ranch to ranch. From Hermann's homestead to the Home Ranch there was a dirt road straight up a very steep hill. It was so steep that one time Adolf's Model T turned over. Luckily, he was strong enough to get out and set it upright. Many people had to climb that steep hill loaded down with lumber to build their houses. In 1910 there was always a man at the bottom of the hill waiting with two horses and a wagon to help lighten their loads. He charged one dollar for hauling their heavy cargo up the hill. The only other route was to go to Bear Creek and get on Hasenwinkle Road. But that, too, was steep—it was where Dora's dishes slid out of the wagon. Or you could go by way of Sisterdale on Number Nine Road. To get to Fredericksburg from the Home Ranch, travelers had to go from one ranch house to the next, passing through twenty-three gates at their pens.

In 1929 Adolf was part of a plan to build Highway 87. He talked his neighbors into giving up land for the highway, as he and his brothers Fritz and Walter had done. He also supplied the caliche from a pit in the Five Hundred and gravel from a quarry in the Camp Shack. Adolf had a good set of working pens right where the highway would come through his property. He let the state cut a highway through his ranch with the stipulation that it build an underground tunnel through which he could safely run his livestock back and forth. He, his brothers, and his neighbors also gave up enough land for the highway to be widened sometime in the distant future.

Black men, an oddity in the area, built the highway by hand using mules and a three-foot-wide iron scoop called a fresno. Hundreds of these workers laboriously scooped and filled, scooped and filled, until the road was finished in 1936. On the big hill, called Stieler Hill, cars and trucks still had to climb it in reverse to keep the gas in the engine, since cars had no fuel pumps in those days. Adolf let the black men water their mules at a big dirt water tank in the Big Pasture. Two miles away, at the Stielers' homestead, Fritz Stieler's daughter, Pluppy, could hear the workers singing and mule bells clanking, a happy, comforting sound.

The work crew provided our neighbors to the north on Bear Creek, the Eddie Herborts, their only income during the Depression. Mrs. Herbort and her daughter Alma baked fifty loaves of bread daily in her woodstove. She used a fifty-pound sack of flour a day and sold the loaves for fifty cents apiece. They also killed a sheep a week for those hungry men, who devoured the fresh bread, then walked singing three miles to work on the hill.

There have been many accidents on the curving steep grade of Stieler Hill. The first fatality was Adolf's own wife, Dora, in 1936. He himself had an accident on that hill, driving carelessly, steering with the stump of his amputated arm on the wheel while playing the harmonica with the other hand.

Highway 87 is now a major artery, and the landscape on Stieler Hill has changed. What used to be remote, quiet rugged hills and canyons choked with cedar and Spanish oak has been ripped through and scarred by caliche roads for high lines. Traffic noises and invisible radio waves clutter the air. Most of Hermann's land is now gone. Rooftops from the Reserve and Falling Water fill the horizon, knock at my door. What would Hermann, the first landowner, think of trading good ranch land for buildings, highways, and cell towers?

Two ugly antenna towers blinking their red lights mark the top of the hill. But when I give people directions to the ranch, my point of reference is not the skyscraper towers but the altitude. When your ears pop, you've arrived.

Cattle Call

You could call it a grand entrance. When Adolf Stieler arrived at a dance, usually late, the band would strike up "Cattle Call," and everyone knew Adolf was there. His mere presence lit up the spirits of the dancers. The band was always happy to see him, too, since he was a big tipper. "We'd be tired and just cranking along," one musician recalled, "and then Adolf would come in and we'd blow it loud!" The crowd thought, "Let the party begin. Adolf's here! Things are gonna be good now!" At the drop of a hat Adolf would play his eight-key ocarina, holding it in his one hand like a roasting ear of corn while dancing a jig to his tune, or he'd sing and yodel "Cattle Call," his theme song. He was a one-man party. Everyone called him Uncle Adolf, whether they were related to him or not.

Adolf had a patriotic face: red, white, and blue. His wavy white hair was like a shock of mohair against his ruddy face, which was always smiling or talking with a German accent. His piercing sky-blue eyes twinkled, friendly and engaging. He always wore khakis, and usually a shirt of fine sheer worsted wool and mohair, the dangling sleeve on his amputated arm held folded up by a rubber band. Adolf was a large, 250-pound figure, more than six feet tall.

When we were small kids, Opa, as we called him, bounced us on his good knee, singing a little ditty in German about riding three different classes of horses. The first one was fine, swaying us gently; the second had a jarring trot; and the third was the bucking one, when he almost let us fall off, singing "Hoopeldybow! Hoopeldybow!" Whenever Opa crossed the threshold of our door, we kids clamored to see him, excited as homesick sheepdogs wagging their tails. His booming jovial voice beckoned all of us. Never one to disappoint, he'd dig deep into his pockets to give every kid there a silver dollar or dollar bill. We never knew then that the strength, joy, and exuberance we saw in this giant of a man was a fierce rebuttal of spirit against the losses and sadnesses that lay deep in his dented heart.

⊢⊃

The Stieler children were fluent in German, Spanish, and English. There were about sixteen people on the telephone party line that nosy gossips loved to listen in on. That's why whenever Adolf and his brother Fritz talked, they'd begin in Spanish and ease in to German, almost never getting to English. Mathilde Real Ingenhuett, daughter of Caspar and Emilie Real and Adolf's aunt, came to the Hermann Stieler homestead to teach regular school to all of the Stieler children, including her son Arthur. Adolf completed the fourth grade. Then he and Felix Real Sr. and Arthur Ingenhuett, Mathilde's son, went to Marshall Training School in San Antonio. It was there that Adolf excelled athletically and held the state shot-put record. That heavy lead ball, our claim to fame, as if it were a degree, has been passed around to all of us to this day. It rests in some dark closet corner as a mysterious symbol of a once-strong right arm that could lift the weight of the world. Arthur Ingenhuett went on to become an internationally famous and highly awarded scholar who taught at Columbia University.

On December 30, 1910, a hunter accidentally killed Adolf's twenty-five-year-old brother, Emil. He had mistaken Emil for a white-tailed deer, misled by Emil's white handkerchief. Later, in remorse, that distraught friend killed himself. Emil was the Stieler's star son; at the time of his death he was a professor of German and a football coach at the University of Texas. This would be a great blow to Adolf, the first of many to come.

After high school graduation in 1912, Adolf was packing his bags to go off to A&M, where Fritz was already a student. His mother, Emma, came into the room and broke down crying, begging her son not to leave. Adolf unpacked his bags and stayed at the ranch to help out and to console his grieving parents.

The lack of a college education would make Adolf feel inadequate the rest of his life. For this reason he never wanted to be president of the Texas Sheep and Goat

Raisers, although he did more than anyone else to develop the industry and the livestock operations in the Hill Country area. His work in national politics, influencing government on a local and national level, was accomplished despite his lack of formal education. He became a leader, one taught by the school of life. His enthusiasm, spirit, and charisma were powerful. Adolf adhered to an often-used phrase from his family: "*Kannst immer 'was lernen*"—You can always learn something.

⊦⟨

"I loved going places with my dad—wherever, whenever!" Mama exclaimed.

It was an honor to be with him. One of my earliest trips was to ride with him in the old Model A bobtail truck to haul a load of goats to the Apache Packing House in San Antonio. We only took goats to Lozano's Apache Packing Plant every week. We watched the owner, Cruz Lozano, negotiate. Both Daddy and he were hard traders. Mr. Lozano would take me on a tour of the plant, explaining each process.

A highlight was to eat with everyone—traders, workers, buyers—at a long table family style in a house that looked like The Argyle [a historic private club] in Alamo Heights. One time one of Louis Faust's truck drivers was hauling a load of goats for us to the Apache Plant. Along the way he would drop off twenty live goats at a time at some pasture on each trip. Our Texas Ranger friend, Charlie Miller, got on to investigating the stealing of Stieler's goats. Sheep and cattle were taken to the Stockyards. I watched how they killed the cattle, in a chute with an ax to the forehead. I never wanted to eat hot dogs after that trip.

Adolf liked to raise the combination of sheep, goats, and cattle. "I stretch my grazing that way," he said. "I put cattle on first to eat the grass, then sheep to eat the weeds and short grass, and follow up with the goats to eat the brush."

Adolf was buying, selling, and trading goats every day. Mutton and nanny goats were used for mohair and meat. "I would love to raise goats as breeding animals," he said in an interview with *Ranch* magazine, "but my land is too widely scattered and vast to be possible. The expense and trouble at breeding time is too great." Each fall during the mid-1930s, Adolf sent a minimum of eight thousand mutton goats to markets, shipping them on hoof to San Antonio, Laredo, Fort Worth, El Paso, and Eagle Pass. One year he sold eight hundred nannies to Oklahoma, purchased by the government to go to Indian reservations. He would replenish his herds by purchasing three-year-old muttons from goatmen in West Texas, holding them for their hair until it got coarse or light. Then he'd sell them to the Mexican market.

As for sheep, Adolf ran several thousand Delaines, all muttons. He kept about five hundred head of cattle, mostly cows, shipping them when they got fat or old, and restocking with grown ones. He shipped more than three hundred calves yearly.

But it was Adolf's love for and fidelity to the Angora goat that was unshakeable. Although he was an astute rancher, he lost heavily in 1929 and 1934, when the Depression hit the goat business. Undaunted, he still continued to believe in goats when others were jumping ship.

"I believe in the goat business," he said. "Raising mohair is the best bet in the livestock industry. Although I lost when mohair was low, and floods and droughts wiped me out, my losses were greater in cattle. For making money year in and year out the average shows that the goat is more profitable."

$$\vdash\!S$$

After Shatzie's mother died, when she was fourteen and a freshman at St. Mary's Hall she often had the responsibilities of an adult. Adolf would call her up with a request, say, to take ranch hand Arthur Eickenloff and his new bride, Stella, shopping to buy furniture for an entire house. Shatzie felt very grown up to get out of school with this assignment. That same year she also felt grown up when her dad invited her to attend the very first San Antonio Fat Stock Show in 1938, which Adolf helped organize.

One of Adolf's most important and passionate works was starting the first livestock show in San Antonio. He worked along with Beal Pumphrey and J.W. Kothmann, livestock brokers at the Union Stock Yards downtown, and Perry Kallison and Mark L. Browne. They got legal advice from Judge Henry Burney, originally from Center Point. Burney was a best friend and wise mentor to Adolf in business judgments.

The first location for the stock show was high on the adobe hill on Hildebrand, above where the zoo is now, and behind the University of the Incarnate Word. It was held under big tents. The Stieler Ranch didn't produce show animals, but

Adolf knew many ranchers who did. There was a lot of organizing to initiate. Every county had to be contacted and invited. "When Daddy invited me to attend, to leave school all day to witness this, I felt very privileged," Shatzie said. Adolf remained a director for forty-one years. In the 1940s, Joe and Harry Freeman from Seguin had drive and a dream to build a coliseum. By 1950 the Freeman Coliseum opened its doors on 175 acres. The San Antonio Fat Stock Show became the San Antonio Livestock Exposition and Rodeo. One of the best and largest events in the nation, it is now held in the even bigger AT&T Center next door to the coliseum.

ᚻ

Electricity had just come to the ranch in 1941, and that spring, on the Ides of March, there was a rare ice storm that paralyzed Stieler Hill. Shatzie, sixteen, now a senior at St. Mary's Hall, had gone with Raymond to shear at the Hicks Ranch. On their way back to the Home Ranch they stopped at Woerner Warehouse on Lincoln Street to load corn. Shatzie looked up the street to the Keidel Hospital and saw her daddy's car parked funny, and she wondered why. "Daddy got hurt!" she exclaimed. "I'm staying here with him!"

The lines were heavily loaded with ice. Adolf had spotted a ewe in the Silo Field. When he walked out to get it, he noticed that an electric line was down. He hit the wire with his sheep cane to knock off the ice, slipped, fell, and landed on the hot wire. Luckily, the weight of his big body broke the wire; the electrical charge was so strong it would have killed a smaller person. Christian Blumenchankel hauled him to the doctor. His right arm and knee were badly burned. "His arm had been burned down to the bone, cauterizing the blood vessels shut," Raymond said.

Shatzie's boyfriend Joe Hedrick drove her in from school every day to sit in the room, ironically called "Adolf's Room" because he had furnished the entire hospital. "Joe supported me through this awful ordeal," Mama said. "The stench, blood, pain, watching Dr. Hardin Perry sew up one blood vessel as soon as another one rotted open." Adolf's life was in danger. Shatzie had just lost her mother four years ago, and now she was afraid she would lose her daddy too.

After five days gangrene set in, and they sent for Dr. Watts from Austin to amputate. He wanted to cut off the arm below the elbow, and the leg. But Uncle Victor said, "No, we're going to work with that leg and save it!" It never healed properly—but that didn't stop Adolf from dancing again.

He stayed in the hospital more than two months—so long, in fact, that he started operating his ranch business from his upstairs hospital window. Raymond would drive a big double-deck trailer under his window to show Adolf the goats. Adolf insisted that he let all the goats out into the street, one deck at a time, to look at them, then reload them after he had decided. Likewise, he had cattle unloaded into the street to inspect before they were sent to the auction.

"I never heard him complain once," Mama told me. "His heart had stopped beating. His arm was severed. But he was always positive. Even before he left the hospital he was trying to learn to write with his left hand. He was always looking ahead."

Dr. Keidel strongly suggested to his brother-in-law that it was time to slow down. So Adolf sold the Schladoer Ranch in Blanco, only to buy a 118,000-acre ranch in Sierra Blanca in West Texas.

It was illegal to burn body parts back then, so the arm was buried under the biggest live oak tree in the backyard of the ranch. To see the tree now, spreading its strong arms, branches reaching out, reminds me that even though Opa lost his right arm early in his life, he still moved forward, maintaining an attitude of strength, generosity, and unrelenting work ethic.

Early on, Adolf's family thought of him as the compassionate one among them. "Daddy was generous to a fault," Mama said. "He never turned anyone away. Strangers were always welcome. We never just had immediate family at the table. It was always full of other people." His mantra was "Be generous. Overgive."

Adolf owned the Faust Hotel in Comfort. The manager's son and one of Adolf's best friends, Pat Faust, a postmaster in Comfort, would hitch up a surrey to ride out to the Stieler Ranch to make homemade ice cream for that crew. "Adolf was a giant of a man in his community," he said, "always doing something for others, and usually anonymously. He was amiable, understanding, and respectful of others. He earned the respect and admiration of all who knew him." Another neighbor, Palmer Giles from the Hillingdon Ranch, credits Adolf with ridding the country of coyotes. "All the ranchers and neighbors could raise sheep and goats safely then, at least until recently. He was a good neighbor all those years."

During World War II Adolf bought war bonds, anonymously, for every baby born in the area, whether he knew the family or not. He also sent many deserving kids to college, with the promise never to reveal their benefactor. Likewise, many parents sent their unruly kids to work for Adolf, and he always gave them a disciplined workout. When the navy needed a new mascot, Adolf sent them one of his finest billygoats. He also donated a nice flock of sheep to roam and graze at the San José Mission grounds during San Antonio's mission restoration project.

"Some of my friends had church bell towers named after their fathers. Not me," Mama said. "Daddy wasn't a gambler, but because of him we have a hell of a good starting gate at the race track! All of his life he supported the oldest fair in Texas, the Gillespie County Fair Association, where he was a charter member."

For all his generosity, Adolf was always broke. He always had several business ventures going on with one partner or another, mainly bankers. He was a risk-taker, always ready to take a chance. "For us it was normal for Daddy to always be starting over," Mama said.

The Open Gate

When I returned to live at the Home Ranch in 1992, the house was empty. Our step-grandmother had Alzheimer's disease, and her caretaker moved her out, took over, and made sure there was nothing left there for us. No furniture or original light fixtures remained. We found family photos torn up, books thrown away. It was a shell with no soul. For sixty-five years, that house had been both the headquarters for a busy working ranch and a gracious gathering place, the hub and the heart. Ironically, the only two items left in the house, the only things that seemed of no value to anyone, were the ranch ledger, a record of the workers and their pay, and the guest book, a registry of the parties of goodwill that Adolf hosted after Dora's death. They were records of the essentials of hard work and hard play. The comment left in the guest book by Mrs. M. Lea from Fort Stockton described the ambience of those days: "A beautiful home and fine dinner and an excellent host. What more could we want."

Fragile yellowed pages are sandwiched between wood covers with tiny metal hinges and bound by a leather thong. The first entry was May 25, 1937. The last entry, written in my father Hondo's handwriting, was June 27, 1948. It said, "The rains came. So we thought we'd better have a party. It may never happen again in this world!"

You didn't need much of a reason for parties or company. Passersby dropped in. There were wedding showers, a Pi Phi rush party, hunters, students from UT and

A&M, always leaving notes of rivalry, and, of course, parties for the Texas Sheep and Goat Raisers Association and Texas Angora Raisers. There was a large barbecue thrown for the campaign of Thomas Dewey for president and Earl Warren for vice president, where speeches and music were broadcast from a sound system.

When I read the long lists of names in that guest book—beloved aunts and uncles, cousins, friends, and neighbors who frequented the ranch—it is as though I'm reading a roll call in the Book of Heaven. Their names return their live presence to me again, these people with whom we used to be so familiar. Charles Ingenhuett, Ione Crouch, Tante Lillie, Julius Real, Ceako Neunhoffer, Julius Neunhoffer, Ruth Keidel, Victor Keidel. I can almost hear their vibrant voices, clinking glasses, laughter, festive conversations. Cousin Roberta Stieler would always give this toast as the guests lifted their glasses:

Der grösste Feind für Menschen wohl das ist und bleibt der Alkohol.
Doch in der Bibel steht geschrieben: du sollst auch deine Feinde lieben.

The greatest enemy of mankind is and remains alcohol.
But the Bible says you must love your enemy.

I can just see again Dora's sister, Tante Talla, burst through the door as she cried, "Let the party begin!" Her festive entrance and cheerful voice lit up the room as she carried her basket of chili con queso dip and Wild Turkey bourbon. Her bright red lips and bright red fingernails were as loud as her voice. "*Wie geht's!* How goes it! Hello! S-M-I-L-E!" Within moments of arrival, she had everyone singing along with her. "*Trink'n wir noch ein Tröpfchen. . . . O, Susanna, wie ist das Leben doch so schön!*" Let's drink another drop. . . . O, Susanna, life is so beautiful!

There were six parties in August 1939 alone. February 11, 1938, was a melting pot of names from South Africa, British Honduras, Venezuela, Mexico, France—and even New Orleans. My uncle Gene always signed in as "DoDo Stieler, Blanco." On Halloween of 1937, his was the first name under the heading "The Morning After, a list of survivors," followed by Dora's friend, timid Grace Martin's "Oh, My!" Beal Pumphrey signed in from "East and West of the Pecos, Union Stockyards, San Antonio, May 6, 1940."

Shatzie's peer Rosie Whitehead came from Del Rio that day. Her mother Della was the originator and designer of the legendary W. R. Dallas ranch-style furniture, a style that filled this house once. Dallas, a shop teacher from Carta Valley, made the furniture for Della. Shins were always bumped on the trademark coffee table in the shape of Texas. The wagon-wheel headboards were iconic. Rosie was one of the first to buy the newest and latest breed of meat goat, four Boer goats from Africa for $2,400. "You ought to get in on this new deal now too, Shatzie," she said when she called her up one day. "You owe it to your father to stay in the goat business, even if they aren't Angoras."

The signature of Alfred Eisenstadt, *Life* magazine, Time Life Building, New York, NY, August 11, 1942, was a surprise find. The famous photographer was there to do a feature on Adolf, "the Goat King." Elmira Menefee from Del Rio reminded me how a party reflects the host's family when she wrote, on June 2, 1942, "I salute you, Adolf, as a sweet person, and a perfect host—your family reflects your noble worth. A perfect visit and a wonderful time."

Shatzie's schoolmates from St. Mary's Hall made frequent guest book appearances. "Authentic. That's how you describe the Stieler Ranch," wrote Gloria Galt, who signed with an "X" from Ardmore, Oklahoma. She and her sister Patsy (Steves) had come from San Antonio on that day, July 8, 1941. Another visitor was Shatzie's roommate at St. Mary's Hall, Mary Nan "Pet" West. She had a lot in common with Shatzie. Both were ranch girls who were half-orphaned. Pet was raised by her grandfather in Batesville. Shatzie spent weekends on their ranch in South Texas. Pet and her grandfather's favorite pastime after dinner was to sit on the porch and shoot their pistols. "That was a shocking and new experience for me," Shatzie said. "We never played with guns like that at home."

The South Texas town of George West was named after Pet's husband. Years later, when Shatzie and Pet were in their late seventies, Pet invited her to the San Antonio Rodeo. The two old ranch girls reminisced about their school days. Pet West was now chairman of the board of the San Antonio Rodeo. In 1984 she was the first female president. She begged Shatzie to meet again at her ranch. But she died soon after, and Shatzie deeply regretted the unfulfilled invitation. Before she died, Pet's greatest honor was to be inducted into the National Cowgirl Hall of Fame in Fort Worth.

Another signer and high school roommate was Jean Sealy, always inviting Shatzie to spend weekends in Galveston. Both girls were tomboys. Visiting the Sealys in Galveston was culture shock for ranch girl Shatzie. Jean's mother never made an appearance before noon. When she did, it was a grand entrance, descending a winding staircase in a long gown for dinner with a long cigarette holder in hand at which Shatzie stared wide-eyed, mouth ajar. "What are you looking at, Shatzie?" Jean asked. Shatzie paused, then replied, "I've never seen such a staircase like that before."

The rowdy bunch that signed the pages in 1941 was made up of Gene's running buddies, on the way back from the popular hangout in Kerrville, the BDI, or Big Drive Inn. They were UT football player Roy McKay, Rooster Andrews, and "Hondo" Crouch from Hondo, Texas, a UT swimmer who was tanned and clean-cut. They had two Pi Phi girls with them, Emily Ann Kennard and Stella Pascal. One would become Shatzie's husband, and the girls, her best friends.

"A Good Time Was Had at Adolf's," read the headlines in the San Angelo *Livestock Weekly* of May 9, 1939. Three hundred members of the Texas Sheep and Goat Raisers had come to a director's barbecue. The men wore suits and ties, the women silk flower corsages and hats. Adolf usually wore a beautiful woman on his arm. "A wonderful ranch. I love it!" signed Mrs. Louis Wardlow of Fort Worth. You could waltz across Texas just by reading the good old ranch towns they hailed from: Junction, Fort Stockton, Comstock, Blanco, Johnson City, San Angelo, Sweetwater, Eden, Llano.

Behind those parties were energy and work. Adolf always had plenty of help with his regular team, who effortlessly and gladly made the preparations: ranch workers Werner and Adelle Roeder, Raymond and Maria Kuhlmann, Shatzie and her aunts. In the screened meat house Werner and Raymond would already have hung three to four butchered carcasses to be quartered, cut up, and seasoned. Starting the fire at four in the morning, they manned the fifteen-foot barbecue pit, on which lamb, goat, and beef sizzled. Raymond sopped the sauce on with a basting mop made of strips torn from sheets and tied to a wooden spoon. Werner sliced the meat with knives worn thin from use. Coals were brought to three tripods. One was for the big iron pot of beans. From another hung the pot of sauce. A three-gallon enamel coffee pot spewed and spattered from the third. Food was served next to the barbecue pit on a twelve-foot cypress plank bar at the cantina. Under the shingled roof were two rock grills where beans, rice, and meat were kept warm over coals. The aunts showed up with huge crock bowls of German potato salad, sauerkraut, loaves of homemade bread and butter, sliced tomatoes, onions, and pickles. Cookies and coffee cakes were lined up. Nothing was catered or store-bought. Tables were made from long boards brought from the shearing barn set on sawhorses, decked with yards and yards of checkered tablecloths. People sat on benches borrowed from local dance halls or pews from churches.

The music was grassroots, as homemade as the food. Hondo sang Mexican ranchero or Sons of the Pioneer songs with his guitar. Paul Pankratz had his accordion, and Adolf his ocarina. But the sweetest music was the words left by the grateful guests. Neighbors John and Anne James from Turkey Hollow wrote, "Another happy day for which to thank the Stielers. The nicest place we know to visit." Dallas F. Wales, the manager of the Cactus Hotel in San Angelo, home base for the wool conventions, counted every minute when he wrote, "Three hours and seventeen minutes of untold happiness."

There is a curious twenty-five-foot-tall cedar post in the backyard at the ranch sandwiched in between the Mother's Day magnolia Shatzie planted for Dora and a huge hovering pecan tree. I noticed two more cedar stumps cut down in the mint and vinca patches. Albert explained to me that these towering cedar posts were put up to hold a huge tent made of wagon sheets that stretched over the patio and backyard for a grand wedding in November 1943.

Shatzie's life at the University of Texas from 1941 to 1943 was marked by the war. World War II molded lives, determined destinies. Every day she would read in the *Daily Texan* that hundreds more had left school to go fight. "It gave me a sick feeling," Shatzie said. She was living at Littlefield Dorm, and then the Pi Phi Sorority House. She was majoring in home economics and was a member of the Bit and Spur Club, for good riders only. She was the only one with a Buick convertible during the Depression. "I should've stayed there," Shatzie said in hindsight. "I had it good." But in the back of her mind was always the thought of how to get back to the ranch.

Shatzie had met Joe Hedrick at a dance at the Schreiner Military School in Kerrville. Joe was from Wheelock, and when he wasn't at school he worked on an offshore oil rig. "He was called off to war," Mama told me. "Before he left he gave me a ring. He said, 'Wait for me, Shatzie. I'll be back for you.'" Shatzie was devastated by the danger and long separation—and angry, too. In rebellion, she decided to marry Hondo, one of Gene's friends, instead. Shatzie was nineteen, Hondo twenty-six.

"What attracted me to Hondo," she confessed, "was that he needed help. I could take care of him." He had flunked out of flight school in the air corps and was hospitalized for psychiatric reasons. He was then assigned to be a basketball and swim coach at Randolph Air Force Base. Mama said, looking back, "I guess what I learned about myself is that my comfort zone was always to help people. Besides, he was my ticket back to the ranch."

H_S

Cousins Victoria and Albert Keidel took over. Shatzie's Pi Phi friends were seen wearing all of her beautiful clothes bought at Neiman Marcus in Dallas, while Shatzie just kept on dressing plain and simple. Now they took her there again to choose her trousseau, even though it was destined for the ranch or Schertz, Texas, the home of Randolph Air Force Base. Albert and Victoria also chose silver, fancy bone china from England, Steuben crystal stemware, and monogrammed linens for her. After all was said and done, Shatzie wanted just one more item from Neiman's: a roasting pan.

Shatzie and Hondo exited the Methodist Church in Comfort as a handsome, elegant couple, she in her long satin dress and veil, he in his army uniform. Six bridesmaids followed, dressed in dark green velvet and carrying gold chrysanthemum bouquets. Hundreds came to the reception at the ranch, dressed in tuxes and cowboy boots. Up on the roof deck and under the big tent in various areas were washtubs of burning coal, little fires for warmth on the cold November night. Another one of Albert's little elegant details were gardenias wired to branches afloat in the fishpond. The band played on, and people danced and ate the bounty of food. Hondo was in his element, with new people to entertain. "In fact, we didn't leave the party until four a.m.," a tired Shatzie lamented.

Aunt Clara, who was inside helping Shatzie with her clothes, decided to take charge. She marched out to break up the guitar playing. "Enough's enough! It's time for you all to go home now!" Shatzie and Hondo drove over an hour to the YO–Weaver Ranch lease at Mountain Home for their wedding night. Bright and early the next morning, Adolf and Gene showed up. Shatzie barely had time to regroup, get up, and fix them all breakfast on a woodstove.

The die was cast. This was more or less how it would be from now on. "Two weeks after the wedding," Mama told me, "I realized I'd made a mistake. But at

least I was back home!" When Joe came back from the war, he went straight to the Home Ranch to find Shatzie married to Hondo, already with a couple of kids. "Joe Hedrick was the first and only true love of my life," Mama confessed. Although Hondo and Mama made a dynamic and charismatic couple for thirty-one years, they divorced in 1974, two years before he died at age sixty.

Years later, as Mama rocked in one of the rocking chairs she'd restored, listening to big band music caused her to reminisce about her teenage years, "the height of her romance." She said with nostalgia,

Joe Hedrick and I shared such togetherness, dancing at the Schreiner dances, sharing our feelings, thoughts. We both had the same work ethic. We were both forced to grow up at an early age, had early responsibilities, learned how to cope. We never lost our sense of humor and could have fun over the smallest things. We were too young when life took a serious turn for us with the war. And now, in my rocking chair, I can swing back to those most beautiful years. And forgive me, Joe, for my arrogance and childish reaction to your sound judgment.

When I came to live at the ranch in 1992, I was enthusiastic about claiming residence, maybe eager to raise a flag with the ranch brand on the forgotten cedar post. But I imagined the canopy the post had once held up, which domed over the backyard that, for a few moments, housed happy people and high hopes.

ⱵႽ

Politics was Adolf's life. Among ranchers around here it was commonly said, "Just ask Adolf." He was always on some committee or panel to shape legislation, develop livestock and game preservation programs. For example, in 1947 he chaired a committee for a game law conference in Fredericksburg, where 325 ranchmen, farmers, and sportsmen gathered. His political work with the Texas Sheep and Goat Raisers and National Wool Growers led him to work with the Republican Party. He established a national tariff for American woolgrowers competing with imports, and from 1952 to 1972 he represented the Republican Party as delegate to six national conventions. He was a prime mover in engineering Dwight Eisenhower's announcement in Fredericksburg in 1951 that he was running for president.

If Uncle Robert Real was a mentor to his nephew Adolf in ranching, Robert's brother Julius Real was a mentor to him in politics. Many of the Neunhoffers and Reals were public servants. Julius Real was Kerr County judge from 1902 to 1906. Julius helped create a new county to simplify the long distances between the towns of Bandera, Kerrville, Rocksprings, and Leakey, which became the county seat.

Real County was named after him. Later, around 1916, Julius worked for the state, becoming the first Republican senator after the Civil War. The Hill Country remains primarily conservative and Republican today. In 1953, Adolf attended the inauguration of Eisenhower and Nixon. As special friends of Ike, Adolf and his wife Tops were invited to the White House. Tops presented Ike and Mamie with one of her handiworks, a felt Christmas tree skirt lavishly appliquéd, embroidered, and beaded with the Republican mascot elephant characters. While in Washington, Adolf also attended political meetings as a member of the Headquarters Committee of the Republican Party. His homecoming back to Comfort was celebrated in February with a dinner given by his fellow directors and officers of the Comfort State Bank at Becky Braun's Corral Café.

As usual, if Hondo and Shatzie were present there would be impromptu entertainment. It's what Hondo had to offer, what he did best. He ran out to the car and grabbed his classical gut-stringed guitar and put on a one-man show playing and singing Mexican songs.

ᚻ

Hondo cloaked himself in self-made humor, in his writing, his guitar playing and singing, his acting and storytelling. The power of his charisma cannot be underestimated. It eventually earned him recognition as a true tall-tale-telling Texas folk hero. *Texas Monthly* dubbed him "Most Professional Texan." *Time* magazine's "Milestones" column mentioned his death in 1976. On hearing he had died, his Nashville friends wrote a hit song: "Let's Go to Luckenbach, Texas."

Humor and a spontaneous, fun-loving spirit have been family trademarks, on both sides, for generations. My siblings have this energy. Juan is a captivating storyteller. His inventions and ideas for fun have an adventurous twist of danger and excitement. My brother Kerry's sense of humor was strong enough to break through the shroud of his mental illness. I remember the morning he came in for coffee. "Don't drink that old coffee, Kerry," I said. "That's okay, Becky," he said. "I'll drink yesterday's coffee. I'm not ready for today yet anyway." My youngest sister Cris survived the tribe by becoming a combination of party clown and good hostess. Whenever Shatzie enters a room she brings an aura of pleasantness and quickness of laughter, usually at herself first. She took Dora's advice to never lose her sense of humor. Ann Joseffy brought her New York City uncle John Armstrong to dinner at the ranch. The long table was set with the good china, and tablecloth and silver. Mama let the boys put their tadpoles in the individual finger bowls. Glasses were filled with raw milk from the cow. When Uncle John accidentally spilled his milk across the table, Mama was quick to react. She purposely knocked hers over too, saying, "See, it happens to everyone!"

On another tableside occasion, her spontaneity was more daring. We were visiting Cris in Virginia, eating lunch at the very nice Williamsburg Inn with six of her southern belle girlfriends. Our best manners were brought out. One girl in particular had been complaining and griping most of the day, at least until she said, "Oh no! I've spilled something on my new blue silk blouse!" Without hesitation Mama said, "Here! This will cover it up!" as she slapped a pat of butter over the stain. We were shocked. The risky impulse proved to be an icebreaker, and cheerfulness ruled afterward.

So open, so quick with her humor. She takes a bold stand in this wobbly world. Only yesterday Mama and Kat, an old friend visiting from Austria, and I were checking in on a family newly arrived from Mexico who had to leave everything behind. Mama was quick to point out the very hill in their background where German immigrant and hermit Peter Berg had lived, saying, "He had it much worse."

We three women stood around a discouraged Angelica giving advice, encouragement, and suggestions. Mama zeroed in calmly. "Geli, all three of us women have failed at some point in our lives. Fallen down. But we picked up and continued. That is why we are so smart and so wise today and can tell you what to do!" We all burst into laughter, knowing well that no one else cared to hear our advice.

⊢S

When Adolf took up residence at Stieler Hill Ranch, everyone knew he had the front gate removed so as to make his ranch accessible to all. In 1950, the open gate at the Stieler Ranch was about to come to a close. Mama, like her mother Dora, had become overburdened at the Home Ranch. She was keeping up with Adolf's social life, her own three kids, and housework and worrying about Hondo not being very responsible with the jobs Adolf created for him in the Sheep and Goat Raisers Association. Hondo could be a slacker when it came to fence repair. He was good with sheep, but he was really not a good rancher in general.

All of this added to Shatzie's stress and embarrassment. To make up for his inabilities, Hondo became a writer and colorful entertainer, his real talents. While sitting at the warehouse, he wrote the column for the *Comfort News*, "The Cedar Creek Clippings," a social satire commenting on local gossip and the politics of the day, under the pen name Peter Cedarstacker. The column was a hit, with subscribers from as far away as Australia. But Mama, with her German work ethic, never understood the artist and entertainer. "Hondo felt it was his calling to entertain," Mama recalled bitterly. "The nouveaux riches of the era, the oil boom rich, were so bored and consumed with their prosperity. He could join in their company with drink and entertaining. I didn't know how to fit in this useless way of life."

Shatzie became overwhelmed by her workload. She became very ill and had a breakdown. She ended up in the Keidel Hospital, where she was in a coma for five days after a reaction to a sulfa-based drug. To help alleviate her chores back at the ranch, Mama Club was brought in to help with housework. But it was Aunt Clara who stepped in and took charge to protect Shatzie. "With a fourth child coming, Shatzie, you and Hondo need to move out of here and get your own place, away from Adolf's Grand Central Station."

When I was six, my parents bought the Borcher Land Ranch from Adolf, five miles down Highway 87, to start their own Grand Central Station. The land, house, and log cabin had been owned and built by the Henry Borchers family in 1879. It is where Cris was born, the "home ranch" of my generation. But that didn't lessen Shatzie's workload. Now she had more kids, no help, and a bigger house, and she worked both inside and outside as a ranch woman. Stieler Hill would always be the only home for Shatzie.

HS

In 1955, after twenty years of being a widower, Adolf married his second wife, Merle "Tops" Porter, at the Methodist Church in Austin, where fifteen hundred guests attended. The authentic Spanish ranch house was changed to a formal gilded Louis XIV French Empire style. Every detail of Dora's style was stamped out. The Mission-style furniture was stashed up in the barns to make way for the golden chandeliers, organ, and lacquered French antique furniture. Mama described the décor as French Brothel.

Their marriage marked the closing of the gate for us for the next fifty years. Adolf's own grandson, Juan, who had been a hand there his whole life, was fired.

Mama wasn't allowed to use the pens, barns, water, or electricity for her cows when she leased part of the ranch. In general we weren't really welcome, especially after Adolf's death. Time brought with it deaths, divorces, and lawsuits, which separated and scattered us. It almost killed our spirit. I thought we were strong enough to rise above it all. Our fun-loving spirit can be present at times, providing a low-grade glow on the horizon whenever at least two of us get together. The powerful family tradition that once defined us is rare now. I miss it. Maybe it will come back again, in some form.

⊢ʂ

A couple of years before his death, after a series of strokes, Adolf was confined to a wheelchair and taken care of by a nurse at the ranch around the clock. Mama came to his bedside, lamenting her regrets and asking for his forgiveness. "I've made so many mistakes, Daddy. So many failures."

"No, Shatzie," he comforted her. "You didn't do wrong. Sometimes things just didn't go right." Those simple words were very liberating to her.

Later Adolf was unable to speak, a harsh fate for a man who never stopped talking. "That man was so interesting!" I would hear him say, though Adolf had done all the talking. Now he only spoke with his smile and teary eyes. On one birthday occasion we visited him in the hospital. What can you do, say, or give to a mute loved one? Juan walked in, said nothing, and threw a big hank of smelly mohair on his chest. Nothing said more between the giver and receiver than eyes that met with smiles and tears.

Adolf died at the age of eighty-eight at two in the afternoon on Monday, July 5, 1979, at the Home Ranch, where he'd lived for sixty years. The *Kerrville Daily Times* offered this eulogy:

> Adolf was not only one of Kerr County's last remaining second-generation residents. He may well stand alone in his contributions to the Hill Country ranching these past 65 years. The public and private deeds of this man affect the lives of all of us who live here today. . . . He was indeed a giant of his times—one of the last breed of proud individualist who may never be seen in our county again.

Mama was quoted as saying, "He did more for sheep and goat ranchers in gaining national legislation than will ever fully be known." Tops paid tribute by saying, "Adolf was the most generous and genteel gentleman I've ever met. There just never was a better person than he. Never had any animosity, never had a grudge; he was a lovable man, kind to everybody and everything he came in contact with."

In fact, Tops had something very similar to this engraved on his headstone. All of it was true. But after her death, after waiting an appropriate amount of time, and after checking with other family members, Mama had someone chisel off all of "that flowery bullshit," as she put it, leaving only his name and birth and death dates: Born April 1, 1893; died July 5, 1979. "Let's just be simple," she said with finality.

As for my monument to my grandfather, it exists in my mind. When I think of the people dear to me that I have lost, I recall a motion: my father Hondo rolling a leather thong on the floor with his tanned bare foot to soften it, my brother Kerry holding anything, as if his fingers were a pedestal showing off some admired or pondered object. I like to think of my son Ren scampering up the stairs on all fours singing at the top of his voice, and my sweet mother-in-law Helen, meticulously ironing clothes with her hands, fingers smoothing out every wrinkled corner as she folded the laundry.

For Opa, it would be how he threw corn out of a five-gallon bucket, feeding the herd of deer that lived on the ranch. He would hang the bucket on the crook of his amputated arm and scatter it with one powerful swing. The flung corn made a giant yellow arc against the blue sky before it landed.

⊦S

The Dance

Shortly after I had moved back to the Home Ranch, I had a new social life. I am an aficionada of the Mexican *charrería*, the original rodeo, born in the 1700s of the challenge to control a cow or horse in the open field. I regularly attended the charro ball at the Menger Hotel in San Antonio. The music, charro clothes, folk dancing, graceful floreada roping exhibition, and genteel people were a feast for my hungry soul.

On Valentine's Day 1997, I gazed out onto the dance floor. One figure in particular stood out. It was the most animated yet elegant silhouette, enthralling to watch in black *gala traje*, the formal charro suit with tight trousers with silver running down the legs. The form was thin and lithe. Dance after dance, it never let up, kept up an exhaustible fast rhythm, shoulders shimmying, legs prancing, hips swinging in Mexican style.

"Who is *that*?" I asked.

"That's Oscar," a friend said. "They brought him here for two years to train horses for a charro family."

Oscar Barrales was a third-generation charro, a champion in Mexico City in the events of *cola* (tailing) and *cala* (reining). I thought that I would love to dance just one time with a good Mexican dancer who took charge. That night my wish came true. He invited me to dance.

A few weeks later I invited some of my charro friends to a Tish Hinojosa concert at Luckenbach. They came right after a charrería. Every head turned when they walked into the dance hall in their charro clothes, big sombreros, and jingling spurs. At the break, to the amazement of the onlookers, the guys performed a dueling floreada roping exhibition out in the street, lit by car headlights.

I filled my dance card that night with Oscar, trying to learn to move like he did, but I never would. "How do you do that?" I asked of his footwork. "It's like making guacamole with your feet," he laughed.

The charros returned the next day to see the ranch. We toured the pastures. At the last gate in the cow pens, Oscar grabbed me and started dancing to the Mexican music blaring from the car, stirring up dust with his boots. So it was, joyous spontaneous dancing—in the cow pens, in restaurants, in parking lots. The dance was on. He didn't just walk across a room to hand me a drink; he danced over. He exuded such happiness and poetry in motion that the mere sight pushed tears of awe out of my sad eyes and heart.

$$\vdash\!\mathcal{S}$$

I thought that knowing Oscar would be a brief song. The odds seemed against us: he was younger, and he didn't speak much English. But just knowing him made me want to be a better person. So to begin saying goodbye to this unlikely acquaintance, I wrote twelve poems to him. The Spanish teacher in Comfort helped me translate them into Spanish.

My fascination started with his voice on a phone. His words were like poetry to me. "*Tu dobles mi corazón.*" You double my heart. "*Tu me flechaste con tus ojos.*" You shot cupid arrows at me with your eyes. "*Contigo todo brilla.*" With you everything shines. "*Voy a acurrucarte, arrullarte.*" I am going to coo to you like a dove, lull you. Then there was "*¡Cálmate! ¡Animo! ¡No te preocupa!*" Calm down! Liven up! Don't worry!

He called me *Tejana Blanca.*

My first love has always been Mexico. I had heard Hondo sing and play the music all my life. So my wounded heart felt at home, took comfort in Oscar, his simple joy, and the Mexican culture he brought with him.

Rosas de noche
Sleepless nights—your voice is

like the rain
to lull me to sleep
that waters the dry flower.
Bring me tranquility.
Keep the stars alive
so I can put them in a jar.

Oscar returned God to me through Spanish. *Adiós* became a new word to me, meaning not just goodbye but, literally, "May God go with you." I needed to learn that the word *esperanza* means both "hope" and "waiting." The word for horse trainer, *amansador*, means "one who gentles"; that gentleness could conquer something big and wild. In those days, every time I returned to the ranch, I faced the tormenting fear of loneliness. From his blue jeans pocket, Oscar pulled out a piece of folded paper, tattered, fragile with wear. It was an ancient prayer for protection, written by a knight in medieval Spain. "Before you go into your house, Becky, put this in your pocket," Oscar said, "and it will protect you." I doubted his advice, accepting the crumpled paper with a gesture of obligation. "You know this piece of paper can't protect me!" "Maybe not," he answered, "but the *faith* you have wearing it will."

He taught me his *oración*, his favorite prayer. I memorized it like a grocery list, as if my life depended on it. The line that struck me was "How blind I have been, Lord, thinking you don't love me for all the pain and sadness that I carry inside me. They are blessings, because it is through them that I know your divine mercy and infinite love." I was starting over from scratch. Because I had to struggle and focus to understand Spanish, the words became new ideas, larger than life to me. They made me listen, believe in new possibilities. I could talk to God in Spanish.

⊢ς

In 1998, when Oscar came to the Home Ranch, he invited me to go with him for six months to Spain, where a friend wanted him to train a quarter horse for an equestrian show in Barcelona.

Before I went, my sister Cris thought she'd better invite Oscar to dinner to check him out. I remember the tense moment for him as our whole family sat at the long table for the interrogation. Oscar stood up and in Spanish said, "Everyone wants to know my intentions with Becky. My intentions are serious. The education I received in Mexico is one of work and manners." Wow, we all thought, we could use some of that. Cris was kicking Johnny under the table to say something. "Oscar," Johnny warned, "the Crouch women, *mucho*"—he pointed to his mouth—"but *no mucho*"—and he pointed to his ears.

In anticipation of Oscar's returning to the ranch, we bought our first horse together, a six-month-old buckskin paint filly we named Tres Colores. Mama went even further. She was crazy about Oscar. She showed him an esperanza plant she planted at the Camp Shack. Its brilliant yellow blossoms waved cheerfully in the breeze. "Oscar," she said emphatically about her self-made omen, "if this esperanza plant is blooming when you come back from Spain, that means you are going to stay here!"

I was not a world traveler and had never been anywhere. The bustling airport in Barcelona was crowded with people meeting arrivals. As I stood at the top of a huge stairway in my boots and cowboy hat looking down at the masses, I wondered how on earth I would ever find Oscar. It wasn't hard. He stood out in that crowd: a body jumping up and down, head wearing the only white cowboy hat in the crowd, arms waving a huge bouquet of flowers. It's as if I was being greeted and welcomed to another world as a brand-new person, away from anything familiar—family, friends, ranch, language, and sadness.

Tu me agitas
With Mexican manners
you stir the cream in my coffee.
You stir the lime in my soup.
You stir the air with your quirt.
You stir the hooves of your horse.
You stir my feet to dance.
You stir the blood in my heart
You stir the feeling in my head
until tears are pushed out of my eyes.
Who knows why we meet.
You stir my world.
¡Disfruta!

H5

Oscar's mantra to me was "*Disfruta*, Becky, *disfruta!* Enjoy, enjoy! This is your time." Barcelona was alive and beautiful with art nouveau architecture. We walked La Rambla, which bubbled with life, art, color. Mimes and musicians performed. Everything was arranged artistically in the open-air markets—fish, vegetables, pastries, breads, nuts, flowers. The blue, blue windows of Antoni Gaudí's cathedral, Sagrada Familia, inspired the windows I designed for the chapel of Comfort's Baptist Church.

We ate outside by the sea, by the statue of Christopher Columbus pointing the way to America. But we were here, on this side of the world, eating *langostino* and drinking *calimocho*, wine mixed with Coke. Along the streets Oscar guarded me from the flow of people or oncoming traffic, even blocking the stares of men's eyes on me. He firmly held my hand everywhere, maneuvering me like a seasoned ship captain navigating through choppy waters. With agility he dragged me, moved me, lifted me. The dance continued.

H5

"This is our *nidito*, our little nest," he said arriving at our tiny one-room cabin. We were atop a hill with a 360-degree view in northern Spain, in between two little towns below: Monzón on the left, Barbastro on the right, a medieval castle in both. Forty miles away, we saw the foothills of the snow-capped Pyrenees.

Color was in my life. The view was breathtaking: green alfalfa fields and acres of yellow-gold sunflower fields. The almond, cork, and olive trees were centuries old. The only fences were human—shepherds, guarding their flocks with their dogs. Oscar trained and cared for eight horses while battling flies and heat. I took care of Oscar, keeping him up and alive to do his heavy work. On my walks on the hill I finally had time to paint watercolors of everything I gathered: eggs, round rocks, grasses, dried sage and chamomile and wildflowers. I painted our food before we ate it, the vegetables from Yolanda's garden and the long sticks of fresh bread they brought us every day.

I embellished the long table with stones, candles, dried weeds, and feathers. Oscar's work was grueling, hot, dusty. But every hour he rode by the door and said "I love you" through the door. He'd enter the house at ten p.m., hot and tired, to food cooking, music, a table set with candlelight. He threw up his arms and shouted, "Thank you, God, for this *gran mujer señora* Becky!" Then at breakfast, as I cooked at the stove, he'd come with his clean lean blue denim body, brown skin, black eyes, and moustache and smoothly, softly dance with me in that rhythm I could never imitate. "*Te guardaré. Te amoré.* I will keep you. I will love you, *mi dama, mi gran mujer.*"

Sometimes sadness swept over me like a wind. I knew it would pass, but I needed to take time out to cry away all the grief that sometimes piled up, from Oma Wilhelmine on down. For now I was insulated by Oscar's comforting Spanish words and the beauty of the landscape. "Don't think of things in the past," he'd say. "Think of today. *Vida nueva.* Our lives together. *Abrazame fuerte! Amame!* Hug me hard! Love me! *Amor con amor se paga.*" Love pays itself with love. Every loving word from him was a nail in the coffin of my insecurities and fears. In English he said to me, "Be smile! I love to hear you smile!" English, which he learned by ear, was a guessing game: "My uncle is swallow" meant "My ankle is swollen."

I looked out the window one day, hearing music. Oscar always played music while riding his horses. As he was bathing a horse, he danced the very difficult La Bamba. He looked weightless, bouncing on his toes, smiling while he was doing his mundane work. His light, fast feet defied gravity in those clunky boots and spurs kicking up the dust.

El lágrima y la estrella
You are a comet,
a star bringing shooting stars.
I am one in need of your fire,
your comfort, a message.
I am a tear.
The star collides with the tear.
and becomes grief of star,
light of tear.

ᛌ

What is old? Here I am in a two-thousand-year-old city, Zaragoza. The name is Roman, from Caesar Augustus. On our hill, we lived next to eight-hundred-year-old olive trees.

I would find myself speechless, staring at ancient crude rock walls made of different-sized rocks, still standing. The tile roofs, coated with yellow lichen, sprouted plants and great nests for storks. It was *time* that had made them beautiful. I saw that it was age, the passing of time, that had created a beautiful patina of enduring beauty.

I was always insecure about the age difference between Oscar and me. Do I have enough *belleza* and energy for him? "I wish I had more years to give you," I told him in the beginning. His answer, "I am here to return the years you lost grieving for your son."

Oscar took me to Seville in southern Spain, where the gypsies dance flamenco in caves. Clapping and tapping as fast as a Gatling gun, they expressed it all: passion, love, anger, flirting, rebuke, and pride. But it wasn't the young beautiful ones in flouncy ruffled dresses with roses in their hair that awed me. It was the older one, the teacher, dressed in simple black pants, white blouse and vest, who danced last. She exuded ageless sex appeal, passion, pride, and beauty that put an exclamation mark on self-confidence.

At a fair in Zaragoza we saw the famous Cuban musician Compay Segundo, age ninety, who sang and played his guitar with energy and passion, not sitting down once. Waiting for a parade to pass by at a festival in Monzón, we stood next to an old man who, after a stroke, couldn't speak. Oscar's friendliness drew him out. Oscar read his silent lips and sign language. He repeated everything the man was trying to say.

The opulent cathedrals, the lush flora of Spain left indelible images in my mind. But what I took home in my heart were the mute man's conversation and the age-defying confidence of Compay Segundo and the flamenco teacher.

ト)

Our Spanish friends Sergio, who raised *vacas bravas* (fighting cows), and Joaquin, a farrier, took us to a finca in Zaragoza to a *tienta*, a test of the bravery of the young female fighting calves. Men tested their bravery by poking them in their sides and drawing blood with a long lance held by the rider on a padded horse. I learned that 80 percent of the meanness of a fighting bull comes from its mama. So you wanted the meanest mamas to breed with the *toros bravos*. The cowardly calf that showed fear, quivering and not fighting back, grew up to be hamburger meat. But the ones who attacked the horse, fought back, got to live in luxury and breed with the fighting bulls. Fear and bravery coexist. The choice is your destiny. Fear, you die. Fear with bravery, you live.

I had come to Spain thinking, "Enjoy the moment, this is not forever." We returned to Barcelona to renew our passports. Later, at the La Dama restaurant, Oscar took his napkin and wrung it, saying, "*Disfrutame*, Becky. Enjoy me, use me all up. You are a *reina*, a queen, you can do everything, *una mujer completa*. Thank God for putting you in my *camino*, road. You need a young man *a tu lado*, at your side. I am not perfect for you but I am the best for you," he declared. I liked his self-confidence.

"*Yo recuerdo todo*." I remember everything, he said of our past two years together. Sitting in a bathtub in Barcelona, he said, "I have nothing to offer you but detail of attention. I can give you my time, my work, my health, my sincerity, my affection, my love." Then he added, "And you better consider me, Becky. I am mentally healthy." How could I go wrong with that smile, that laugh? *Brava* does not mean brave. It means aggressive, attacking, wild. Like the little fighting calf, *la vaca brava*, fighting my fear, I slowly raised my hand and said, "I'll take it." You have to be brave to be in love. We tucked away our promises for another place, another day.

Yo recuerdo todo
Memory—do not mute Spanish whispers.
Do not fade the face, cool the fire,
dry the lips. Stay.
Be my memory—do not leave.
Continue watching me, lips smiling at me,
even from far away.

I don't know how the townspeople of the pueblos had the endurance for parades, bullfights, and all-night dancing for two weeks. The fiesta in Monzón literally started with champagne running down the streets' gutters. Everyone brought a bottle to break. The all-night street dances beckoned young and old, rich and poor, all well dressed. A twenty-piece orchestra always played a variety: chacha, waltz, rumba, tango, rock and roll, but mostly paso doble, a quickstep to bullfighter music. Oscar especially shined in the Jalisco and Rancho Grande numbers. His unique Mexico City style garnered comments: "Where are *you* from?" We danced holes in our boots on the rock streets into the *madrugada* hours all those summer nights. I've never seen such an overflow of happy energy, gusto, and joie de vivre collected all in one place.

The horse show in Barcelona was a huge success. The Spaniards loved anything western. Oscar came galloping into the arena on a paint quarter horse to the music of *Bonanza*, wearing cowboy hat, boots, and chaps and riding a western saddle. The spectators were enthralled by the reining exhibition, but they broke into applause when he unexpectedly dismounted, unwound his rope, and performed a floreada roping demonstation while walking.

⊢S

When we returned to the Home Ranch in November 1998, the first thing we did was run to check Mama's esperanza plant. It bloomed radiantly! We remembered that Mama had told Oscar that if it was, he was to stay. Mama pulled me aside and said, "It died, Becky. Froze. So I planted another one." I hoped that wasn't an omen also.

The hills were alive with the sound of happy music, whinnying horses, jangling spurs. In April 1999, on the birthday we shared, Oscar gave me a hundred roses, red and yellow, the colors of Spain. In May we married under a gazebo at the Plaza Hotel in San Antonio with family members and friends. Oscar and his friends dressed in gala charro dress, and I wore a Spanish mantilla. The women wore gardenias in their hair. We ate and danced at Mi Tierra Restaurant to four hours of mariachi music. Oscar requested the "Marcha de Zacatecas," to which we danced the paso doble.

Romance for One

Eight years later, on February 25, 2007, Oscar left the ranch. When he left, he took all his horses, tack, boots, and spurs. He left me for a better barn a friend was loaning him. He was overwhelmed by the work here, but he was leaving me also. Things had to be renegotiated. I still had some lessons to learn about facing fear, fear of loneliness and abandonment. It paralyzed me, stymied creativity. The Peaceable Kingdom turned once again to Rancho de Viudas. The string that held my heart together was beginning to unravel.

In the hot summer of 2006, a coldness was gathering around me as I anticipated Oscar's decision to leave. Would I die a quick or slow death? I started to grieve what I hadn't lost yet. I would have to dig deep down to hone beauty out of pain again.

I brought Oscar his usual Gatorade in a jar and sat under his barn accompanied by flies and swishing horsetails with my cat and dogs. I saw his lanky blue denim form, cream cowboy hat bowed, spurred boots clanking, as he led a wet horse toward us. I was already missing him. The ranch without Oscar would become a silent vacuum, oppressive and dead. The house would have a cold hearth, with no soul or purpose. I could not exist without them, I thought. I said this knowing I would survive yet another loss. But this one would suck me up like a tornado and drop me lifeless on my concrete patio, unable to lift a broom or one more spoonful of beans.

ᛟ

I ordinarily started my days in calm and gratitude, anticipating the sunrise from my rooftop deck, drinking coffee, with cats Poncho Pantera and No Fear and dogs Copie, Vacita, and Oso at my feet. But in my new single life, the little crises were magnified. Early one morning, after feeding the horses that were left here, I went to scrape up the dead raccoon, baked on my hundred-degree patio for twenty-four hours, to put in a plastic bag. I drove out on the highway to dump it into a canyon. All this, still in my nightgown, before my first cup of coffee. Another morning, covered in chigger bites and anger, I pulled mounds of huge horehound around a fence line just to be able to open and close gates before I could feed the horses. I tugged and strained at the hedge of weeds. They gave way, spattering mud and manure into my shoes and hair. When I stopped, looked, I saw in the forest of horehound another ecosystem. There stood a beautiful yellow grasshopper. Black crickets escaped. Poncho and Lefty, the yearling colts, were thrilled with their new freedom as they ran into the field, munching blindly. I felt productive, for a while. I'd freed the gates. They could now open and close.

At dawn-thirty, I went out in my nightgown again, a lazy habit now, to feed Poncho and Lefty. Panic. Where's Poncho? I heard a distant faint whinny and found he'd jumped a barbed wire fence and couldn't get back. Today I couldn't afford any setbacks. Wading through four feet of wet weeds full of stickers, halter in hand, I tried to figure out how to get through our grass leaser Rick's maze of heavy cow panels with no gate. Poncho seemed eager to cooperate for once. In the foggy dawn I doctored his wounds and got him home.

That evening there was a glorious gold-orange-pink sunset so beautiful it'd make you cry. I cried for beauty but also for the loneliness that comes with that time of day. I saw Alfredo up at the barn, putting up the tractor. Thank God, a human being. I confessed to him I couldn't live here by myself and asked him not to abandon me also. Without making eye contact, he said, "*No se desespere.*" Don't despair. Don't give up. On my way back from the pens my eye lit on one half of a battered butterfly wing lying in the horse manure. Torn and tattered, grounded, but still showing evidence of its once beautiful being.

The next morning, as I walked to Three Colors's pen, I saw her three-month-old colt White Lightning happily nibbling grass at her side. I knew this was the moment I was going to separate them forever. As I approached the contented pair, I remembered walking ever so slowly up the stairs to tell Kit and Sky that their brother Ren had died. I thought, in a few seconds none of us, our whole family, will ever be the same again. Now separation was about to befall White Lightning and his mama. Later, I went to the house to pull weeds. I guess pulling weeds was better than raking rocks—another ranch girl, Lesa Whitehead at her Sonora ranch, had said her father told her to rake rocks all the time, and in a relentless wind.

Romance came to me that night as five little does in the paved lane. I got five gallons of corn and dribbled it on the road. When I drove back by later they didn't even move, just stood there looking at me, not afraid, trusting me. No moon. Dark. I sat in my bedroom, Poncho Pantera on my lap, the dogs at my side. I said, "I love you" to my dogs. I left a message on Oscar's phone, saying, "Every living thing needs salt—and love."

⊢ϟ

Yesterday on TV Barbara Walters was interviewing Bill Clinton. She asked him if he thought he had made a difference in the world. He answered, "In some places." When I go to feed the colts I always check the water trough at the wool barn to gauge the water level, clean out hay and moss, maybe remove a drowned field mouse or grasshopper. This morning there was one tiny bright red spot—a ladybug—clinging for life to a piece of hay. I strained it through my fingers and returned it to familiar ground. I'd like to feel that I made a difference today.

Slowly, mechanically, each day I trudged up to the barn to feed the horses. I had no enthusiasm or energy. Copie, our oldest sheepdog, ran at my side looking up at me with her smiling pant, cataract-clouded eyes, wagging tail. She had a giddy-up in her step despite her crippled old legs. "Thank you for your company and enthusiasm, Copie! You and the battered butterfly wing helped me get up and moving."

Every morning as I sat on the water trough full of ten or more frogs, I sang "Siete Leguas" to Lightning in hopes that he'd at least get to know my voice. He wouldn't let me get closer than a foot from him, his blue eyes fearful and wary. In anger and sadness, I started to clean out the water trough. Three Colors stood by, waiting for a clean drink. I'd sling out the mossy green slime soup with rotten cricket legs, grasshoppers, chips of red barn paint floating on top, peppered with black frog-egg specks. I tossed out the water with a coffee can. The stringy moss and water hit the flat rocks, my shoes, the dog. One desperate frog clung to the float. Finally, it made a jump that landed him out on the driveway. The next day I saw him smushed flat, the result of his leap of faith.

Winter came, and trough cleaning turned into ice breaking. One night I saw Mama had covered my begonias with her own red coat. There wasn't a soul on the ranch, and I could feel the stillness. In the morning I sang "Siete Leguas" louder than ever to chase out the quiet. The Mexican Revolution song is about Pancho Villa's horse, Siete Leguas, who could run seven leagues. Seven leagues, literally eighteen miles, really means "can go on forever." Poncho, Lefty, and Lightning gathered at the trough. So did twenty frogs. They had become my new listeners. "*Oye tú, Francisco Villa, que dice tu corazón. Ya no te acuerdas valiente?"* Listen, Villa, what does your heart say? Don't you remember being brave? You chased away the Federales and returned the land back to us!

I broke the frozen water and checked on the frogs. Under all that ice and moss, they had survived.

Like Monet's haystacks painted in different light on different days, I looked down on my familiar scene every morning from my rooftop in different seasons, weather, light, and moods. With coffee, cat, and dogs I surveyed a pen with one horse, one crooked tree, the wool barn and its crooked rooster weather vane, and the miracle of sunrise.

$$\vdash\!\!\zeta$$

Whenever I was depressed, I learned a new Mexican song. They were sadder than I was. I sang at the top of my voice from my rooftop. The songs filled the air like prayers that connected me to eternity. I sang every song I knew while mockingbirds flew screeching past me: *"Me gusta cantarle al viento porque vuelan mis cantares."* I love singing to the wind because it carries my songs: "Feria de las flores," "La palma," "Una página más," "El as de oro," "Carcel de Guadalajara," "Caballo prieto asa-vache," and the homesick "Canción mixteca." I sat inside their revolutions, train stations, palm trees, bullfight rings, desolate ranch landscapes, singing about their bravery, fidelity, infidelity, deceit, unrequited love, passion, heartache. Their words were my life, too, here at the ranch. Says one of those songs, "Dos arbolitos," "My tears run between the furrows of the field. My only friends are my animals, to whom I sing my sadnesses. Two little trees, I'm so lonely. If God doesn't send me a companion, keep me company under these heavenly skies until I die."

$$\vdash\!\!\zeta$$

Of all things, a plastic doll leg became my version of a prayer tool. I found it among other unusable junk in my studio. Others have used pocket crosses, worry beads, rosaries, candles, as spiritual aids. The journey back to God and myself was like a journey into a new world. I wanted to trust God again, and make friends with the world. In the middle of a sleepless night, tormented, I'd grab the doll leg by the heel like Jacob wrestling with God. "Don't let me go!" I'd say to God. "I won't let go

of you if you won't let go of me. But I'm barely hanging on to your heel, and you've barely got me by the toe. Keep me! Bless me! Change me!"

I looked for answered prayer anywhere. Today Charles put in a new air condition-er unit called "Comfort Maker," and my cat No Fear slept on my chest that night.

ʜꜱ

I spent another sleepless night, not knowing which way the sun would come up. In a dream I drove over all the stained glass windows I had made, which were lying in the threshold of a gate. All five dogs barked throughout the full-moon night. I finally heard that bark of pain, and I knew they had a porcupine out there. When I went out into the full moon light to check, they had it cornered under Sky's car, no chance of escape. I put the dogs in.

First thing next morning I looked out and there it was, sitting in all its bushy sunshine glory in a frozen pose underneath the pomegranate tree by the rock entrance steps, perfectly still, oblivious to the dogs' relentless yapping. The sun was coming up over the Highway Field and wool barn in a soft yet blinding in-your-face light. Its brilliant orange-rose glow created a halo, an aura, around the porcupine. It sat as if it were meditating on a new day.

"We've got to kill it!" Mama said. "I'll call Jimmy to bring his gun."

The porcupine's in his own world, I thought, but mine too. Jimmy came with his rifle, a small flashlight taped underneath the barrel for nighttime varmint shooting. I left the scene. I heard a pop and Mama yelled, "He *got* him!" She scooped the limp clump up with a pitchfork and put it in the back of her truck for disposal. Up close, I noticed thousands of sharp quills along with long silky hairs that had created the seemingly soft mane—protection and beauty intermingled. The ground underneath the granada tree was strewn with quills, proof that in one moment it had been there and in the next was gone.

For much of the day I was sad over this. There, finally, was the cool untroubled dawn.

I bonded with the porcupine. I wanted its beauty and aura camouflaged among my defenses too. Not knowing if this could be our last day, and before confusion sets in, we'll be brave, wait, and face the light.

⊦)

Oscar had been gone a year without word or talk of return. He had politely called every morning and evening, wishing me good day and good night. Often we would comment on the moon, a connection that at least put us under the same sky. I needed more words. I yearned for the return of his words, *"Que bonito es llegar a casa!"* How good it is to come home!

As I was turning onto the caliche road from taking soup to a sick Sky, a red-tailed hawk flew from an oak tree right down by me. I felt low. It flew low. I took the hawk sighting as Kerry, the sweetest spirit of all, and thanked him for his little blessing.

I remembered Dora's quote from Goethe, "There's something genius about just beginning." So I began. I finally began to take Mama's advice: "Enjoy being alone, be proud of yourself. Love yourself."

I was always looking down the road for a return, listening for a sign. A word. I reminded myself of Tante Talla's insistent voice: "S-M-I-L-E!" I could hear a faint echo of her lively song, *"Wie ist das Leben doch so schön!"* How beautiful life is!

The bitter edge of loneliness had softened. I finally reached the point that I could live with Oscar or without him. But with him would be nice. I just waited, learned patience without expectations. I even planted another esperanza plant. It grew, towered, bloomed, dominated everything, was overwatered and underwatered. Then it froze, died, got lopped off. I gave up on it. The word *esperanza* stopped meaning "hope" and became "wait."

I remembered the advice Albert once gave me about watering a bougainvillea: "Let it get dry. When it struggles to survive, it will bloom." After a two-and-a-half-year drought, Oscar came back.

The Camp Shack

For a short time, Mama had leased the Home Ranch from her stepmother for ranching. After Tops died, Mama had it all to herself. She was finally in her own home place. I saw her, now at seventy, in the cow pens, ankle-deep in muddy dung surrounded by her bellowing cows. "There's Harold," she said, finding the bull. "And where's Big Tit?" A paisley wool rag covered her Angora white hair. She wore an old ratty sweater gleaned from ninety-year-old Tante Talla, her arm sticking through a big hole in the elbow, leaving the rest of the sleeve to dangle in the wind. Upstairs in the barn, her rough hands wrestled twenty bales of hay. She threw them down through a hole into four mangers on the ground level. I cautioned her not to slip down into them. "If I do, I'll die a happy old woman!" she said. "Just think, *anything's* possible in life! We have our own barn, our own hay, and our own cows!"

Wiping the cow dung off my boots, I could scarcely share the ecstasy. With joy, she struggled to be a rancher with no money, no good equipment, and no predictable help except her unpredictable son Kerry, business partner Bob, and Esequiel, a ranch hand who spoke no English.

In January 1995, from down at the Shack where she and Kerry lived, she wrote about the events of the day:

It's been another one of those full days of being out and around in the pasture.
I started it with a slow fire—no coals left. Pot roast and vegetables in the oven.

Esequiel and I go back in the Salt Lick; one cow all alone—maybe today is her day! But here we are—feeding on the frosty ground. Sun shining on the crystal grass. We spread the hay. The cows are gentle and contented in the pasture. Baby calves all around—three new ones this week. The old Brahma South Texas cow had her little jackrabbit calf.

Back to the barn and home—pot roast is ready and so are we. A quick trip to town for cow cake and spray for cows before we can eat. What a chore to ready the spray. Need oil, need gas, and spark plug. Then another trip back to town—need nozzles. Then Esequiel hassled to get Briggs-Stratton sprayer going. It's now after four. Kerry figured out how to move the back seat of the pickup to get the jack out to jack up the trailer so we can take off the tire to take up to Jimmy's air compressor, only to find lug wrench didn't fit. Forget that one. So Esequiel used a hand pump and fixed tire. Finally we sprayed 10 heifers, 6 cows! Only 53 more cows to go. Got to get that Briggs-Stratton going better on its own.

She kept detailed notes on her little herd scrawled in her checkbook from 1993 to 1998: a history of what was sold, bought, worked, born, lost, sprayed, moved. At her highest count, she reported fifty-nine cows, two bulls, eleven heifers, and thirty-seven small calves. Her rotation records, written on tiny lines, were along the lines of "All cows into Section, 8 heifers into Camp Shack, 5 heifers into Section with bull (need to put bull back December 15), all cows from Section into Windmill." She knew her cows like her own kids: "Black and white cow slipped calf, lost '93 heifer calving; white-faced black heifer to calve for first time, sold red Pedolla cow with funny teat, had black calf. Removed cancer eye from black white-faced cow and butchered it." She knew of every loss: "Lost 1 small calf, trampled in barn; pulled a dead calf; gave Mulie red heifer to Sky." In 1994 she bought out her partner, Borchers, and continued ranching by herself.

H)

We are from the tribe of fire builders and pecan gatherers, steeped in the longtime tradition of pasture worship and dinner on the ground. So for Mother's Day, when my son Kit said he was taking me out to eat—out in the pasture—I knew it would be a rejuvenating experience.

From years of picnicking, I have learned to make do. This lesson was learned early on the famed family *rote Decke*, or red quilt, when my toddler brother Kerry fell, wet cotton diaper first, into a beautiful bowl of guacamole. Mama casually scraped off his bottom. Not a spoonful was wasted. Then there was the time Mama made stew on a campfire and forgot to bring any utensils. We all took turns sliding the stew from the one butcher knife into our mouths.

Bouncing around in the back of a pickup was magic to me. We were told to keep our "eagle eyes" peeled to see the first deer. Picnics in the pasture were some of my happiest memories.

And here we were today, nine of us piled into two pickup beds, off to the Six Hundred pasture. Sitting on the tailgates, swinging our feet, we could smell the pungent spongy grass from recent rains. The pasture had on its "Sunday clothes," as foreman Raymond would have said. Tall grasses, leafy post oaks, lacy mesquites, and blooming prickly pear made a collage of every shade of green. The dusty gray-green agarita had changed from yellow blossoms to red berries.

From a tailgate you can see the smallest and meekest vegetation: the tiny yellow flower Scrambled Eggs, the small delft blue Star of Bethlehem; the gray fuzzy ground plant that looks and feels like cotton swabs and ends up in bird nests. The dove weed, used medicinally by the Indians, smells like camphor when crushed.

Halfway back in to the pasture, at an underground spring, Mama decided that she and her dog Lucky would get out and walk the rest of the way. We were too lazy to join her. To arrive at the Birthday Springs, you have to cross a treacherous dry creek bed of boulder-sized rocks and four-wheel-drive over a seepy muddy marsh until you come, gratefully, to a canopy of live oaks and the most perfect spring-fed creek. Except for slippery surprises, the creek is user-friendly, ranging from ankle- to waist-deep.

Kit thought of every detail. He quickly set up a card table and tub for drinks. He'd brought a rich feast: prosciutto ham, cheese, melon, and crackers for starters. Red wine and Bailey's Irish Cream on the rocks. There were deviled eggs, fried chicken with biscuits, corn on the cob, coleslaw, tossed salad, fruit drinks, and bottled water. "Store-bought water!" shrieked Mama in protest. Mama's contribution was a marbleized three-layer flintstone, which she plopped down on the buffet table, saying, "Here's the Rock of Ages."

Thankfulness was the theme of Kit's prayer. He thanked the mothers present for their love and strength. "In spite of all the bad we've been through," he said, "we are still richly blessed in our lives and each other. I am rich having a grandmother like Shatzie who continues to amaze me through all the good and bad. She is a mentor to me. In all of our disappointments she is strong, sympathetic, funny, nonjudgmental, and conducts herself with energy."

Sky bathed both sheepdogs in the creek, despite the presence nearby of a water snake snapping at fish. My grandkids walked and slipped in the ankle-deep water. Mama slept, not on the quilts we had spread out but on the grass with her dog, her paper plate and napkin tucked under her. I tried to throw it away, but she clung to it to save it. Later, to the delight of grandson Kitito, she lit it and sent the tiny barge aflame down the creek. The sun was like balm poured onto my head. We hated to break the spell, pack up and leave.

These were moments that connected us to eternity.

In tailgate conversation on the way back, Mama pointed out the unusual landscape. From the air, one would see strips of trees and then strips of grass. "Before government agents would tell you what to do, we cleared the land in strips so you can get through the pasture. Opa did this to have grass for livestock, but also trees for the deer to hide among. I just recently talked to the old man," she said, "who cleared all this by hand in the 1930s. He showed me all the worn-out, dull ax heads."

As we looked at the grassy pasture, it was hard to imagine more trees and thousands of goats following us. She continued, ever the taskmaster, "And when are you going to get this group back together again to chop cedar and take down the old barbed wire fence in the cline grass field?"

Back at the shack, Mama cautioned Sky, "Don't mow over these pink coneflowers or the red salvia for the hummingbirds. I saw an old buckhaw tree in the Six Hundred, almost dead," she reported. Up at Oscar's horse barn before the picnic, she'd already pulled a pile of weeds at her "state park," her favorite viewpoint, where Maria's ashes are buried. Two blue herons flew overhead, choreographed in perfect duet. "They used to have a nest down in the canyon," she said. "Look! They're putting on an air show."

She continued to give orders: "Chop the thistles on that side of the road, Sky. I've already chopped 'em on this side. Don't let 'em spread."

"But that's where rattlesnakes live," I warned, "in all those prickly pear."

"Oh, well," she shrugged. "Everyone's gotta be somewhere."

My brother Kerry was the most creative and remarkable person I have ever known. Kerry was our family favorite. When we lost Kerry to schizophrenia at twenty-one, it was a blow the entire family never recovered from. We learned to accept that his creative personality was more cultured yet primitive, more sane yet insane, more constructive and destructive at once. Despite our ignorance of mental illness, I give credit to my parents and the survival skills Kerry learned at the ranch from the way we lived, genteel and yet wild. It was his exposure to art, nature, humor, the discipline of good schools and athletics, that allowed Kerry to cope as gracefully as he did when handed this assignment from hell.

Kerry was good-natured, diligent, and independent. He was voted most popular camper and counselor at summer camp. At St. Stephen's Episcopal School he was dorm counselor and captain of the football, basketball, and swim teams. He'd ride his Italian racing bike from Austin to the ranch, eighty miles, on weekends. He was in the Math Honor Society. His near-perfect math SAT score got him accepted to MIT. But he went to the University of Texas instead, maintaining a 3.8 grade-point average in the school of architecture and engineering. While there, he was completely financially responsible, held two campus jobs, and sold his fabulous pencil sketches.

The most remarkable accomplishment while he was a student of architecture was to build his own house on some land Mama had bought in Austin. He drove the family tractor, at twenty-five miles an hour, to Austin, used rock from the ranch, and only spent a total of seven hundred dollars. The house had five levels. Kerry said, "You fit in it, like a piece of furniture." Yale professors of architecture saw it and said it was the best-designed house they'd seen in twenty years.

There was no physical endurance test not dared or challenged by the brazen brothers, Juan and Kerry. The athletic feats you didn't tell your parents about were like the time Kerry and Juan and daredevil cronies jumped from the top of the spans on a three-span bridge into the Colorado River near Burnet. One false angle would kill you. During the 1960s, news from the Red Cross broke Juan's long silence from Vietnam: he had suffered injuries in a helicopter crash. Then Kerry's dear Tante Butta died of cancer. For a conscientious nineteen-year-old, these burdens caused stress enough for him to lose focus and break down. He hitchhiked the countryside, was in and out of jails and hospitals. The greatest damage was caused by twenty electroshock treatments with no follow-up therapy or care.

Hondo had encouraged Juan and Kerry to camp out solo, survival style, in parks and pastures. That was good training, because when society no longer accepted Kerry, he went to live in the Big Pasture at the Home Ranch in a polyurethane tent, eating what he killed: snakes and armadillos, mostly. In his letters from jail he wrote, "The best and hardest I ever did was cross country at the ranch. I can still feel the bounces in my feet." For someone who could draw sensitive line drawings, figure out a Rubik's cube in minutes, or glue a smashed jar back together, one day he simply announced, "I have confusion in my fingers."

↳)

Before Mama and Kerry came to live at the Home Ranch, they lived in one of Mama's houses next door to her log cabin on Mistletoe Street in Fredericksburg. Living with a schizophrenic was hard. Mama buried the silver out in the yard to protect it. Kerry would put a chicken to bake in the oven with no pan. Cris and I tried to clean up Mama's yard with ecological sensitivity. We left the coyote tail Kerry planted sticking out of the row of onions. We left the wire funeral flower tripods to hold up the soon-to-be vines. But we did dump eight dollars worth of ant poison on the wide trail of red ants leading up to her back door. "Oh no!" she shrieked. "Now my horned toads won't have anything to eat!"

Kerry discovered Joanie, a homeless woman living with her bike under a bridge in town. It was cold weather, and Kerry begged Mama to let her come to the house. She was down and out, lost and found. She was so thankful for a roof, a table, a meal, kindness. She carried in her purse a picture of her family's home, lost to eminent domain. It was a prominent hacienda on a Spanish land grant. Going to the Christmas Eve service with Mama and Kerry at St. Barnabas, she said, changed her life, was a turning point for her, renewed her faith. Through compassion and Kerry's reaching out to her, she regained her confidence.

Our family went to eat dinner at My Blue Heaven restaurant. As we were going in, we saw a blind beggar standing to the right of the door. He was so pitiful-looking that we averted our eyes. It might ruin our dinner. Only Kerry stopped and said, "How's it goin'?" Kerry didn't follow us in. He just hunkered down and stayed with him, offering him a smoke, conversation, and kindness when no one else would.

Living down at the Shack with Kerry, her dog, and her cows, Mama found contentment among the chaos and unpredictability. In the occasional notes she wrote to herself, at seventy-five, she reflected one Saturday morning, comforted only by her dogs and childhood memories.

I fed the calf and Copie. I take in the fall misty morning view of the canyon. I count six stages of hills past Comfort. Peaceful from here. Thank you, Lord! How I love my animals around; adoring and simple demands. Takes me back to my beautiful childhood, surrounded by love and total security—wonderful, because until now I didn't know it! Memories of coming home from school to the smell of fresh baked bread, homemade butter with a sprinkle of sugar. There was always somebody at home! The warmth of the big wood heater in my bedroom. Love abounded, as I curled up in the evening with my mother reading adventurous and exciting books to me. Thank you, Lord, for giving me time to count my blessings!

What a beautiful fall evening. Madle on her pallet, Buzzer spread-eagle on the grass. Kerry's happy and contented with his new radio. He's hanging on a thin thread today. It's getting late—head to the house—wash Mac [the bulldog], bathe Lucky. I rock and hold Lucky all wrapped in the best bath towel in front of the fire—what could be more content.

What blessings I have! A full day of doing what I love most. I have fantastic children. As I sit before the fire I think of all the bustle and struggle to insure the inheritance, etc. We cherish each rock and each inch here, but without the *spirit* we all share from each generation and from each other, there is no need to inherit. Where is the innocence, the magic, the unconditional love, the simple, the humor? How we can laugh at ourselves, at each other? Get over the grudges! There's too many doors opening. Oh dear Lord, if only half the good I have had thrust on me could go on for these next ones to enjoy. Please let it be! I wonder what will happen tomorrow.

Kerry had once written on a scrap of paper, "Face fear not death," a quote from Alexander the Great. Time passed, and the years went by. Perhaps due to a new and improved medication, Kerry now seemed sane, settled down, functional. It's as if he'd been Rip Van Winkle waking up after twenty years and realizing he had missed so much of his life. Thinking he had leveled out and improved, we ignored his repeated pleas to go back to the state hospital. He would come to Mama's bed in the middle of the night, worried. "Who's going to pay the taxes, Mom, when you're gone?" He said to a guest at Cris's house, "Life has passed me by." On March 4, 1999, Kerry was sitting on my couch. "Becky," he asked, "what's the purpose of my life?" I was brief and simple. "Kerry, first we are here just to say hello to God, to acknowledge him. Then we need to have a thankful heart, no matter what comes in our life." Maybe that was too little too late. Kerry's lifestyle exhibited more godly kindness and thankfulness than anyone could muster up. The reality of losses and pressures of the real world became overwhelming to him. Despite his strong, anxious efforts to participate in society, lack of concentration, shaky nerves from medication, and loneliness turned Kerry to giving up.

The next day, Mama and Kerry were working side by side in the yard, planting geraniums. "Go in the house and fix us something to eat," Mama told him. After an hour passed she decided to go in and join him. As she passed the garage door, she noticed her dog sitting there, strangely staring at the garage ceiling. Curious, she went to look. She saw Kerry hanging from the rafters. She struggled to take him down herself, lifting the dead weight of a grown man with one arm while fumbling to untie the rope knot with the other.

The emergency medics and sheriff were already down at the Shack when Sky and I flew down the caliche road. Mama's main concern at this point was that they hurry up and get his body on ice because she'd promised to send his brain to the Harvard Brain Tissue Bank for research.

On that same day, Cris discovered that Mama's dogs had run off on a spree, crossed the boundary fence of the Camp Shack, and killed fifty of Kenneth Spenrath's goats. Mama called him, apologizing sincerely. "We lost control of our dogs," she confessed. "We will pay for the goats."

"How gracious of you to call, Shatzie," Kenneth responded, "but that's nothing compared to what you lost today."

We sent this announcement to the newspaper.

The family of Kerry Stieler Crouch would like to thank all the people of the community who, over the years, befriended Kerry. It took understanding, courage, and love on your part to step across the barrier and stigma of schizophrenia. Every smile, hello, handshake and kind word from a stranger or a friend made his world a little less lonely and frightening. In this difficult assignment he was given—he maintained a spirit of kindness, gentleness, and thoughtfulness that leave us all with a profound example.

We took Kerry's ashes to the Laughing Tree on Hondo's ranch, the same place we'd put Hondo's ashes. More friends of Kerry's than I thought existed gathered to join us. Where had they been when he needed them? In Crouch style, we did things our way. Cows gathered. Sandhill cranes flew over in homage, dark gray rain clouds showed appropriate somberness. The Rev. Jane Lancaster Patterson, with her special insight, was the perfect one to officiate a service for us in this most difficult circumstance. Kerry's ashes were passed around in a crock with a wooden spoon for everyone to take part in scattering. Oscar took a handful of ashes, kissing them before he released them into the wind. Juan knew of nothing else to do but to squat down and build a little fire in honor of his lifetime camping buddy. "Because that's what Kerry and I did," he explained. Sky remembered Kerry's poetic response to a prayer my ex-husband Dow once prayed: "Good patch kit, Dow," he'd said. Out in the pasture, as we huddled in the circle offering up prayers, Sky repeated it by way of an amen.

In the circle, we comforted ourselves with fond Kerry stories. Cousin Mary Lee mentioned the time Kerry's big Chesapeake dog Buzzer was left tied to a parking meter in town on a fifty-foot rope, barking in the middle of Main Street for hours. Everyone tolerated it, knowing it was Kerry's dog. The policeman who drove Kerry to the state hospital because he'd been turning cartwheels on the courthouse lawn said that Kerry had educated and fascinated him on the trip with stories about the history and architecture of Fredericksburg. "After he got out of the car at the hospital, he thanked me."

The St. Barnabas Episcopalians recalled how they accepted Kerry with unconditional love and tolerated his antics. The church was the only neutral place where he could hang out in those days. There was the time he wired the toilet's flush handle and pulled it from outside, under a window, surprising whoever entered. The Rev. Dean Pratt didn't even crack up when Kerry pulled out a coffee-stirring sipping straw to take wine at Communion. There was the gift he'd made while in state hospital rehab for his friend Marian, who had multiple sclerosis and couldn't walk

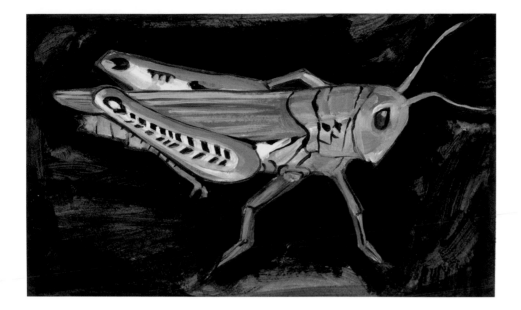

well. It was a crude pair of moccasins made out of tire inner tube laced with colored electrical wires. "Here," he said, handing them to her. "These are so you can walk on water."

Wook Avery said she had a dream about Kerry running through a field. He told her, "I'm all right." When it was my turn to take out some ashes, I remembered the time Kerry came running up excitedly to tell me about the magical qualities of a grasshopper.

"Becky!" he said. "I found this big yellow grasshopper dead, buried underneath some grass. I looked at it and everything was quiet and still. When I picked it up and put it in my hand it alerted all the birds and squirrels and they all started chattering!"

I took some of Kerry's crushed, burned bones in my hand and let them fall, sifting into the tall yellow grass. The chattering of all the squirrels, birds, cows, trees, and people stopped.

⊢⟨

Now it was my turn to take Mama down in the canyon, to see the wonder, to heal, to remember, to learn, and to work. The descent was steep. We had to be sure-footed, choose our steps carefully to avoid loose rocks. It was late August, hot. We checked on the spring. It was dry. "I want to show you where the rocks are because no one knows how to clean out this pipe." She moved away big rocks, dug in the mud, pulled weeds, scraped out gravel with her fingers as if she was searching for a treasure. Soon we heard a gurgle. A trickle, a flow of water started to fill two big cement troughs Raymond had made decades ago. "Oh, we should've cleaned out those first!" she said.

We scrambled back up the canyon to get buckets, shovels, dustpans, a coffee can to clean out the leaves, mud, tree limbs, and gravel in the neglected troughs. I knew that Mama would bring hundred-year-old shovels—too big, too wide, too heavy. I carried a lightweight plastic dustpan that did the trick. "We need to cut this limb that's hanging over the trough, Mama." She nixed that idea. "No need. Doesn't bother anything." I guess I was remembering as kids sitting in the lap of luxury in our underwear, cooling off our bottoms in the three-inch-deep mossy pools.

"Let me show you the source of the spring," she said. "It starts up there under those trees." The spring is almost hidden, revealed only when we moved some rocks in the creek bed. After Mama cleared away some debris she knelt down to drink, Indian style, with cupped hands and her face in the shallow water. There she was, surrounded by dried cow patties, drinking from the *ojo de agua*, the holy place. "It doesn't get any cleaner than this!" she said, encouraging me to kneel down, too. "Pure clean water. Here, drink some. Raymond used to keep a tin cup down here."

I wanted to share the experience, the taste, the knowledge, the reward, to be more like her. But I didn't. Too much trouble. Getting down on my knees and the cow patties were my stumbling blocks. Being witness to this image, however, of Mama face down in the rocky creek bed sucking up water from the earth would come to haunt me, and I promised myself that I would return someday to get down as she had.

Now we had to carefully cover up the *ojo de agua* with flat rocks to protect it from clumsy cow hooves. Mama looked around, always finding rocks that were too big and heavy and half-buried in the ground. "Too heavy, Mama," I warned as she tugged on a boulder. "That's okay. I'll just roll whatever I find."

As we trudged back up the hill out of the canyon carrying our heavy tools, I thought surely we'd have a heart attack. "I was gonna clean my house today, but I'm outta chi," I panted. "Oh, that's okay," was her tired answer. "Who cares? We do what satisfies us at the time. It'll all even out. We're never finished."

As we topped the hill, we saw a red-tailed hawk darting across the cerulean blue sky near the shack. "Look! There's Kerry!" Mama pointed out. "His spirit is in that

red-tailed hawk." On unexpected occasions we'd see the red-tailed hawk making rare appearances, flying right in front of us, perched on a fence post or near our houses. It called out its shrieks as it darted or stared. We came to accept the hawk as Kerry, coming around to check on us, to say, "Remember me."

HS

Now Mama and I would impart our maternal sentiments to every animal on the ranch. When Rick Franzen took his cows away to rest the range, he told me he left two cows that were probably going to calve soon. One cow had lost her calf, and she stood by her dead baby for two weeks. Still protecting her baby, she fought off twenty buzzards. "There's nothing like the mother instinct of a cow," Rick said. Another time, Mama and I were cleaning up Werner's rental house. When we entered the yard gate, a tragic sight shocked us: there lay a newborn fawn no more than hours old, its insides totally eaten out, legs crushed, its sweet head perfect and untouched. "There's a sad mama out there somewhere," Mama lamented. The yard was totally fenced in. Was it a coyote or a mountain lion we'd seen here recently?

Mama continued cleaning for four more days. "Every day the mama doe returned," Mama said. "She just stood at the gate staring at me, stomping her feet and snorting at me."

We both knew how she felt. It's the rending, the detachment, the emptiness. The long, long longing that is so long it never ends.

$$\vdash\!\!\!\!\!\!\zeta$$

On Labor Day, September 6, 2004, Lucky followed Kit and the kids out into the four-hundred-acre Windmill pasture and ran off. Lucky was a stupid city dog, unfamiliar with the land. Mama, Sky, and I drove out into a wet muddy pasture to search. I drove fast over the rocky road, my anxiety in high gear, and got stuck in the mud at a rocky creek bed.

We got the wheels unstuck from the mud by putting logs behind them. Along the way, Mama pointed out the sunset, shining on the lush grass. "That guajillo bush is not indigenous to this country," she said. "Its seed was planted by the cow dung of Opa's South Texas cows he brought here." We bounced back home.

At eight o'clock that evening, we ate and tried not to act worried. When it was almost dark, I watched Mama walk back out into the Salt Lick by herself in the waist-high beggar's lice to look for Lucky. I caught up with her in her truck. More bouncing: we searched for nonexistent roads to avoid washouts, marshy bogs, rocks, and cactus. We called and called. We waited, waited. On the way back, on top of a layer of sadness and lost hope, Mama made us notice: "That's buffalo grass. Look how the cows top it off. And the KR bluestem. Gene seeded the whole place. It was a big deal in the '50s. But it's not so nutritious, takes over." Then, "What's that bird?"

"Maybe a whippoorwill," I said. "A Poor Willie's Widow," Mama corrected.

The sea of Mexican Hat scraped and rattled against the bottom of my car. "Stay on the high ground," Mama directed. "Don't worry, Becky. The dog will either come back or not. Why worry?"

"Because he's your best friend," I sympathized.

"I've had a lot of best friends I've lost before!" she replied.

In my dreams Lucky would return. In the morning there was a note pinned to my screen door with a bobby pin. "Lucky came back at 2:30 a.m. I hope you can sleep in—Mama."

$$\vdash\!\!\varsigma$$

May 29, 2006, Memorial Day. I went down to the Shack, now Sky's house, where Mama and Kerry used to live. I found her down there, hot and sweaty from pulling a truckload of beggar's lice. To catch her breath, we sat down on the couch. There was a nice breeze. "I planted those native Texas trees so the house would be totally hidden from view," she explained. "Then Alfredo cut 'em all back and lopped off too many limbs. But it's coming back now. I put a string on the north rock wall so that vine can grow and cover it all up, but it's been cut back too. I planted buckthorn and blackhaw. They're rare. And redbud, cenizo, mountain laurel, and Spanish oak. I pulled up all the beggar's lice because once that gets hold you've lost your whole yard. Sky let it all go to seed. He has to be taught how to live here."

Sky and Mama lived together at the shack after Kerry died, and she tried to teach him some survival skills—or just how to grab hold. The hunters always killed her a doe and would leave the whole carcass in her house on the kitchen chopping-block table. Since that was full, she told them to lay it on the bed on the porch, to cut up later. When Sky came home late that night, seeing a dead body on the bed scared him half to death. Next morning they moved the deer to the kitchen, and Mama got her hacksaw out. She wanted to teach Sky how to cut up a deer. "Sky," she said as they were butchering, "don't tell anyone Frida [her dog] was chewing on this deer. They'll never know."

Mama found Sky in the garage with the chainsaw out. Oh, good, she thought, he wants to learn to use the chainsaw. Her spirits fell when she realized Sky was making an art film, with the chainsaw chasing a gallon of paint around. Always feeding, always pushing food at people, she asked, "Sky, do you want something to eat? I bet you haven't eaten all day." "No thanks." "Come on, Sky, eat something!"

"No, I'm okay." "How 'bout a sandwich?" She wore him down. "Well, okay," he said, "I'll eat something." "Well, get in here and make it yourself! I'm not gonna make it for you!"

Returning to the clutter, I asked, "Mama, no matter how much you sweep here, the pill bugs are back the next day." "I always had a barrier of diatomaceous earth sprinkled across the threshold," Mama advised. "You have to just step over it. I think it's made of crushed snails. They eat that and it cuts up their insides." I wondered how much more she could tell me—where the ironstone plates are from, why she salvaged the one lonely andiron from the fireplace at the big house. Where she found those huge cypress beams she put in the ceiling. Sky had been painting his walls a Mexican rose, but one day he left suddenly, leaving them unfinished. "Why do we keep coming here to clean up? Seems useless," I asked Mama. "Because we care," she said. We discussed trivialities nonchalantly, even though a sad pallor mixed in with the dust motes floating through the sunlight. We tried not to notice the notch Kerry's body weight left in the garage rafters, or wonder where Sky had gone for so long.

It got to be late in the evening, and I turned on the light over the couch to continue our talk. "We can't sit here," she said. "We have to go outside. The mama wren is coming to feed her babies that are in a nest on the light fixture, and we'll disturb her." The ordinary facts we talked about were insignificant. Yet they would become famous to me someday because Mama, who once lived here, told them to me as we sat together that day talking on the couch.

I visited the Shack another day after she had been there. On the table I found her offering of the day. Out of a turquoise soda bottle sprouted a pungent sprig of dill like a lacy umbrella. The table was covered with small fragrant peaches ripening. The peaches had come from a scraggly tree outside. Kerry had casually tossed a seed pit outside one day, and it volunteered to take root, grow, and produce sweet fruit.

Unkept upkeep. It's a constant fight against weeds, overgrowth, drought, invasions of pill bugs, scorpions, and spiders. There's no rug under which to sweep them. Cobwebs and dust mingle with nostalgia, memories, and longings. The amputated trees offer no more camouflage. The vines' severed arteries left a wall of dead leaves. All is exposed: our messes, disappointments, hurts, and failures. Remains that remain, compost waiting for a better day.

ⱅ

A Conversation on the Patio

On August 5, 2001, I had morning coffee with Mama, and we had the following conversation.

"You know," I said, "you learn something about the mind of Raymond with just the shortest conversation with him."

Mama agreed. "He is so observant, always inventing, always thinking—so much common sense."

"We were sitting on the patio at the Camp Shack yesterday enjoying a little breeze," I told her.

Finally, in the summer heat he said he noticed a little beginning of fall this morning at the nursing home. Indian summer, I said. Then he said it'd be even cooler if your mom would put a big suction fan in the garage that would draw the air over here on the patio. And then in front of you, from the grape arbor, you could hang a sprinkler upside down and you have yourself a cooling system. I mentioned to him that this weather was almost as bad as the drought of the 1950s that lasted seven years, and he laughed and said, "No way!"

Raymond mentioned the roof on the tenant house, near my house, where he'd lived seventy-two years earlier. "I lived on the divide," he said. "A divide marks the separation of water when it rains." He told me his roof was the only one on the ranch facing parallel to the highest point on the ranch. The water that ran off his roof on the front side ran down the hill into the canyon to North Creek, then collected in the Guadalupe River. The water running off the back side ran into the horse trap and ended up in Bear Creek and then the Pedernales River.

Mama asked, "Now, who'd ever notice that?"

"Last night I watched the movie *Isadora*, with Vanessa Redgrave," I said. "Isadora Duncan lost her two children in a car wreck, and she said that from then on she never would experience natural joy again the rest of her life. I know what she means."

"I can relate, too. Yes, she's right. With our sons gone, Becky, we'll never quit thinking what could've been. I wonder what Kerry could have done by now. He was so far ahead of himself!"

"Ren's been gone fourteen years now. It's just that I have busied myself with doing for others—Kit's family, Sky, Oscar—and I still feel the need to do for Ren. That's why I killed the grass I planted on his grave. Remember? Overwatering and overfertilizing it, as if I still have to nurture and feed him as a swimmer."

"You will always feel that need. I do too."

"I drive by the cemetery running my busy life. I don't even stop at his grave anymore. It's too painful."

"Don't look down at his grave. Look up at those fiery sunsets. That's where he is!"

"I will *never* get over the pain of *him* missing *his* life! No matter what anyone says to me."

"And I'll never stop feeling guilty that I didn't do enough for Kerry or that I didn't listen to him when he begged me to take him to the state hospital. Why didn't I listen better than I did? Am I listening better now?"

"The hardest and saddest thing," I said, "is to realize the *pain* Kerry must have felt to cause him to end his own life."

"Oh, I think of how much he must've hurt. The humiliation and degradation of it all. Life is so fragile!"

"What gets me is that schizophrenia is the most insidious of trickery because being out of touch with reality *is* your reality. And then when you finally realize you *are* crazy, you're sane, because you can think rationally."

Mama agreed. "And we'd be so impatient when Kerry wouldn't answer a question, not realizing it takes so long for a schizophrenic to process words through all the static in his head."

"You know, when Ren died . . . I have different definitions of God, faith, eternal life now. I'm sorry, but all I know is this sentimental life here on earth. It's nostalgic, dazzling, beautiful—so beautiful I can't stand it."

"I'll never forget how unlifelike it is!"

"Do you mean death, or when you found Kerry hanging in the garage?"

"I'm talking about Ren, when I saw him in the casket at the funeral home. I touched his hands, those beautiful hands. I was shocked. They were so cold and stiff. To see him lying there and then remembering how full of life he was—singing everywhere he went. Like the time his whole art class was watching him and laughing because he was singing out loud with his headphones on as he painted."

"And Mama, how could you ruffle up his too-combed hair in the casket? I thought you'd run into the cracked open wound where he'd landed on the street pavement!"

"Because his hair was *never* combed!"

"And how can you ever get that image of Kerry out of your mind, Mama, when you struggled to take him down, single-handed, from the rafters? He was so heavy, and staring you in the face?"

"I never will. I never will. All I wanted to do was hug him. It's all he wanted me to do when he was alive."

"We couldn't become a one-family social work team for him."

"Oh yes, we could've! If we only could've understood this mental illness better and how it works. He always said, 'Mom, you're selfish. You get to do whatever you want, but I can't.'"

"Mama, you've never been selfish. You're like the mama scorpion that carries her babies on her back 'til they eat her up. You know, we both had the most superb sons. Ren's swim coach at UT commented on how well adjusted, happy, and people-loving Ren was for a nineteen-year-old. Not many kids were. And Kerry was our talented genius and trendsetter to his peers. Who else would've made a pair of Indian moccasins for his girlfriend from the hide he tanned in chemistry lab from a deer he'd shot himself?"

"Juan still hasn't gotten over losing Kerry. I forgot how close they were as brothers. Kerry told him once, 'Juan, I have lights in my fingers.'"

"Ren would be thirty-three now. And it hurts when I see his friends going on with their lives. There will always be a part of me that is so cruelly hurt. Betrayed, untrusting of happiness."

"Well, what are you going to do? Doctors, pills, roses won't help. We are all just a collection of feelings."

"I don't know. I lost my rudder. When Ren was alive I had energy. I lost my way when he died."

"I lost Kerry twice. My only comfort is that at least we had that wonderful man. What blessings, what anxieties! I remember his intuitive candid insights. He taught us so much.

He demanded nothing. How special and unique they both were. I'll never pass that Ford sign at the Rumpel without thinking of Ren up on a ladder painting it, two weeks before he died—in shorts, that gorgeous body, laughing, so alive! We are constantly carrying our ghosts and torments with us. At times we might as well mention them, laugh about them."

"Yeah, we have to choose what to give meaning to or not. Mama, do you know what I can do about all these grasshoppers eating my kumquat tree?"

"Sprinkle Sevin Dust, I guess, or get some geese."

"Then who'd clean up after the geese?"

"The tree just has to grow faster than it can be eaten up, then!"

A Texas Star

In December 2002 Mama received the prestigious Texas Star Award from the state of Texas and the Gillespie County Historical Society in appreciation for her labors, outstanding achievements, and contributions to preserving Texas historical culture. Mama took home the award, a beautifully carved limestone star. I soon noticed that it was being used as a doorstop instead of being proudly displayed on a shelf. That wasn't disrespect, I decided, but just another sign of Mama's practicality.

The four other honorees gave impressive and articulate speeches. They had enriched Texas with their culinary skills, humor, and art collections, or had restored buildings that required great monetary investment. When it was Mama's turn to talk, she got up, didn't say much, and quickly sat down.

"I chickened out," she said. "I had planned to pull out of my purse the things that to me represent a pioneer spirit—the one we should all be working to preserve. It's the *spirit* of the people—not so much the things—that we should remember. I was going to show them Minna Fishbach's long black hand-knitted stockings and Louisa Hellmann's little rusted tin candleholder. These women stood for bravery, hard work, and perseverance in times of hardship. They had a simplicity of lifestyle that we've lost touch with. But seeing all those people, I felt silly and thought maybe no one would care or understand."

Yes, Mama collected and restored antique cars, houses, and furniture. But those were just symbols of her real collections—namely, of antique people.

"You should've done it, Mama," I said. "Everyone needed to hear why these people are your heroes." So here is what Mama really wanted to say when she was honored on that December day in 2002.

$$\vdash\varsigma$$

Mama told me that the humble relics she cherished more than any fine expensive antiques were that little fragile rusted tin candleholder and a small ten-by-twelve-inch broken mirror. They had belonged to the first woman ancestor Mama admired, the widow Frau Louisa Hellmann, her maternal great-great-grandmother.

Louisa was born in Berlin, Germany. She and her husband and an eleven-year-old daughter, Emilia, were on the shipping list of the *Galliott Flora*, which left Germany in 1849. Only Louisa and her daughter arrived at the Texas coast at Indianola on November 8, 1851; she had been widowed at sea. They made the hard journey to New Berlin, in Guadalupe County, on foot, their few belongings carried by primitive oxcarts.

Accustomed to a more refined life in Germany, Louisa walked with her young daughter into an unknown world. The threat of Indian attacks and disease, which had wiped out thousands in the pilgrimages of German immigrants, always loomed.

Among Louisa's very few belongings in her trunk was the little tin candleholder, with a base smaller than a saucer and a handle barely big enough for a finger. One night on the journey, staying in a house along the way, Louisa placed a lighted candle near a small mirror on a dresser. The heat from the candle broke the mirror. Evidently the mirror's owner wasn't very forgiving. She wanted ten dollars for the damage, an enormous amount for widow Louisa to pay. Louisa paid for the mirror, it seems, but then took it out of its frame and took the broken glass with her.

The mirror, never used, remained in her bottom drawer. The mirror and the candleholder were passed down in the trunk of relics until one recent "outsider" wife threw all the "treasures" out, including the Indian arrows that had pierced Adolf Rosenthal's hand and chest. But the candleholder and the story remained.

At New Berlin, Emilia grew up and married Adolf Rosenthal, who became a remarkable pioneer of the Hill Country. They moved to Comfort, where he became the town's first schoolteacher, and they had six children, three boys and three girls. One of the girls, Clara Rosenthal Neunhoffer, became Mama's grandmother. To Mama,

Louisa's pioneer spirit was a standard of endurance that would be an inspiration years later. Frau Louisa Hellmann was the first to walk across Texas. She was a strong-willed woman. From her came the families and communities we are today.

H S

The other item Mama had in her purse that day was a long misshapen black stocking finely hand-knitted out of cotton. Minna Strackbein Fishbach was another one in Mama's collection of old German women. "From only a few moments of conversation," Mama said, "I learned so much wisdom."

During the 1970s, Mama visited with Minna a few times. "I could tell about her lifestyle from these things," Mama said. "She was self-sufficient, didn't whine or complain or live on welfare. But she had her self-pride and her faith. She drove her Model T only two miles to the Zion Lutheran Church and back every Sunday. Her simplicity and independence is what I admired most. I thought, if she can do it, I can do it."

Minna, at age forty, had answered an ad in the paper for a mail-order male from Germany. Mr. Fishbach came, married her, and then sat around giving her orders. He only burdened her lifestyle more. Minna lacked nothing. She had her milk cow, chickens, and garden. But Mr. Fishbach was so strict and thrifty that he wouldn't let Minna put milk on her cereal. The milk was to sell. So she used water.

Minna did beautiful needlework. Mama has her finely knitted stockings, the fingerless black gloves embellished with cable stitching on top. There were sheets made out of soft flour sacks and a monogrammed banquet tablecloth out of finer cotton. She had only two dresses, a black one for church and a calico one for everyday wear. She had a cotton bonnet for summer and one for winter. Inside her winter bonnet she had knitted a delicate, soft angora wool lining, as if a bird had feathered its nest.

Her undergarments especially attested to her resourcefulness and frugality. Pantaloons, camisole, petticoat, and underwear were all made of crude cotton sugar and flour sacks. The faded printed words "sugar," "pure as snow," and "50 pounds" were written all over her body like a jumbled crossword puzzle. "Evaporated milk" was printed on the camisole. In this throwaway society, the underwear spoke volumes to Mama.

Minna was a widow when Mama befriended her. Mama, too, was alone, living on a meager income restoring furniture. She was amazed to hear Minna was living on four dollars a month, which she received from the German government. After Minna died, Mama bought Minna's Model T and proudly drove it down Main Street in Fredericksburg, happy that it was getting a good airing out. Just a few blocks from home, but still on Main Street in full sight of everyone, the whole drive shaft dropped out. There she sat. She doesn't remember how she got it home. All she said, repeatedly, was "If she can do it, I can too!"

In the 1960s Mama bought a gem from Bertha Krammer, an old *fachtwerk* (half-timber) and plaster house at 512 West Creek Street. It was one of Fredericksburg's original pioneer houses. Another of Mama's collectibles, Mrs. Nehr, was renting it. She still spoke only German. Leaning over the fence one day talking to her, Mama asked how old she was. "*Ach, achtundneunzig oder neunundachtzig, macht nichts!*" "Oh, eighty-nine or ninety-eight. Makes no difference!" Mama laughed. "You know, she's right! What difference does it make?"

In 1960, Mama was president of the Gillespie County Historical Society, which had always been run by her Keidel family members. Conservation efforts had no power, no money, no public awareness. Businesspeople thought the conservation-minded people were unrealistic to invest in the Hill Country's history mainly to attract tourists. But with Lyndon Johnson's presidency in 1963, suddenly it was noticed. Under Mama's leadership, a small band of dedicated warriors made a grand turning point in historical awareness. Important landmark buildings were rescued and saved because of her. Some of the highlights were buying and restoring the Kammlah House and wagonyard for the Pioneer Museum. She took an active part in the cleanup and restoration project. She also brought the public library up to state standards during its transition from being merely her aunt Clara's book collection in the Vereins Kirche to a library at the old courthouse. In 1964, when the Gillespie County Courthouse was to be restored into the library, it was through Mama's quick insight and strong leadership that the restoration was rerouted through correct hands for architectural authenticity.

She even remembers the buildings that weren't saved. "Over there," she pointed out, "is where the church tore down that house where the woman lived who used to bake bread for the Indians."

Mama was proud that she owned, at one time or another, six original pioneer houses. All were on town lots deeded by the German Emigration Company. She never had any money, but through wily finagling she borrowed or financed her way to buy these houses to "save" them. There was the Strackbein-Roeder Sunday house, a weekend townhouse for farmers, at 411 West Austin Street on town lot 25, built in 1854. In 1972, she bought the Jenschke Sunday house at 406 West Travis, built in 1851. Mama lived there a couple of years right after her divorce.

In 1971, Mama and my brother Juan bought the Pape-Dangers log cabin and rock house at 213 West Creek. The first immigrants in 1846 had quickly built the tiny log cabin for the minister Fritz Pape and wife, who had lost three of their four children on the long trip from Germany. The surviving daughter, Dorothea, ended up marrying a local miller, Carl H. Guenther, who founded the Pioneer Flour Mill, now in San Antonio.

The urgent motivation to buy and save these houses in the 1960s was that they were on the demolition list for their rock, which was to be used to build the museum at the LBJ Park in Stonewall. Next on the hit list was the Schumaker-Leyendecker House, the oldest two-story house in Fredericksburg.

So in 1969 Mama bought that whole town lot, naming her homestead and place of business Rumpelkammer, which is German for "junk room." In order to buy that property, Mama had spent hours talking to the previous owner, Mr. Klein, buttering him up by—well, bringing him homemade butter. It was here that she refinished primitive furniture, caned chairs, collected Texas crockery, sold antiques, and restored Ford Model T cars with her partner Bob Borchers for the next thirty-six years.

That same year, Mama became owner of house number six, the Heinrich Cordes house, where she lives today. Her ownership broke the longest-running heirship of that original family since 1857. The house is built on what were originally eight town lots, a huge area deeded to Johan Alsenz II by the German Emigration Company. The property consists of a wood frame house built in 1922 and the log cabin built in 1857 by Cordes.

Heinrich Cordes was a stonemason, carpenter, and *baumeister*, or master builder/architect. He helped build the Nimitz Hotel and old St. Mary's Catholic Church.

When he built his log cabin home, Crockett Street was little more than a footpath; their henhouse and pig-pen were where the street is now. Mama bought the property for a restoration project with two friends, Dottie Leslie and Ruthie Shafer. When Mama got a divorce in 1971, she left her china and crystal behind and moved to the primitive barnlike log cabin, then later to the frame house, with her son Kerry. The log cabin is located behind the Girl Scout building on Mistletoe and Crockett, sitting dangerously close to the banks of Town Creek. The creek didn't always run there. When Mama and Bob Borchers were look-ing for old original car parts, Bob's father Henry explained why there were none left. Town Creek ran close to Main Street, blocking what now is Austin Street. At the turn of the last century, the townspeo-ple wanted Austin to run straight through from east to west. They al-tered the creek's course by filling it in with everyone's old car parts.

Seat of Wisdom   Becky Patterson '05

At eighty, Mama finally moved back into the 150-year-old cabin, now owned by her grandson Kit Patterson. She has adjusted in comfort and simplicity to its four small rooms and antiquated condition, along with the primitive indigenous pieces of old furniture in it.

HS

As president of the historical society, Mama oversaw the writing of the first volume of a book about the original pioneer families of Fredericksburg, *Pioneers in God's Hills.* She wrote the foreword, as well as a story about eccentric Peter Berg, who was known as "the hermit of the hills." The story of Peter Berg hauntingly parallels the life of our brother Kerry. Both were ingenious, creative, resourceful, building something out of nothing. Both had talents that went unnoticed, and eventually both turned to despair, solitude, and suicide.

Peter sailed from Germany in 1857, when he was twenty. When his fiancée didn't follow, he withdrew from society and built a hermitage on land he didn't own. He skillfully constructed a shelter in a ravine, and a Dutch windmill that pumped water, ground corn, and served as his lookout tower. He operated his own still and sold whiskey at thirty cents a gallon.

But his cleverest invention was a clear-sounding pipe organ built out of boards, sheets of brass, and cones of rolled-up newspaper for the pipes.

Shatzie collected and restored pieces for the Witte Museum in San Antonio and Ima Hogg's houses at Round Top and Bayou Bend. Furniture she owns or has restored can be seen in Lonn Taylor's *Texas Furniture* and the *Early Texas Furniture* books. But her main concern in restoring and collecting needlework, textiles, tools, machines, cars, Texas crockery, and furniture has always been, she says, "to keep what has been made in Fredericksburg in Fredericksburg. By placing these symbols of our heritage in museums, libraries, and homes in Gillespie County, we can continue to feel the charm of the past and the spirit of the people who worked so hard taming this land."

On Juneteenth of 2008, we were walking through the Institute of Texan Cultures, admiring the beautiful historical vignettes. "I'm inspired about history again!" Mama said with childlike enthusiasm. "I guess I live more in the past than the present. I cherish. I cherish my ancestors, what they did and what they stood for."

Erbteil: Inheritance

The price of nostalgia is high.

Washtub Canyon and Turkey Hollow in the James Section, and the Five Hundred next to it, were so precious and sentimental to Adolf that when the James sold he had a mandate drawn up by his lawyer prohibiting the Five Hundred and its water rights from ever being sold. He told Gene and Shatzie to never sell it. It was beautiful, he said, but more important, it had springs and water. Two weeks after Adolf's death, Tops and Gene were eager to sell it, and Gene begged his sister to release the hold their father had put on it, with the promise that later he would give substitute land.

She let them have their wish. The Five Hundred and its water rights were sold immediately. Shatzie never received reimbursement in money or land later. She regretfully remembered the day the new owner, Mr. Davis, who'd also bought the James, drove through the gate smiling and saying, "Your dad would be glad I own this!"

The loss of this sentimental piece of land was the first of many regrets that would pile up and haunt her dreams sixty years later. Shatzie lived with other expectations promised to her for years. But they were all eventually wheeled-and-dealed away from her and otherwise sold off. In the end, Mama's stepmother wouldn't even let her visit her father on his deathbed when she came to the door.

When an attachment to the land is born in you, the detachment, as with people and animals you love, comes with broken dreams and eternal longing. Shatzie wrestles with the bitterness of broken promises today.

ƕ

When our beloved Aunt Bertha Neunhoffer Ingenhuett died, Mama was in charge of dismantling her estate in Comfort. Her and Uncle Charlie's house was on High Street. Their backyard neighbors, Gretchen and Poodle Flach, had to get to their own house by walking up Bertha and Charlie's gravel driveway through Bertha's chicken and pigeon coop. Mama sold Bertha's chickens, but one had escaped. Poodle called and said they had found the lost hen at their house.

Mama went to pick up the hen in her car. She doesn't remember where she took the hen or what she did with it. But as it sat on the back of her car seat by her head, Talla, who was with her, laughed and said, "This is your *Erbteil*—your inheritance!"

ƕ

From my father I inherited arrowheads, the white fluffy ends of cow tails, and a rusted belt buckle for my craftwork. From my mother I will inherit—along with some crocks and wooden spoons—symbols, images, and words. Symbols strong enough to prime a broken heart into life-pumping action again; images so real they'll sail you over the cactus and rocks for a better landing; words with enough humor, wisdom, and creativity to reduce monsters to mice.

Mama's like a big powerful bird, flying best against the wind. I remember an image long ago. I saw her riding horseback, up to her knees in a flooded swirling creek saving drowning kid goats. She can take bad situations and make the best of them with her creative resolve. If you are her child, your own children will not receive the usual birthday or Christmas gifts from her. But some day at five in the morning, unbeknownst to you, she will have climbed your backyard fence and thrown pebbles against your sons' windows to wake them and take them deer hunting. When you wake up, you will have no idea where they are. But by now she will have wrapped the bloody kill of the day in her new Christmas jogging jacket. Later in the day she will have lost at least one of your son's shoes. She'll say to the kid, too embarrassed to go into the grocery store wearing only one shoe, "Oh, just limp and everyone will think you have a sore foot!" When it thundered at my eight-year-old's birthday cookout, Mama comforted the trembling little city slickers: "Oh, listen! I didn't know we were going to have *Indian* music for dinner!"

After a sheep hunt at the Home Ranch with my boys one day, Mama left a gift, some beautiful findings to keep. On my doorstep I found a rusted sheep bell, a small cactus to replant, and a branch covered with delicate green, gold, and rust lichen moss, which, on closer scrutiny, revealed a whole other world.

Mama's purse was either an emergency repair bag or a source of embarrassment. But she was always prepared for any situation. Security guards at Rusk maximum-security mental hospital rifled through it once when we were visiting Kerry there. It was his birthday, and we were bringing a fabulous picnic. I'm sure our presence seemed even more bizarre to the guards. In a sudden downpour, we arrived wearing garbage bags, Mama's emergency raincoats. From her purse they took out one hunting knife, an ice pick, a corkscrew, a needle and thread, a hammer, and a golf tee used in caning chair bottoms.

I flashed back to happier times when the ingredients of Mama's purse had once saved the day. We were at a muddy lake with a pitiful sailboat that kept sinking. From Mama's purse came dental floss to sew up the sail, a screwdriver to act as a pin to hold the rudder, and duct tape to patch the leaky bottom.

Mama has no sense of self-importance. She's an image to be felt. And she feels real. At one of my art shows, she surprised me with her presence. Standing around my wine-sipping, culture-conscious friends, she put her hand in her pocket, only to find some dirt and lint there—and two little worms. Astounding my circle of friends by her nonchalance, she said, holding the worms in the palm of her hand, "Oh, I wish I had some chickens!" One time when she was turning a corner in downtown Fredericksburg too wide and fast, four bulldogs hanging out of every porthole, some bratty boys shot her the finger, yelling, "You crazy damn fool granny!" Mama leaned out to respond, "Oh, you're so right!"

Just as she can pull out repairs for breakdowns from her purse, I may someday have to pull out a few of her quotes from the grab bag of her blatant advice. Her ninety-year-old cousin Albert came to cry on her shoulder about the destruction and changes his Keidel cousin did to his beautiful showplace house after he sold it to him, thinking he would get the usual sympathy from Shatzie. "He bashed out all the beautiful blue and yellow Mexican tile in the kitchen and the handmade tile in the bathroom that Harding Black and I made!" Albert cried. Her form of compassion was this cold response: "Well, that's what you get for living so long!"

To me she has said, "Find life and go for it!" Or "We're gonna take it like it comes." And when I complain about people, I get "People are like they are for a reason." And the hardest one to follow: "Remember the people you idolize—like Bertha. She was poor but self-sufficient. Her calm, simple, basic lifestyle—*these* values rather than attention and materialism. You'll mope on like this," she warned, "until something bad happens, and then you'll appreciate what you *do* have. *Simplify! Simplify!*"

It's hard for me to simplify. When the bright light faded again, she found me in my studio disheartened, overwhelmed by clutter, confusion, and exhaustion. She stepped in the door long enough to hand me a tiny flower, a Johnny Jump-up. She laughed about the clutter and said, "Think nothing of it!" Then she was gone.

Her kindness and thoughtful actions spoke louder than words. One time she drove up with a truckload of firewood for my tea party. Another time I was sick and found a note on my table that read, "I came by because I care. Call me if I can just *be*. Roast in oven. Mama." When I'm discouraged about a lost day she says, "That's life. It's all batter, batter, batter! We do what we can today."

⊦S

When I moved back to the Home Ranch in the 1990s, I was trying to clean out the barn full of old tools and buckets of rusted nuts and bolts stockpiled from the previous save-everything generation. More than that, there were old treasures, valuable keepsakes accumulated. Looking at it was overwhelming. All of the things here were dear to me, owned by people dear to me who were gone—Hondo, Ren, and Kerry.

What do I keep? What do I throw away? There were old vinyl records, boxes of decaying newspaper clippings from Hondo's fame, his early artwork cartoons on bulletins, Mexican songs written on silverfish-eaten paper, broken frames, tarnished trophies, all links to a person. I had saved special cards and letters from special people.

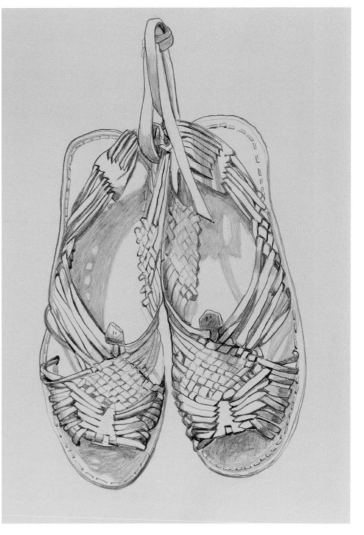

Then there were the last precious remnants of Ren, school notebooks and artwork from his few last days at UT. When I looked at his unique handwriting, I could hear his voice. There were folders of his colorful and ingenious line drawings from age three, poems, random thoughts and songs he wrote, bags of swimming medals. There were fragile faded newspaper articles on swimming I'd so proudly clipped and saved. I hadn't revisited them for twenty years. There was always a lot of press during the state meet time in March. Ren, Kit, Sky, and the Churchill team were among our city's best, state champions who were watched closely. The headlines said it all.

Then there was my little yellow water-stained Post-It grocery list: Sani Vac, Mr. Clean, Scrub Free, Lysol Toilet Bowl Cleaner. At the top I had scrawled so proudly

Ren's latest swim time—"100 (yard) fly/50.6!" The *Austin-American Statesman* clipping from June 1986 reported that the latest signee by UT men's swimming coach Eddie Reese was Ren Patterson, a sprinter-butterflier from San Antonio Churchill, adding that he was the grandson of Hondo Crouch. The coach was quoted as saying, "I recruited him because he can swim."

I could relinquish their dreams, hopes, goals. This was nothing compared to the stabbing anew of my heart on seeing the two UT vouchers refunding a total of $1,532 for Ren's room and board, for food uneaten, a bed in a dorm room vacated, empty. A sudden exit, with no return, dated September 25, 1987.

Kerry's hands had skillfully carved designs on boards, intricate chains and puzzles out of wood he'd learned from master woodcarver Lynn Ford. He had Picasso-like drawings and poetic lines in sketchbooks. These were all things representing those I idolized and loved most. But the loss of my men added up to be collectively larger and more painful than the collection of things could bear. I was the keeper of their archives, the saver, the historian of their lives. When I surveyed their accomplishments, their incredible talents, their wonderful potentials and what they stood for, I felt bottomless pain from dashed hopes. They kept me from the freedom of healing.

All of a sudden I could no longer carry, keep, or store the precious relics that marked their existence on this earth, that kept them alive. I am 99 percent nostalgia. I like to be surrounded by things that remind me of where I've been, who I love. Ren's huaraches, for example, are still hanging on my wall. They used to bring pain when I looked at them, but now they bring me peace. There's something beautiful about passing by something that belonged to a person you loved and lost.

Sometimes nostalgia has to be put on or taken off at will. Shifting into that cold-blooded but life-saving robot gear, I built a fire in the place where we burn trash. Into the flames went trash and boxes and, individually, many of the keepsakes of Hondo, Kerry, and Ren.

I felt as if I were killing them off all over again. I felt sacrilegious, sinful, rebelling for the last time over their untimely deaths. Aren't we all reduced to ashes anyway? What's left of us? Are they farther from me now? Or closer? I felt sad, but a burden of grief lifted.

Also lifted, sailing and dancing on the wave of heat, was one black charred paper trying to escape its death sentence. I grabbed it lest it alight on dry grass and spark a fire. It was one of Talla's birthday cards to me. Rescued from the ashes, all that was left legible in her handwriting, therefore her voice, said, "Dear Becky, Remember, S-M-I-L-E ! Love, Talla."

A spark ignited in me. I said to myself, "Okay. I get it. Finally. Thank you, Talla. You have the last word!"

$\mathsf{H}\mathsf{S}$

Our Lady of the Weeds

"It's no good unless you get the roots," Mama said on her hands and knees down at Werner and Adelle's house. "It's futile, remember. Futile. But eliminating two or three weeds a day makes a change, small, but a change. And change is always good. Just leave me alone here. I want to reveal the violets."

The weed pulling started in August 2008 with the passing of three of her lifelong friends, who died within months of each other. First it was Cathy Joseffy, followed by Arthur and Stella Eickenloff, original ranch employees in the 1930s. The weed pulling was never-ending, went on over two years, every day with fervor, for an exhausting eight hours a day. Mountains of weeds were pulled and hauled off in flatbeds, tractors, trucks, from acres of pens and fields. Mama waged war over thorny *Fuchsschwanz* (foxtail), stubborn ragweed, and beggar's lice, ever-present horehound, deep-rooted thistles, caliche-hugging ground cover, and enduring prickly pear. It was turning into such a commitment, such a monumental task, that I started keeping track of it.

Now, at eighty-five, crossing over a threshold to a new territory, Mama, as Our Lady of Sorrows, was harvesting memories of vanished days, pulling sadness, regret, and anger up out of the earth, revealing light, reconciliation, and forgiveness. One time when she didn't quit until after dark, I went out to find her. "That's how mad I was!" she said. But she was also crossing this threshold clothed in thankfulness and love of the land. "I may not own this land anymore, but I still have the *dirt*!" It was a natural instinct for her to return to the familiar, to return to herself, to return home.

Һ𝒮

On August 15, 2008, Mama went to see Cathy Joseffy on her deathbed. The impact of that visit sent Mama straight home to her little log cabin. "I'm so at peace in my cabin bed," she said, "with the whitewash from the ceiling falling down on me like flakes of snow. I thought, I don't have to impress anyone, do anything, go anywhere, be somebody. All I have to do is face myself."

The next day she came out to the ranch to pull thistles in the hundred-degree heat at high noon, with no shade. I'd check on her now and then for fear of heatstroke. Mother returns to Mother Earth, I thought, feeling the dirt, trying to rearrange the impossible force of nature a little. Then she washed my dishes and left, sweaty but satisfied.

On September 25, Mama came to pull weeds again. "I thought it'd be easy after that half inch of rain, but it wasn't," she said. "Hard, damned old caliche." She looked pretty in a salmon linen blouse with her white cottony head sticking out above in the tall ragweed. Today she was going to Stella's to take care of her at her Blanco ranch. Stella's husband Arthur had died at ninety-four a week earlier, and Stella was told that now she had only three weeks to live. "My prayer has been answered. I prayed I'd outlive Arthur. So now it's my turn," Stella said so matter-of-factly. She was ninety-one and battling stomach cancer. "I don't want any more transfusions," she told the nurse. Stella was a supreme gardener and artist, never went to school but knew so much. "No one has been to check on her," Mama said. "She's so brave, never complains."

"I used to run away from situations like that, Mama," I said. "Do you have the energy for this?"

"I did too," she answered, "but not with her. I don't need energy for this. There's something special about Stella, and I'm going to learn from her!"

On October 7, Mama was back on the weed campaign. Stella had taken a turn for the worse. Mama had been pulling weeds by the mare called Three Colors, side by side. The minute Mama pulled a weed, the mare eagerly nibbled the exposed grass.

"When I move she moves. We're two mares. One mare recognizes another. She's just lonely." I remembered a line out of one of Dora's 1917 books, *Aunt Olive in Bohemia*: "Only women know the loneliness of women."

"Solitude. That's all I want," Mama said. "I don't have to think, just let my hands be busy so I don't have to think."

"Who will care if Stella was the Tasha Tudor of Blanco? What's it all about in the end, Mama?" I asked.

"I've thought of the same, Becky. Made one mistake after another, hurt people. I've come to think that living is in the now, the moment. We have nothing to show for it in the end. We can only be proud we are ourselves—our authentic selves. I don't have to impress people."

That night, at seven thirty, Mama was still out there, sitting in the weeds, scooching around, her faithful dog Lucky at her side. "I've gotten it down. You have better leverage pulling sideways. The ground is soft now—we had an inch and a half last night. I have to hurry and pull them while it's still easy. Just don't tell me how to pull weeds!"

In Blanco the next day, Mama asked Stella if she wanted to go outside in her wheelchair and see her beautiful gardens. "No," she answered, "I'm through with outside." The day she moved out of her house for the last time was on her ninety-first birthday. She was wheeled out of her home, leaving a freezer full of food, jars full of preserves, an icebox full of leftovers, books on gardening and conservation, ranch histories. She did not look back. She left a job well done, a nest well feathered, family devotedly cared for, and a garden left to seed, not in its glory anymore.

Mama brought me Stella's *Family Circle* magazine with dog-eared pages of recipes she'd tried. I went and bought every ingredient and cooked the meals she'd cooked. Mama and her sister-in-law Odette went to see Stella on October 17. When they entered her room, Mama noticed the strange stare on Stella's face and realized she wasn't there anymore. Another woman showed up with a little vase of beautiful lavender-blue plumbago blooms, saying, "Stella brought me this plant, and I wanted to show her how it bloomed!" When Mama told her she was gone, the woman shoved the vase into her hand, turned around, and left without a word.

The next day Mama came out to pull weeds around six in the morning. Said she didn't want to be in her house. She remembered Stella saying she grew a bumper crop of turnips one year and gave them to everyone. "No one knew how to cook turnip greens, so she taught them. They didn't know how good they could be." Mean-

while I continued cooking Stella's dog-eared recipes. "It's the people who've made this ranch. Arthur, who came here at fourteen," Mama concluded. "How long the threads continue. It's the people, not the trophies or accomplishments, that have come and gone in our lives. The love that lingers is what continues."

When Mama came in from pulling weeds, she said, "I've conquered it! It gave in to me! The bad corner of horehound, thistle, and ragweed yielded, surrendered. I won!"

If I didn't know Stella very well, I at least wanted to know what she cooked and what grew in her garden. Her son Rickie took inventory and called me. What he recognized were marigolds, zinnias, geraniums, daylilies, begonias, impatiens, iris, columbine, red yucca, rose, petunia, daisy, larkspur, snapdragon, concflower or Echinacea, and plumbago, to mention a few.

Stella's cancer doctor was Dr. José A. Lopez. Mama never told me of the editorial he'd written about her for the *Fredericksburg Standard-Radio Post*; someone else did. He wrote about visiting Mama's antique furniture shop one day but kept her name anonymous.

I see something hidden behind furniture, a very Hill Country painting. It's an old barn, colors faded, but still showing some lonely tranquil approach to the subject. I got closer and recognized the name of the artist, Stella Eickenloff, in the corner. I wanted the picture but the owner [Shatzie] had a major attachment to it having lived there. The painter was a life-long friend. Clearly, the canvas was not for sale.

We introduced each other, talked some and said good-bye. Later that afternoon, the painting arrived at my office, with a warm note. It was a gift. This became a very touching moment. I am sentimental all over again. This is what Fredericksburg and its people do to me. These are experiences that make one not want to ever leave this little paradise.

ᛏᛋ

On June 20, 2009, Mama ran over her beloved dog Lucky. At the caliche Angora Lane she turned left when Lucky turned right. "Let's bury him right away before I think about it," she said. "I'll never forget how he looked up at me and then closed his eyes. I feel such shame."

We buried Lucky with the other five dogs we lost that year, under the huge pecan tree Dora had planted eighty years earlier. First there was my new border collie puppy Oso, then Smokey, Copie, Simón, and Cinco. There is a saying in Mexico that if you want to have a fruitful pecan tree, you need to bury a dog under it. We already had the pecan tree. It was just old and tired, waiting to embrace our dead dogs.

For the next two months Mama was on her hands and knees, paying her dues, in the muddy ground at Werner and Adelle's little house next to the pecan tree, pulling weeds and chopping thistles. Werner and Adelle had also been charter employees and caretakers for several generations. Mama watered the ground to make it soft enough to pull the stickers, dock, clover, *Fuchsschwanz*. This loss would take a lot of weed pulling for such a great healing. It was 100 degrees every day. She was out there from six thirty in the morning until five in the afternoon.

She got to know the ground like a road map. "Look! I'm making a connection from this plot to another. They're all connected, like a colony of people. Get rid of one group and up comes the next to gang up on you. I love it! There's so much bad in the world. I'm pulling up all the bad!"

In that yard, we sat on Minna Fishbach's rusted bed, the one that Mama had rescued long ago. No mattress, in the shade, outside, too tired and sad to talk. Beautiful clouds billowed overhead, and sunset glowed. There was a sadness floating in the air that touched us as a cool breeze. Tending the old yards of dead people she once knew and loved was better than tending their graves at cemeteries.

Mama pulled weeds without gloves, not caring that her arms and hands were tattooed with ant bites, her face swarmed by gnats. All along she thought of Adelle and Werner as she cleaned their yard on her hands and knees. At the end of the day she came up to the house in wet muddy pants, so baggy and raggedy-looking that the dogs barked at her. After pulling weeds for two months at Werner and Adelle's house, Mama presented me with five figs. "Adelle sent you these. She had the best fig tree on the ranch."

"I'm at the end of the trail and I'm not at the end of the trail," Mama said. "I feel worthless, unsettled. I have lists of hurts from Hondo and I'm bitchy and mean and blurt out. I took on too many responsibilities for everyone. I reached a boiling point two years after we married and it just got bigger over the years. Hondo was immature, selfish, unappreciative, stingy, mean. But I took it, didn't rise up and do anything about it. I wanted a man to take charge, stand up and face things. All I wanted was his attention and love."

Such was Mama's litany of confessions, regret, and resentment over her life with Hondo. Now Mama, as Our Lady of Reconciliation, didn't want to take this bitterness to her grave. Sixty-eight years later, like the light that a pulled weed reveals on new grass, light was shed on her. "I finally realized he couldn't do all that I expected. We don't get what we want. It was easy for him to receive praise and admiration from an audience, but not from me. I was unattractive, selfish, domineering." In January 2010, Mama brought me a book she found while browsing at a used bookstore, *On the Banks of the Blanco* by Blevin Vernon. A chapter in it portrayed a sensitive side of Hondo. "I needed to read this for me," she said. "It helped my bitterness." Vernon called him "one of the great living shows of the Texas Hill Country, an original production, a primitive whose artwork was already there, a mirth." He also described Hondo as a "most courtly genteel person, *not* a professional character, egotist, braggart or loud-mouth." Vernon saw him as soft-spoken, gentle, reflecting an inner peace. Mama finally understood Hondo's limitations and his artistic side, his true talents, and that he had a genuine gift for turning sadness and loneliness into limitless possibilities of laughter. When Vernon offered Hondo a new parking meter for Luckenbach, he turned it down. "Luckenbach couldn't support two parking meters," he said. "The truth is, when a big car parks parallel in Luckenbach, both the tail lights and head lights stick out past the city limits."

On Sunday, August 31, late afternoon, Mama sat in the sun cleaning the ground like it was a carpet in her house. She was using her fingernails like a rake, cleaning up even the seedlings around the big weeds.

There was a big drop of sweat at the end of her nose waiting for the law of gravity to take effect. "Why don't you sit in the shade, Mama?" I encouraged. "Because it's beautiful to see the sun shine through the grass, like looking into a gleaming forest," she said. The horse pen was an immense two acres. It looked overwhelming. "Little by little. Look at what we've *done*, not at what's not done," she said.

From my rooftop perch I saw the rooster lightning rod on the wool barn pierce the sky like a church steeple. I looked down at the field of weeds Mama had been working on for two weeks, one-third cleared and free. The cleared land was like our souls, so happy to breathe, be free, relieved of regret, unfairness, hurts, deceits. The grass had been waiting in the dark, eager to see the light, saying, "Pull me next! Don't forget me!"

A few days later, I went into San Antonio. I was eager to get back from a long hot day there to check up on the white-headed figure in a field of weeds. And there she was. I saw her white crouched form from the highway. Heck, you could probably see her figure from a satellite in space, on her knees, pulling, painted in mud. She had been there for more than eight hours. As I drove up to her, I saw her sitting cross-legged like an Indian chief facing the soon-to-be-setting sun. "It's 102 degrees in San Antonio, Mama! Why are you in the sun so long?"

"Oh, it's pleasant here! Delightful!" Shielding her eyes from the sun, she said she had seen three young deer tripping past her. She threw up her arms victori-

ously and said, "Take my picture! Yes, like Lady Bird in her field of bluebonnets!" We laughed. Yes, there she was, the First Lady of Weeds.

After dark, Mama quietly appeared in my bedroom. She looked like she'd been in a battle, white hair flying, face red, sweaty, shirt wet, pants muddy at the knees and seat, socks full of burrs, shoes untied, hands and fingernails weathered and raw. She made a sober announcement. "Now, at my age, Becky, I want to tell you I'm finally getting to know myself and love myself. Next, I want to tell you to do the same, to love yourself. Don't beat yourself up so much. You've accomplished and done wonderful and beautiful things. Don't talk of your failures and regrets. This is what I want to say to you." Then she left, driving home with her muddy hands.

The next morning at six o'clock I was sitting on my roof deck with my coffee, dogs, and psalms. Her words, "You do the same," echoed in my mind. I looked at the same silhouetted crooked tree I see every morning, leaves like black lace against the strip of hot orange horizon, the sun waiting to burst forth over the hills. It held a cool, peaceful silence. Only a mourning dove mourned.

$$\vdash\!\!S$$

Mama, Our Lady of Conservation, on a windy day in April, red bandanna on white head, was collecting tin roof pieces that had blown around in the well lot. She'd been chopping thistles with Oma's little woman-sized hoe for eight days now. She had been concentrating on thistles in Werner's Lot and was about to quit after a long hot day when a second wind energized her. "I hit pay dirt!" she exclaimed. "They're blooming already. Dirt's soft. Can't stop." I took her a glass of water and one glove. She was chopping around a mott of dead oaks when she made a discovery. "Look at these little new trees, Becky, only three inches high!" She put rock circles around these sprigs that had only two leaves. "This is our new beginning! We'll never see them full grown in our lifetime. How can we protect them from the deer? Just let me try."

This became her next obsession—to protect every little oak sprig she found, cluttering up fields by hauling truckloads of dead brush to throw over and protect them. In my backyard, I tripped over a whole pathway of coat-hanger croquet hoops stuck in the ground. Each one was protecting a three-inch oak twig. Alfredo came to the door and handed me a mysterious note. He was bulldozing, then sawing and burning dead oak trees. The note was warped and bleached by sun and rain and had been tied to one of the felled trees. "Please save this tree like it is for a bench at the cantina." On several other trees, notes read, "Keep these for kids to play on."

One morning I found a right-hand red ski glove in the driveway, like Cinderella's lost glass slipper, but fitting only the hand of Our Lady of the Weeds. Anyone else's hand would find it full of prickly beggar's lice seeds and sticker burrs.

"I love the dirt!" she said. "I love the iron punky smell of it. It's healing. Solitary. This poor grass underneath is so glad to breathe and see daylight. It'll take over. Just give it a chance. Don't fuss at me in this 99-degree heat. I have to hurry. Tomorrow it'll be dry and hard. Don't worry. I know my limits."

Pulling weeds over at the shearing barn, we both uncovered archeological finds, two rusted broken shearing blades. Her hands now became a very stubborn oily black she couldn't wash off even with soap and a brush. "I wonder what this oily black dirt is that I can't wash off," she said. Was it from animals? From the poisonous dipping vat that once dipped thousands of goats half a century ago?

She was getting tired. She'd go back to her cabin, crash and burn, sleeping for days. "I work till I fall over. At my age I'm falling apart anyway, so it doesn't matter." Her hands would get so crippled she'd have to rest them for days.

After one hard day of weed pulling, Mama drove up the road in her beat-up old truck, her leg sticking out of the open door. I suspected trouble. When I asked her why she was driving like that, she said, "I was just too tired to put my foot in to close the door." She eventually lifted her tired leg up into the truck and closed the door. "I better keep going," she said, "before I crash." On another Mother's Day picnic, May 10, 2009, we all waited at the Birthday Spring in the Six Hundred for Kit and Mama to show up. They'd decided to walk in the 90-degree heat. "What took y'all so long?" I asked. "Well, I didn't want to leave Shatzie behind," Kit said. "She took her hoe along and was stopping along the way chopping weeds in a six-hundred-acre pasture. She said she knows it's useless, but it's her obsession."

"They're like buzzards flying over, Mama," I told her one day. "Those eager real estate salesmen who send me mail with maps of our land on their letters!" "Do what you feel is right with this land, Becky. You can't stop the towers coming, eminent domain, gated developments. This ranch used to be a big outfit with a lot of help. Now we feel desperate. Everything's falling down. That's country life! Don't be sentimental over heritage. Everything's changing. You can't stop it.

"The love of the land and sentimental ties are a burden. I guess that's what enough weed pulling'll do to you!"

That September, Hurricane Ike, a Category 2 storm, hit the Texas coast and destroyed Galveston. The stock market fell worse than in the Depression of the 1930s. Three Colors got her foot cut so badly in barbed wire that we feared she'd be lame forever. But the biggest news was a call from Mama late that night. "Go out and look at the moon!" she said. "It's a big orange pumpkin!"

Coming Home

On July 29, 2009, Mama had the task of getting rid of a mama raccoon and her four babies. They found the cat food on her open windowsill at her cabin near the creek in town. She was tough and heartless about catching them one by one each night in a Havahart trap. "We need balance!" she said coldly as she sent each one off to its execution at the dog pound. However, when she trapped the fourth baby, it was on a Sunday and the pound was closed. So she took her captive down the highway to a creek at a roadside park and let it go. "It ran and ran and ran, free!" Mama told me. "Then I thought, it's never been away from home before! Where will it go? And I got so depressed I couldn't drive away. Where did I go? Home. Home to the Home Ranch. It was seven a.m. and I didn't want to disturb you. So I just sat in my truck. I came back later to pull weeds."

You don't quite realize the strong pull of home until you leave and return to it like a swallow returning to the nest after a long trip. The ranch that is us formed our individuality, created who we've become. Our roots lead us back to our childhood kitchens and bedrooms. Mama now had the Home Ranch available to come back to, this place where things, no matter how run-down, are glad to see her again and can give her the same simple welcome.

There, in August 2007, Mama was recuperating from surgery in the same room that had been hers as a little girl. "I have been so peaceful here," she said. "After years, I can sit and feel again, the happy times I had as a little girl. For the first time,

I can talk to Mama, hear her voice. I never could before. I do feel like there's a Great Spirit that we can connect to, that we inherit the spirits of our ancestors. I'm satisfied with that."

After healing from surgery, Mama was back to pulling weeds in the shearing barn pen. I was inside the house rummaging through old yellowed letters Adolf had written to her at St. Mary's Hall. I came upon a treasure, one from Dora written on June 11, 1935. I ran outside to read it to her. I saw her lying down, prostrate, in the grass. Was she dead? My heart stopped. No, she was only napping, face down on the bare ground. Startled, she sat up. "I didn't know you were coming. It's wonderful here, a cool breeze."

"I have a letter here your mom wrote to you when you were eleven!" I said. Shatzie and Talla were visiting Talla's relatives that summer in New Braunfels.

Seeing Dora's handwriting was hearing her voice. Addressed to Helen Ruth Stieler, it read: "Dear Shatzie, Tiny [Shatzie's dog] is still looking for you. He camps right on my foot all day long. Daddy's shearing down at Sisterdale and the Franklin ranch today. Tell Talla I picked the prettiest bunch of rosebuds—about a dozen—to put in her room here at the house."

"Oh?" Mama interrupted with tearful voice and shaky smile, her face embracing her mother's every word. She listened with the ears of an eleven-year-old.

I continued reading. "Raymond and Rosa and I worked in the garden [the three-acre Werner's Lot] all day, and you wouldn't know the old garden any more, we pulled so many weeds. I cut the long grass that goes down to the tennis court. Then it began raining and is still raining . . . a big hug and kisses to the sweetest little girl in the world. Love, Mom."

The old letter, sent for three cents and re-sent seventy-two years later, brought Mama to life. It was sunset. A golden glow covered everything and held us together as if we were in a time warp. There we were, the three of us together for the first time: thirty-nine-year-old Dora, eighty-three-year-old Shatzie, sixty-three-year-old Becky. All of us were united by pulling weeds, with no time separating us. Dora's garden in Werner's Lot and the shearing pen were separated by only the lane. We could look over there and imagine the life and color Dora had brought to it with her vegetables, flowers, and short-lived tennis court. It was as if Dora's absence had come alive in her hidden presence of that letter. For a moment, nothing was lost or forgotten.

With every weed Mama pulled, it said thank you and she said thank you. More and more, Mama's heart was filled with peace and thankfulness. Even in the midst of her crises and confusions, Mama was able to follow the path to the home in her heart. Being at home with herself gave her balance and poise. From her little bedroom in the log cabin she wrote a psalm of gratitude:

Thank you, my Creator. I am grateful to be on this earth long enough to reach an age that I am not forced to a schedule of commitment. I can honestly await the happenings of the day without fear or misgivings. I know in my heart and mind that the Power above will guide and care for me *if* I will accept and listen. May the peace of the early morning outdoors stay with me throughout the day.

In spite of her bad memory, she listed all of her teachers from first grade on. Her most memorable in Comfort elementary school was Mr. Arthur Bergman, simply because of his long, long glare at her. She had popped off some smart-aleck response to him like, "Well, that'll be the day!" The whole class froze along with her. Mama never changed her outspoken ways, but she remembered how a stern, silent stare could demand respect. Then she made a list of "folks to whom I am forever grateful for their love, support, and inspiration: Mama & Daddy, Maria Kuhlmann, Aunt Clara, Talla, Aunt Bertha, Oma Clara Neunhoffer, Mrs. McManus (piano), Vera Flach (reading & drama), Ruth Matlock (dance), Albert Keidel, and Joe."

Mama had always said, "I should have never left the ranch." But when she left she took with her these people and all she learned from them. In leaving, she found home within, her real self, and it sustained her through the many great and hard challenges of life. "With all that's happened to me there's always been a little bit of survival, support, friends, life around me. Growing up, I had the best of everything. My life has been 98 percent happy."

She has only one good eye now, and her hands are numb from weed pulling. Still, she continues to cane the seats of two or three rocking chairs, just to see if she still can. Now she is more homebound, and she doesn't drive anymore. "I give thanks even for these handicaps," she says. "I hope you can feel this way, too, someday, Becky. We don't need to feel useful always. I am thankful where I am now."

I had one last view of Our Lady of the Weeds on March 8, 2010. It was dusk. Mama was leaving after pulling weeds all day. Tired, she walked to her beat-up truck over muddy ground in her stocking feet. Her knees and the seat of her khaki pants were wet and muddy. In one dirty hand she held a beautiful stargazer lily stem like a scepter. In the other mud-caked hand she held her muddy shoes, a hoe, and her supper, a small bowl of salmon. She carried a heavy stinky bag of trash in the crook of her arm like a purse—or like Opa had carried his bucket of corn out to the deer all those years ago. It made her lopsided. I knew she took our trash so she could go through it to separate whatever was recyclable. I couldn't stop her, and she would not let me help her. She drove herself home like this.

She was comfortable being uncomfortable.

H5

Hands Listed in Ranch Ledger, 1943–1946

Poncho Aguilar, Homer Alexander, Manuel Ayala, Eugene Bauta, Alfred Boos, Cates Burit, Arthur Eickenloff, Slim Ely, Charles Everett, Red Everett, Bartolo Garcia, Clarence Gay, Clyde Hatcher, José Herrera, Puddin Stieler Heyland, George Keilman, George "Honey" Koester, Alfred Kuhlmann, Herbert Kuhlmann, Otto Kuhlmann, Raymond Kuhlmann, Roland Kuhlmann, Tillie Kuhlmann, Joaquin Longoria, Leandro Longoria, Paula Longoria, George Lopez, Bob Lott, Leon Merritt, Andres Muñoz, Kunt Norman, Paul Pankratz, Buck Pantemuel, Bob Paulson, Albert Reck, Red Rees, Melesio Reyna, Owen Roberts, Oscar Roeder, Werner Roeder, John Rotge, Clifford Rushlow, Adolf Schlueter, Frank Schultze, Kenneth Carl Scott, Max Sens, Christian Breeman Shenle, Rat Smith, Tom Sperger, Robert Stieler, Emil Uecker, Willie York Watts, Walter Wehmeyer, George Wellington, Emil Wieters, Herman Whitney

THANK YOU

Raymond Kuhlmann   age 88
      foreman
1917 - (1935) — 2005
  " I'll never forget....."

H5

Special Thanks

This book exists because of blessings and gifts. First, thank you, Maureen Barrett, whose Robert M. McNamara artist residency gave me the gift of time and opportunity to paint about people and lifestyle we've loved and lost. Naomi Shihab Nye and Barbara Ras, on seeing the artwork, invited me to put words to it. They were the first to speak the idea for this book.

Raymond Kuhlmann is like Thunder Mountain. He will always be there. I am blessed with the treasure of his memory and amazing stories. He was the very blood and sinew of the ranches. We will never forget you, Raymond.

Other stories, like little strings saved from feedbags, I crocheted into a banquet tablecloth on which we can all feast. Thank you, storytellers Arthur Eickenloff, Odette and Gene Stieler, Felix and Lillian "Pluppy" Real, Allen and Karen Stieler, Julius Neunhoffer, Juan Crouch, Jimmy Kuhlmann, Kit and Sky Patterson, Anne Stewart, and JoAnn Pankratz Stiles.

Reginald Gibbons, at Gemini Ink, said three words to me. "Write. It. All," he said of my ancient history—the good, the bad, the beautiful. I also thank the Trinity University staff, Sarah Nawrocki and Tom Payton, for rolling up their sleeves for me on this project.

I am indebted to my right-hand woman, Caren Richardson, who transformed my scratched-out yellow legal pages into fresh typed white ones. I found a friend and a sister. Blessed are the offerings of time from Francis Worley and Angelica Suarez, who retyped the typed.

The hawk feather Gregory McNamee handed me on our first meeting was enough to get me airborne, and I continue to fly. In good faith, I gave him a knife with a deer antler handle, and he carefully cut, carved, and sculpted these pages into a book. A talented word craftsman, he speaks many languages—German, Spanish, Greek, and hawk. With his keen expertise and direction, I learned so much on this adventure.

To interpreters of German, Bridgette Neidre and Chris Wickham at UTSA, *danke*. To camera artists Ansen Seale and Susan Riley, thank you for capturing my images.

My sons Kit and Sky Patterson and my husband Oscar Barrales are gifts who inspire and encourage me. They give the greatest purpose to my life. Thank you, my God, for blessing me with my eyes blinded or open. I am humbled.

I breathe thankfulness every day for the blessing and gift of Helen "Shatzie" Stieler Crouch. Mama's examples of graciousness, wisdom, humor, and humility, in good times and bad, are an inspiration to many. She has taught me how to cherish what we have and what we have lost.

Published by Trinity University Press
San Antonio, Texas 78212
Text and illustrations copyright © 2012 by Becky Crouch Patterson

Book design by Kristina Kachele llc

Trinity University Press strives to produce its books using methods and materials in an environmentally sensitive manner. We favor working with manufacturers that practice sustainable management of all natural resources, produce paper using recycled stock, and manage forests with the best possible practices for people, biodiversity, and sustainability. The press is a member of the Green Press Initiative, a nonprofit program dedicated to supporting publishers in their efforts to reduce their impacts on endangered forests, climate change, and forest-dependent communities.

The paper used in this publication meets the minimum requirements of the American National Standard for Information Sciences—Permanence of Paper for Printed Library Materials, ANSI 39.48-1992.

Library of Congress Cataloging-in-Publication Data
Patterson, Becky Crouch, 1945–
The ranch that was us / text and illustrations by Becky Crouch Patterson ; foreword by Willie Nelson.
p. cm.
ISBN 978-1-59534-138-9 (pbk. : alk. paper)
1. Ranch life—Texas—Texas Hill Country. 2. Texas Hill Country (Tex.)—Biography. 3. Texas Hill Country (Tex.)—Social life and customs. 4. Crouch, Helen Stieler. I. Title.
F392.T47P39 2012
976.4'885—dc23   2012010494

16 15 14 13 12   5 4 3 2 1

Printed in Canada

© Susan Riley

Becky Crouch Patterson is the author of the Texas best seller *Hondo, My Father*, a memoir of life with her folk-hero father, Hondo Crouch, who was a rancher, storyteller, humorist, and self-proclaimed mayor of Luckenbach, Texas. A textile artist for more than forty years, Patterson has sewn appliquéd tapestries for many businesses and individuals. She is also a liturgical artist and designer and has created stained glass windows and furnishings for churches throughout Texas. She is the owner, with her sons Kit and Sky Patterson, of Stieler Hill Ranch, near Comfort, Texas, where Sky is an artist and Kit continues the family's 135 years of ranching. Patterson helps out with the activities of the ranch, including the Texican Single Action Shooting Society, the hunters, art workshops, and her husband Oscar Barrales's horse training business.